TX
714
.N43
2004

MMANNI

Chicago Public Library

P9-DES-949

Recipes for our daughters

DISCARD

THE CHICAGO PUBLIC LIBRARY

Mabel Manning Branch
6 S. Hoyne
Chicago, IL   60612

RECIPES *for Our* DAUGHTERS

◆

RECIPES
for Our
DAUGHTERS

NAOMI NEFT AND

CYNTHIA ROTHSTEIN

BALLANTINE BOOKS

NEW YORK

A Ballantine Book
The Random House Publishing Group

Copyright © 2004 by Cynthia Rothstein and Naomi Neft

All rights reserved under International and Pan-American Copyright
Conventions. Published in the United States by The Random House Publishing
Group, a division of Random House, Inc., New York, and simultaneously in
Canada by Random House of Canada Limited, Toronto.

BALLANTINE and colophon are registered trademarks of Random House, Inc.

Recipe for "Oprah's Potatoes" copyright © 1994 Harpo, Inc. All rights reserved.
Reprinted by permission of Harpo, Inc.

www.ballantinebooks.com

Library of Congress Cataloging-in-Publication data is available.

ISBN 0-345-46800-7

Manufactured in the United States of America
First Edition: May 2004

10 9 8 7 6 5 4 3 2 1

TEXT DESIGN BY DEBORAH KERNER/DANCING BEARS DESIGN

RO401633753

Mabel Manning Branch
6 S. Hoyne
Chicago, IL   60612

Recipes for Our Daughters is dedicated to our families: David, Michael, and Debbie Neft and Jerry, Michael, Lori, and Meryl Rothstein. We wish to express our love and thanks for their encouragement, support, ideas, assistance, and patience, and especially for their good humor throughout the entire process, particularly when we enlisted them for our many taste tests.

We would also like to express our love and appreciation to our mothers, Ida Silver and Pearl Pincus, who introduced us to the joys of happy mealtimes, and to our fathers, Bernie Silver and Morris Pincus, and our brothers, Steve Silver and Jerry Pincus, with whom we shared those times. Naomi also thanks Steve for the many times he helped her clean her plate, and Cynthia is grateful that Jerry no longer kicks her under the table.

CONTENTS

INTRODUCTION

Our daughters Debbie Neft and Lori Rothstein were the inspiration for this book. The girls met many years ago when they entered kindergarten at P.S. 158 in Manhattan. They soon became very close friends and could usually be found together—at school, the playground, drama club, ballet class, day camp, birthday parties, sleepovers.

A few years ago, the girls graduated from college, embarked on new careers, and moved into their own apartments. We soon found ourselves receiving many phone calls and e-mails asking for our opinions and advice. Often, they asked cooking questions and wanted the recipes for their favorite dishes. Thus, we decided to create a "user-friendly" cookbook for the girls, pooling many of our favorite family recipes as well as the cooking wisdom we had accumulated over the years.

While gathering our recipes, we also reflected on what a wonderful time it is for young women today—a time when they can be and do anything and everything. We thought about the importance of role models in their lives and decided to include in our collection a number of recipes contributed by many of today's exceptional women.

These women, all greatly respected and admired for their notable successes and achievements, are truly role models for today's young women. We are deeply honored that they have contributed to this book and we wish to express our sincere appreciation and gratitude to them:

JOAN BAEZ, folksinger, songwriter, social activist, author

BRENDA CZAJKA BARNES, business executive; former president and CEO, Pepsi-Cola North America

CATHLEEN BLACK, president, Hearst Magazines; former publisher, *USA Today*

"LINDY" BOGGS, former congresswoman from Louisiana, former ambassador to the Vatican

CAROL MOSELEY BRAUN, former U.S. senator from Illinois, the first African American woman elected to the Senate

BOBBI BROWN, professional makeup artist; founder and CEO, Bobbi Brown Cosmetics

DR. JOY BROWNE, psychologist, author, radio talk-show host

BARBARA BUSH, former first lady; founder, the Barbara Bush Foundation for Family Literacy; author

ROSALYNN CARTER, former first lady; vice chair, the Carter Center

SUE CLARK-JOHNSON, senior group president, Gannett Co., Inc.; publisher and CEO, *The Arizona Republic*

BEVERLY CLEARY, author, winner of the American Library Association's John Newberry Medal and Laura Ingalls Wilder Award

GLENN CLOSE, actress, producer, winner of three Tony Awards and one Emmy

SUSAN M. COLLINS, U.S. senator from Maine

KATIE COURIC, coanchor, NBC News' *Today;* contributing anchor, *Dateline NBC;* cofounder, National Colorectal Cancer Research Alliance; winner of two Emmy Awards and a George Foster Peabody Award

LOIS B. DeFLEUR, president, Binghamton University–State University of New York

ELIZABETH DOLE, U.S. senator from North Carolina; former president, American Red Cross; former secretary of Transportation; former secretary of Labor

NANCY S. DYE, president, Oberlin College

NORA EPHRON, author, essayist, director, producer, screenwriter

CHRIS EVERT, tennis champion; winner of 18 Grand Slam singles titles, 3 Grand Slam doubles titles, and 157 tournaments

DIANNE FEINSTEIN, U.S. senator from California, former mayor of San Francisco

GERALDINE A. FERRARO, vice presidential candidate, 1984, the first woman to run as a major party nominee for national office; former congresswoman from New York

PEGGY FLEMING, figure skater, winner of the Olympic gold medal, winner of five consecutive U.S. skating titles and three world championships

JANE FONDA, actress; author; social activist; winner of two Academy Awards, one Emmy, and five Golden Globe Awards

LUCINDA FRANKS, journalist, author, winner of the 1971 Pulitzer Prize for National Reporting

CAROLEE FRIEDLANDER, jewelry designer; president and CEO, Carolee Designs, Inc.

CLAIRE GAUDIANI, senior research scholar, Yale Law School; president and founder, New London Development Corporation; former president, Connecticut College

TIPPER GORE, photographer, author, wife of former U.S. Vice President Al Gore

JENNIFER M. GRANHOLM, governor of Michigan

AGNES GUND, former president, Museum of Modern Art; recipient, National Medal of Arts

JANET GUTHRIE, professional race car driver, the first woman to compete in the Indianapolis 500 and the Daytona 500

JOAN HAMBURG, radio talk-show host, consumer reporter, author

KAY BAILEY HUTCHISON, U.S. senator from Texas

LADY BIRD JOHNSON, former first lady; founder, The Lady Bird Johnson Wildflower Center

PERRI KLASS, M.D., author; assistant professor of pediatrics; winner of five O. Henry Awards

JUDITH LEIBER, designer; founder, Judith Leiber Inc.

MADELEINE L'ENGLE, author, winner of the American Library Association's John Newberry Medal and Margaret A. Edwards Award for lifetime achievement

SHIRLEY MacLAINE, actress, singer, dancer, author, winner of one Academy Award and three Emmy Awards

JUDY MARTZ, governor of Montana, member of the 1964 U.S. Olympic Speed Skating Team

BARBARA A. MIKULSKI, U.S. senator from Maryland, former congresswoman from Maryland

NICOLE MILLER, fashion designer; president, Nicole Miller, Ltd.

RUTH ANN MINNER, governor of Delaware

LISA MURKOWSKI, U.S. senator from Alaska

PATTY MURRAY, U.S. senator from the state of Washington

JOSIE NATORI, fashion designer; founder and CEO, the Natori Company

ROSIE O'DONNELL, actress, comedian, author, winner of six Emmy Awards

MERYL POSTER, copresident of production, Miramax Films

ALMA J. POWELL, vice chairman of the board, John F. Kennedy Center for the Performing Arts; author

JUDY RANKIN, champion professional golfer, sports commentator, winner of twenty-six Ladies Professional Golf Association tournaments

DIANE RAVITCH, historian, author

NANCY REAGAN, former first lady

DEBBIE REYNOLDS, actress, singer

ANN RICHARDS, former governor of Texas; author; member of the board of directors: Brandeis University, JCPenney, Aspen Institute

COKIE ROBERTS, journalist, author, televison and radio news analyst, winner of the Edward R. Murrow Award and two Emmys

PAT SCHROEDER, president and CEO, Association of American Publishers; former congresswoman from Colorado

KATHLEEN SEBELIUS, governor of Kansas

JEANNE SHAHEEN, former governor of New Hampshire

DONNA E. SHALALA, president, University of Miami; former secretary of Health and Human Services

BEVERLY SILLS, chairman of the board, Metropolitan Opera; opera star; recording artist; former chairman, Lincoln Center for the Performing Arts; winner of one Grammy and two Emmy Awards

JANE SMILEY, author, essayist, winner of the 1992 Pulitzer Prize for Fiction and four O. Henry Awards

OLYMPIA J. SNOWE, U.S. senator from Maine, former congresswoman from Maine

NADINE STROSSEN, professor, New York Law School; president, American Civil Liberties Union

MARLO THOMAS, actress; producer; author; winner of four Emmy Awards, one Golden Globe Award, and a George Foster Peabody Award

KAITY TONG, television news anchor, winner of the Edward R. Murrow Award

LILLIAN VERNON, founder, Lillian Vernon Corporation; author

JUDITH VIORST, author, poet, winner of one Emmy Award

ADRIENNE VITTADINI, fashion designer; former chairwoman, Adrienne Vittadini Enterprises, Inc.

DIANE VON FURSTENBERG, fashion designer; chairman and founder, Diane von Furstenberg Studio

WENDY WASSERSTEIN, novelist, playwright, screenwriter, winner of the 1989 Pulitzer Prize for Drama, the first woman to win a Tony Award for Best Play

DIANA WILLIAMS, television news anchor

JODY WILLIAMS, coordinator, International Campaign to Ban Landmines; winner of the 1997 Nobel Peace Prize

OPRAH WINFREY, actress, producer, author, creator and host of *The Oprah Winfrey Show*, creator of O, *the Oprah Magazine*, winner of seven Emmy Awards

PAULA ZAHN, CNN television news anchor and host, winner of one Emmy Award

EUGENIA ZUKERMAN, flutist; author; arts correspondent, CBS News' *Sunday Morning*; artistic director, Vail Valley Music Festival

MANY THANKS

In addition to our extraordinary role models, we have many other wonderful people to thank. First and foremost, our incredible literary agent, Julie Barer, whose expertise and guidance were so valuable in bringing this project to fruition. Her encouragement, energetic enthusiasm, and endless patience always kept us going. We are equally appreciative of the help and support we received from our talented editor at Ballantine Books, Maureen O'Neal, and her terrific assistant, Johanna Bowman.

We are also indebted to innumerable friends and relatives and would like to extend special thanks to the following people for sharing their culinary expertise: Madeleine Barbara, Helen Barer, Bettye Beaton, Janice Bernhardt, Dorothy Buxbaum, Linda Carner, Janet Davis, Suzie Davis, Linda Dzuba, Melissa Feldmesser, Judy Fradin, Christine Burton Glickman, Kate Headline, Rita Hodos, Karen Jakes, Evelyne Johnson, Sharon Korman, Ann Levine, Sally Lockwood, Linda Mandle, Linda Marabell, Susan McFaden, Michael Neft, Arline Norkin, Janet Pincus, Pearl Pincus, Gail Raybin, Gail Reisch, Ann M. Rhodes, Jane Rifkind, Anne-Marie Rosaler, Gert Rothstein, Bernie Silver, Annette Siskel, Marjorie Siskel, Deb Vineberg, and Judy Weinstein.

We want to express our deep gratitude to a number of other friends for the special help, support, and guidance they generously provided: Donna Bascom, Barbara Colodner, Joan Easton, Carole Gitnik, Sari Singer, and Ann and Fred Yerman.

And, of course, we especially thank Meryl Rothstein, Cynthia's younger daughter, for her invaluable research, fact-checking, and fax-checking. Although still a college student, Meryl will soon enter the world of young career women for whom this book was created.

PROLOGUE

WORKING MOM'S BREAKFAST

from **PAT SCHROEDER**
President and CEO, Association of American Publishers;
Former Congresswoman from Colorado

♦

1. Find a bowl—if it's on the floor, wash it!

2. Find cereal—hopefully a sugar-coated one so you don't have to pound the dried sugar in the bowl.

3. Check spoil dates on the milk in the refrigerator; if okay,

4. Assemble and go for it!

♦

"No pressure on my daughter!"

RECIPES *for Our* DAUGHTERS

◆

BREAD AND BREAKFAST

TIPS AND HINTS ON...

BUYING AND STORING EGGS

+ Eggs are generally available in five sizes, from small to jumbo, but unless otherwise specified, the word *egg* in a recipe refers to the large size.

+ Shell color is a matter of personal preference, since brown and white eggs are the same in quality and flavor. The color of the shell is related to the variety of hen.

+ Always buy eggs from a refrigerated case and check the carton for the expiration or "sell by" date.

+ Jiggle each egg in the carton and do not buy any eggs that are cracked or leaking. Damaged eggs may be contaminated and should never be used.

+ Store eggs—blunt side up—in their original cartons toward the back of the refrigerator, where they will be kept colder than on a door shelf, where they would be exposed to warm air every time you open the door.

+ Refrigerated eggs generally last from thirty-five to forty days after the "sell by" date. Once an egg has spoiled, you will be able to tell right away by the terrible "rotten egg" odor it gives off when cracked open.

+ Older eggs are just as flavorful and nutritious as fresher ones. The main difference is that once they are cracked open, older eggs tend to spread out; their yolks are flatter and their whites are looser. Since older eggs have larger air pockets under the shell, they make better hard-boiled eggs because they are easier to peel.

+ If you are unsure about the freshness of your eggs, place the uncooked eggs in a bowl of cold water. The freshest eggs will lie flat on the bottom. The older ones will stand on end, and the really old ones will float because they have the largest air pockets.

+ Always handle eggs carefully, as there is a very slight chance that they have been contaminated with salmonella bacteria. Wash your hands after handling eggs and be sure you also wash the countertops, equipment, and utensils you used. It is also because of this possible contamination that you should *never eat any food containing raw eggs.*

+ If you see any small dark spots in an egg yolk, don't be concerned about them. They are perfectly harmless and can easily be removed with a spoon or the tip of a knife.

+ If you have some hard-boiled eggs in the refrigerator and can't tell them apart from the raw eggs, give them a spin. Cooked eggs will spin smoothly, while raw eggs will wobble.

HOW TO BOIL AN EGG

+ A boiled egg should not really be boiled—it should be gently simmered to prevent it from getting too hot and becoming rubbery. Vigorous boiling might also crack the shell.

+ After lowering the egg into simmering water, wait for the water to come to a second simmer and start your timer: three to five minutes for a soft-boiled egg, twelve to fifteen minutes for a hard-boiled one. The exact time depends on the size of the egg.

+ As soon as the egg is ready, plunge it into cold water to stop the cooking. This also prevents a dark green rim from forming between the yolk and the white.

+ Here's another foolproof way to hard-boil eggs: Place them in a pot of cold water, bring the water to a boil, and immediately cover the pot and take it off the heat. After fifteen minutes, immediately plunge the eggs into cold water.

+ When peeling hard-boiled eggs, it is easier if you start at the blunt end, where the air pocket is located.

+ When slicing hard-boiled eggs, dipping the knife in water will prevent the yolk from breaking.

BUYING AND STORING FLOUR

+ Recipes tend to call for one of three types of flour: *all-purpose flour,* which is used for practically everything; *cake flour,* which gives cakes a lighter texture; and *bread flour,* which is ideal for making bread, as it produces a tastier, lighter loaf. Unless otherwise specified, the word *flour* in a recipe refers to all-purpose flour. Never substitute bread flour or self-rising flour for all-purpose flour in a recipe.

+ If necessary, you can interchange all-purpose flour and cake flour:

> 1 cup cake flour = 1 cup minus 2 tablespoons all-purpose flour
>
> 1 cup all-purpose flour = 1 cup plus 2 tablespoons cake flour

+ Flour should not be stored in the bag in which you bought it but should be transferred to a glass or plastic canister.

MAKING YEAST BREADS

+ Many bread recipes do not specify an exact amount of flour, since the amount needed may vary by as much as 1 or 2 cups. Add the flour slowly and stop when the dough reaches the right consistency—it should be smooth and somewhat elastic and not stick to the bowl or your fingers.

+ When shopping for yeast, do not confuse baker's yeast with brewer's yeast, which is sold as a food supplement in health-food stores and should never be used in baking bread.
+ Most bread recipes call for active dry yeast, which comes in handy 1/4-ounce (scant-tablespoon) foil packages. If you are using quick-rising yeast, be sure to follow the package directions for dissolving it.
+ If you like bread with a soft crust, brush the top with melted butter before baking. If you like a shiny crust, use a beaten egg. For a crisp crust, use a spray bottle to spritz the preheated oven or place a pan of water in the bottom of the oven to increase the humidity while the loaf is baking.

MAKING QUICK BREADS AND MUFFINS

+ Quick breads and muffins are leavened with baking soda or baking powder, not yeast. Follow the recipe directions carefully and do not substitute one leavening agent for another.
+ Shiny metal loaf pans are best for baking quick breads. If you use a dark pan, lower the oven temperature about 25°F to prevent the bread from browning too quickly.
+ For an easy cleanup, bake muffins in paper or foil muffin-cup liners placed in the muffin tin.
+ If you don't have a biscuit cutter, you can use the rim of a drinking glass or cup to cut the dough.

DELICIOUS HEALTHY BREAKFAST DRINK

from ANN RICHARDS

Former Governor of Texas; Author; Member of the Board of Directors: Brandeis University, JCPenney, Aspen Institute

◆

"This is a great breakfast or lunch high-energy strength-builder. Other kinds of health powders may be added as desired, as well as other fruits."

MAKES 1 PORTION

2 to 3 frozen strawberries
3 to 4 slices frozen peaches
$^1/_2$ frozen banana
$^1/_4$ to $^1/_2$ cup protein powder, such as MET-Rx or SPIRU-TEIN
    (available at health-food stores and many supermarkets)
1 cup flavored or plain yogurt
1 cup apple juice, plus more as needed
Crushed ice (optional)

1. Place all of the ingredients in a blender and process until smooth.
2. Add more apple juice if the mixture is too thick.

GRANOLA

◆

SERVES 8 TO 10

8 tablespoons (1 stick) butter
$^1/_2$ cup honey
4 cups rolled oats

Continued

2 cups shredded sweetened coconut

1 cup sliced almonds

1 tablespoon dark brown sugar

2 cups mixed dried fruit, such as cherries, cranberries, chopped
apricots, currants, or banana chips

1. Preheat the oven to 350°F.
2. Melt the butter and honey over a low flame.
3. Toss the oats, coconut, and almonds in a large bowl.
4. Drizzle the butter-honey mixture over the oat mixture and toss thoroughly to coat.
5. Spread the mixture on a large baking sheet and sprinkle the brown sugar evenly over it.
6. Bake, tossing the mixture at least once, for 45 minutes, or until everything is well toasted and brown.
7. When done, allow the mixture to cool for 10 minutes on the baking sheet, add the dried fruit, and mix well. Store in an airtight container.

DUTCH BABIES

from **BEVERLY SILLS**

Chairman of the Board, Metropolitan Opera;
Opera Star; Recording Artist; Former Chairman,
Lincoln Center for the Performing Arts; Winner of
One Grammy and Two Emmy Awards

◆

"This makes a wonderful Sunday brunch or midnight snack."

SERVES 2 TO 3

3 eggs
1/2 cup flour
1/2 cup milk
1/2 teaspoon vanilla extract
1/2 teaspoon salt
3 tablespoons butter, melted

1. Preheat the oven to 450°F.
2. Place an 8-inch iron skillet in the freezer.
3. Put the eggs, flour, milk, vanilla extract, and salt in a blender and blend at low speed.
4. Pour the melted butter into the cold skillet, follow with the batter, and bake for 10 to 12 minutes, until the crust is brown. The batter will puff up like a soufflé.
5. Serve immediately with jam, stewed fruit, maple syrup, or butter.

BREAKFAST PANCAKE

from **JUDY RANKIN**
Champion Professional Golfer, Sports Commentator,
Winner of Twenty-six Ladies Professional Golf
Association Tournaments

◆

SERVES 4

4 tablespoons (1/2 stick) butter
1/2 cup flour
1/2 cup milk
2 eggs
A few dashes of ground nutmeg
Powdered sugar, for dusting

1. Preheat the oven to 425°F.
2. Put the butter in a large pan and place it in the oven. (Make sure the pan is suitable for oven use.) Do not allow the butter to burn.
3. While the butter is melting, whisk together the flour, milk, eggs, and nutmeg.
4. Tip the pan so that the melted butter covers the bottom and pour in the batter.
5. Bake for 15 to 20 minutes, until the batter bubbles and the edges of the pancake are lightly browned. (I prefer it a little browner.)
6. Pour off the excess butter and dust the pancake with powdered sugar.
7. Place the pancake on a platter and cut it into wedges like a pie. Serve with syrup or, before cutting, fill with fresh peaches by topping one side and folding the other side over.

LEMON–POPPY SEED PANCAKES

SERVES 4

2 cups flour

1 teaspoon baking soda

1¹/₂ teaspoons baking powder

2 teaspoons sugar

¹/₂ teaspoon salt

2 cups unsalted buttermilk (or use regular buttermilk
  and omit the salt)

2 eggs, beaten

1 tablespoon light vegetable oil

Grated zest of 2 to 3 lemons

2 to 3 teaspoons lemon extract, more or less depending
  on how lemony you like your pancakes

2 teaspoons poppy seeds

1. Sift together the flour, baking soda, baking powder, sugar, and salt into a large bowl.
2. Mix the buttermilk, eggs, and light vegetable oil and add to the dry ingredients. Stir just until the flour is wet; don't overbeat. If the batter seems too thick to pour, add a little regular milk to thin it out. (If it's too thick, the pancakes won't cook thoroughly.)
3. Mix in the lemon zest, lemon extract, and poppy seeds.
4. Preheat a heavy griddle or skillet until a few drops of water sprinkled on it sizzle away instantly. Grease the pan by smearing it with a piece of paper towel with a pat of butter on it.
5. Using a very large spoon, ladle pancake-sized portions of the batter onto the pan.
6. Cook the pancakes on one side until the edges start to look dry and bubbles form. Then flip them. It helps to press down lightly on the pancakes with your spatula. Once the second side is nicely browned, flip them over one more time for a few seconds to cook any residue of uncooked batter that may have come up through the holes in the pancakes.
7. Serve immediately with maple syrup.

TIPS AND TIDBITS

+ Even though it's more expensive, try to get pure maple syrup, not maple-flavored syrup, which contains only a small amount of maple syrup mixed with other sweet syrups, such as corn and sugar syrups. Many "pancake syrups" have only artificial flavorings and no maple syrup at all.
+ When buying maple syrup, keep in mind that the paler syrups ("Fancy" and Grade AA) are milder and the darker ones (Grade A and Grade B) are more flavorful.

GRAPE-NUTS PUDDING

◆

4 cups skim milk

3 eggs, or 1 egg and 2 egg whites

¹/₃ cup sugar

1 tablespoon vanilla extract

1 cup Grape-Nuts cereal

1 tablespoon ground cinnamon mixed with 1 teaspoon sugar

1. Preheat the oven to 375°F.
2. Butter a 1¹/₂-quart (7 × 7 × 3-inch) casserole dish.
3. Heat the milk in a saucepan until it almost comes to a boil and a skin forms on the surface.
4. Beat the eggs in a blender, adding the sugar and vanilla extract and processing until incorporated.
5. Pour the blended egg mixture into the casserole dish.
6. Pour the Grape-Nuts over the egg mixture, sprinkle with the cinnamon-sugar mixture, and follow with the scalded milk.
7. Place the casserole dish in a large roasting pan containing 2 inches of water.
8. Bake in the middle of the oven for 1 hour. When done, the top will be crusty and the custard in the center will be solid. Serve hot or cold.

TIPS AND TIDBITS

✦ This also makes a great dessert or snack, and it keeps in the refrigerator for several days.

✦ If you don't have the exact size casserole dish called for, you can substitute a similar size (such as 7 × 5¹/₂ × 3 inches) or use a 2-quart casserole—just be sure it is at least 3 inches deep.

HUEVOS RANCHEROS
(Ranch-Style Eggs)

SERVES 4

¹/₂ onion, minced

1 large green bell pepper, seeded and minced

2 cloves garlic, minced

¹/₄ cup olive oil

¹/₄ cup hot salsa, or more to taste

2 cups tomato sauce

1 teaspoon dried oregano

¹/₂ teaspoon salt, or to taste

8 eggs

1. In a large skillet, sauté the onion, bell pepper, and garlic in the olive oil until the onion is golden.
2. Add the salsa, tomato sauce, oregano, and salt.
3. Simmer the mixture for 3 minutes and then break the eggs over it.
4. Cover the skillet and simmer for 7 minutes, or just until the eggs are set.
5. Serve with fresh fruit, English muffins, or a basket of interesting bread.

EASY EGG SOUFFLÉ

from **JENNIFER M. GRANHOLM**
Governor of Michigan

"Impress/fool your in-laws! Makes even the lousiest cook (like me) look like Julia Child!"

SERVES 4 TO 6

2 cups milk
6 eggs
1 teaspoon salt
6 slices bread, cubed
8 ounces English Cheddar cheese, grated or sliced
4 tablespoons (¹/₂ stick) butter, melted

1. Grease an 8 × 8 × 2-inch baking dish.
2. In a large bowl, beat together the milk, eggs, and salt.
3. Add the bread cubes.
4. Pour the mixture into the prepared baking dish, cover, and refrigerate overnight.
5. When ready to cook, preheat the oven to 375°F.
6. Place the cheese on top of the bread mixture and drizzle with the melted butter.
7. Bake for about 45 minutes, or until the cheese is golden brown.

SAN FRANCISCO–STYLE BERRY-STUFFED FRENCH TOAST

SERVES 9 TO 12

12 slices sourdough bread
8 ounces low-fat cream cheese
1 cup berries, your choice, fresh or frozen
10 eggs
¹/₃ cup maple syrup
2 cups low-fat milk

BERRY SAUCE

1 cup water

1 cup sugar

2 tablespoons cornstarch

1 cup berries, your choice, fresh or frozen

1 tablespoon butter

1. *To prepare the French toast:* Oil a 13 × 9-inch baking dish.
2. Trim the crusts from the bread and cut the slices into ³/₄-inch cubes.
3. Place half the cubes over the bottom of the prepared pan.
4. Cut the cream cheese into ³/₄-inch cubes and sprinkle the cubes over the bread layer.
5. Spread the berries over the cream cheese and place the remaining bread cubes over the top.
6. In a medium bowl, beat the eggs, maple syrup, and milk together, and pour over the bread.
7. Cover the baking dish with aluminum foil and press the foil down to make sure all of the bread is soaked. Refrigerate overnight.
8. When ready to bake, preheat the oven to 350°F.
9. Bake with the foil on for 30 minutes, then remove the foil and bake until the center is set and the top is lightly browned, about another 30 minutes.
10. Remove from the oven and allow to cool for 10 minutes before slicing.
11. *To prepare the berry sauce:* Stir the water, sugar, cornstarch, and berries in a saucepan over medium heat until thickened, 4 to 5 minutes. Add the butter and stir until melted. Serve warm.
12. Serve the French toast topped with the berry sauce.

TIPS AND TIDBITS

+ This dish is somewhat like a bread pudding in that the longer it is allowed to soak before baking, the fuller the flavor.

CRÈME BRÛLÉE FRENCH TOAST

◆

SERVES 8 TO 10

8 tablespoons (1 stick) unsalted butter
1 cup packed brown sugar
2 tablespoons light corn syrup
6 slices challah bread, plus more as needed
5 eggs
1½ cups skim milk
1 teaspoon vanilla extract
1 tablespoon ground cinnamon
½ cup raisins (optional)

1. Combine the butter, brown sugar, and corn syrup in a small saucepan over medium heat. Stir constantly until the mixture is smooth. Pour into a 13 × 9-inch baking dish.
2. Trim the crusts from the bread and arrange the slices in 1 layer on top of the warm mixture.
3. Whisk together the eggs, milk, vanilla extract, and cinnamon in a small bowl. Add the raisins if desired.
4. Pour the mixture evenly over the bread, cover the dish, and refrigerate overnight.
5. When you are ready to cook the French toast, preheat the oven to 350°F.
6. Remove the dish from the refrigerator and allow it to warm to room temperature.
7. Bake uncovered for 35 to 45 minutes, until the bread is puffed up and golden brown. Serve immediately.

TIPS AND TIDBITS
+ Light brown sugar is milder than the dark variety, which contains more molasses. Unless a recipe specifies either one, use whichever you prefer.
+ This recipe is easy and delicious and smells terrific while baking.

BAKED SAUSAGE AND APPLE PUDDING

♦

SERVES 4

1 cup flour

1 cup milk

2 eggs

1 teaspoon salt

A pinch or a grind of pepper

12 ounces of your favorite sausage (do not use small breakfast-
style links or any sausage that is very spicy)

6 small to medium apples, peeled, cored, and cut into slices
about ¼ to ½ inch thick

1 tablespoon butter

2 tablespoons brown sugar

1. Place the flour, milk, eggs, salt, and pepper in a blender or food processor and mix well. Scrape down the sides and mix again. Cover and allow to rest for 1 hour.
2. While the batter is resting, place the sausage in a large pan with 2 to 3 tablespoons of water. Cover the pan and cook for 4 to 5 minutes. Remove the cover and continue cooking, turning the sausage, until the links are brown. Remove from the pan and drain on paper towels.
3. Pour some of the sausage drippings into an 8 × 8-inch baking pan and set aside. Use enough of the drippings to cover the bottom of the baking pan.
4. Cut the sausage into chunks and set aside.
5. Place the apple slices, butter, and brown sugar in the same pan in which you browned the sausage. Cook, stirring often, until the apples are tender, 10 to 15 minutes. Stir in the sausage chunks and set the pan aside.
6. About 10 minutes before the batter is ready to use, preheat the oven to 450°F.

Continued

7. Place the baking pan with the sausage drippings in the oven until it is hot. This takes just a few minutes.
8. When the baking pan is hot, remove it from the oven and pour about one-quarter of the batter into it. Place it back in the oven and bake for 5 minutes.
9. Remove the pan from the oven and spread the apples and sausage over the cooked batter. Pour the remaining batter over them and place the pan back in the oven.
10. Bake for 15 minutes, lower the oven temperature to 375°F, and bake until the pudding is puffed and crusty, about another 15 minutes. Serve warm.

TIPS AND TIDBITS

+ This is a great dish for breakfast, but you can also make it for dinner, accompanied with mustard and served with a green salad. It is a version of the traditional English dish called "Toad in the Hole."

GAMOO'S BAKING POWDER BISCUITS

from **GLENN CLOSE**

Actress, Producer, Winner of Three Tony Awards and One Emmy

◆

MAKES 16 TO 18 BISCUITS

2 cups flour

¹/₂ teaspoon salt

4 teaspoons baking powder

¹/₂ teaspoon cream of tartar

2 teaspoons sugar

8 tablespoons (1 stick) butter (butter is best, but margarine or even Crisco is a possible substitution)

²/₃ cup milk

1. Preheat the oven to 425°F.
2. Sift together the flour, salt, baking powder, cream of tartar, and sugar.
3. Cut the butter into small pieces and add to the flour mixture. Using a fork or your fingers, crumble the pieces until the mixture resembles coarse crumbs.
4. Add the milk all at once and stir until the dough follows the fork around the bowl.
5. Place the dough on a floured surface and pat or roll it out until it is about ½ inch thick.
6. Cut the dough into rounds with a biscuit cutter and place the rounds on an ungreased baking sheet.
7. Bake for about 10 to 12 minutes, until golden brown. The biscuits should be crisp on the top and bottom but tender and flaky inside.

BANANA MUFFINS

MAKES 12 MUFFINS

8 tablespoons (1 stick) unsalted butter, at room temperature

1 cup sugar

2 eggs

4 ripe medium bananas, mashed

2 cups flour

1 teaspoon baking soda

1 teaspoon baking powder

½ teaspoon salt

1. Preheat the oven to 350°F.
2. Grease a 12-cup muffin tin.
3. With an electric mixer, beat the butter and sugar until smooth.

Continued

4. Add the eggs and mashed bananas, beating until blended.
5. In a separate bowl, combine the flour with the baking soda, baking powder, and salt, and gradually add to the banana mixture.
6. Pour the batter into the prepared muffin tin and bake for about 35 minutes, or until a toothpick comes out clean. Remove to a wire rack and allow the muffins to cool.

TIPS AND TIDBITS

✦ For a nice variation, add some fresh blueberries to the batter.

✦ For an easier cleanup, use paper or foil cups to line the muffin tin.

✦ As bananas ripen, their skins may blacken. Don't worry; they are probably fine for eating and may even be sweeter.

CRANBERRY BREAD OR MUFFINS
◆

SERVES 8 TO 10

2 cups flour

³/₄ cup sugar

1¹/₂ teaspoons baking powder

¹/₂ teaspoon baking soda

1 scant teaspoon salt

³/₄ cup orange juice

2 tablespoons unsalted butter or margarine, cut into very small pieces

1 egg

1 tablespoon grated orange peel (optional)

1 cup cranberries, washed and coarsely chopped

¹/₂ cup chopped walnuts

1. Preheat the oven to 350°F.
2. Prepare a 9 × 5-inch loaf pan by greasing it only on the bottom. (If you are making muffins, similarly grease a muffin tin or place paper or foil muffin-cup liners in the tin.)
3. In a large bowl, mix together the flour, sugar, baking powder, baking soda, and salt.
4. Stir in the orange juice, butter, egg, and orange peel, if desired.
5. Stir in the cranberries and nuts, and pour into the prepared loaf pan.
6. Bake for about 55 to 60 minutes (muffins take about 40 minutes), until the top is somewhat crusty and pale brown and springs back when lightly pressed.
7. Allow to cool for about 15 minutes before removing from the pan.

TIPS AND TIDBITS

✦ Here is a quick, easy way to prepare the batter in a food processor:

1. Place the flour, sugar, baking powder, baking soda, and salt in the processor bowl. Process for a few seconds.
2. Add the juice, butter, egg, and orange peel, and process until blended.
3. Add the whole berries and nuts and turn the machine on and off very quickly a few times. Don't let them get too finely chopped.

✦ Cranberry bread stores well in the freezer. Defrost at room temperature and reheat (unwrapped) before serving.

MONKEY BREAD

from **NANCY REAGAN**

Former First Lady

◆

MAKES 2 LOAVES

1 package active dry yeast
1¹/₄ cups milk
3 eggs
3 tablespoons sugar
1 teaspoon salt
3¹/₂ cups flour
12 tablespoons (1¹/₂ sticks) butter, at room temperature
¹/₂ pound (2 sticks) butter, melted

1. In a large bowl, combine the yeast with about ¹/₄ cup of the milk (warmed up a little) and stir until dissolved.
2. Beat in 2 of the eggs.
3. Mix in the sugar, salt, and flour, and add the remaining 1 cup of milk, a little at a time, mixing thoroughly.
4. Cut in the 12 tablespoons of butter until it is well blended and the dough comes together to form a ball.
5. Knead the dough until it becomes elastic, and let it rise until it has doubled in size, 1 to 1¹/₂ hours.
6. Knead again and let the dough rise for another 40 minutes.
7. Preheat the oven to 375°F.
8. Butter and flour two 9-inch ring molds.
9. Roll the dough onto a floured board and shape into a long log. Cut the log into 28 equal pieces and shape each piece into a ball.
10. Roll the dough balls in the melted butter and place 7 balls in each ring mold, leaving some space between the balls. Place the remaining 14 balls on top, dividing them between the ring molds and spacing them evenly. Let the dough rise in the molds.
11. In a small bowl, lightly beat the 1 remaining egg and brush the tops of the loaves with it.
12. Bake for 15 to 25 minutes, until golden brown.

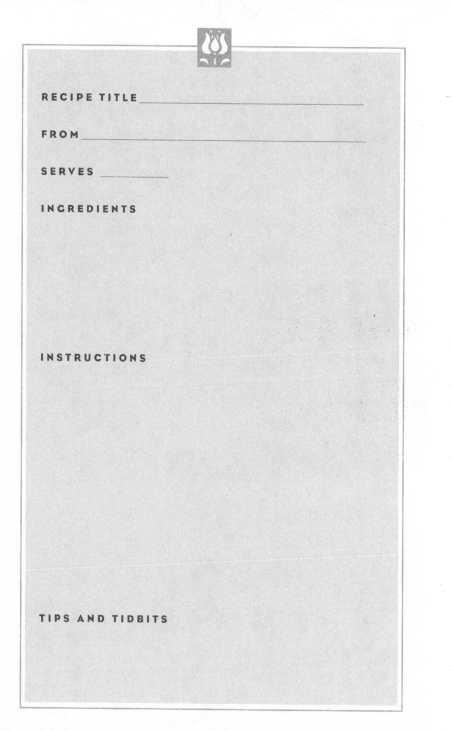

RECIPE TITLE

FROM

SERVES

INGREDIENTS

INSTRUCTIONS

TIPS AND TIDBITS

RECIPE TITLE_____

FROM_____

SERVES _____

INGREDIENTS

INSTRUCTIONS

TIPS AND TIDBITS

APPETIZERS
AND SNACKS

Also check out:

LOW-FAT SNACKS

Low-fat snacks can be delicious and satisfying. Here are some of our favorites:

+ Fruit (you knew we'd say that!).
+ Frozen fruits: Try putting some loose grapes in a plastic container in the freezer. They won't stick together and you can pop them a few at a time. Blueberries and chunks of banana are also delicious frozen.
+ Dried fruits: Although apricots, prunes, raisins, and the like may be high in sugar, they still make healthy snacks because they contain many vitamins and minerals as well as fiber.
+ Fat-free ices or sorbets and low-fat or nonfat frozen yogurt or ice cream: These are always better choices than their regular counterparts, which often have as many as 16 grams of fat per serving. And they are now available in a wide variety of interesting flavors and combinations.
+ Pretzels: Because they are baked, pretzels are always a healthier choice than potato chips and other snacks that are fried. But since some brands of pretzels are lower in fat than others, be sure to check the label.
+ Air-popped popcorn (of course, skip the butter): This is always a good snack. But if you can't live without the taste of butter, a good substitute is I Can't Believe It's Not Butter! spray.
+ Toasted frozen waffles: Try the low-fat, whole grain varieties, which are delicious topped with jam (preferably the "all fruit" kind), maple syrup, or your favorite frozen yogurt.
+ Sweetened cereal: While not great as a daily breakfast food, this can be a handy snack.
+ Fat-free or low-fat crispbread, flatbread, and corn or rice cakes (which come in a number of flavors, including caramel, chocolate, and popcorn): These are all good snack choices. But do read the labels, since many similar-looking products are high in fat.

HEALTHY SANDWICHES

+ Whole grain breads, which provide more nutrients and fiber, are a better choice than white bread.

- Pita bread is another good alternative to white bread or rolls and can easily be stuffed with leftovers or salad. For added fiber and flavor, use whole wheat pita.
- Mashed avocado is a great alternative to butter, mayonnaise, or margarine as a sandwich spread. It adds a delicious creamy flavor, has some nutritional value, and is lower in calories and fat.
- Slices of fruit and vegetables (especially tomatoes) are also wonderful substitutes for mayonnaise or butter, adding moistness and flavor.

QUICK DIPPING SAUCES FOR FRESH VEGGIES

Fresh vegetables—carrots, celery, cauliflower, cucumber, red, yellow, and green bell peppers, green beans, zucchini, scallions—make wonderful healthy snacks, especially when served with a flavorful dipping sauce. Keep the cut-up vegetables in bowls of cold water, but pat them dry before serving.

- The old classic: a package of Lipton onion soup mixed well with 2 cups of sour cream or plain yogurt.
- Your favorite salad dressing thickened with a little plain yogurt or sour cream and, if you like it hot, a pinch of cayenne pepper, minced garlic, or other spices.
- Equal amounts of tahini and plain yogurt, seasoned to taste with lemon juice and cumin.
- A can of black bean soup blended into a puree and mixed with plain yogurt or sour cream and seasoned to taste with cumin or Tabasco red pepper sauce.
- One cup of plain yogurt or sour cream mixed with 3 tablespoons of drained white horseradish, 1 teaspoon of Dijon mustard, and salt and pepper to taste.

Naturally, using low-fat sour cream or yogurt makes these dips healthier.

EASY CLAM APPETIZER

One 8-ounce can minced clams, liquid reserved
4 heaping tablespoons bread crumbs
¹/₄ cup olive oil
³/₄ tablespoon garlic powder
³/₄ tablespoon minced onion
Dried oregano to taste
1 tablespoon grated Parmesan cheese

1. Mix the clams and half the liquid from the can with the bread crumbs, olive oil, garlic powder, minced onion, and oregano.
2. Spoon the mixture into 2 scallop shells (each about 3 inches wide) and sprinkle with the Parmesan cheese.
3. Just before serving, heat in the broiler for about 10 minutes, or until browned.

TIPS AND TIDBITS

✦ You can buy scallop shells in many supermarkets or kitchen supply stores.

OYSTERS À LA OLIVIER

from **"LINDY" BOGGS**

Former Congresswoman from Louisiana,
Former Ambassador to the Vatican

◆

"This recipe is from my great-aunt, Anita Olivier Morrison."

SERVES 6

1 tablespoon chopped scallion (green onions)
½ teaspoon chopped garlic
One 8-ounce can mushrooms, drained and chopped
2 dozen large oysters, shucked
Flour (enough to powder the oysters)
12 tablespoons (1½ sticks) butter
½ teaspoon salt
½ teaspoon black pepper
6 to 8 ounces dry sherry
1 tablespoon Worcestershire sauce
6 slices buttered toast
2 tablespoons chopped fresh parsley

1. Combine the scallion, garlic, and mushrooms and rechop them together.
2. Dry the oysters and powder them with the flour.
3. In a heavy frying pan, heat 4 tablespoons of the butter until bubbly. Quickly brown the oysters in the butter until their edges curl. Remove from the heat.
4. In another pan, place the chopped scallion, garlic, and mushroom mixture and add the remaining 8 tablespoons butter. Fry until the butter is melted.
5. Add the salt, pepper, sherry, and Worcestershire sauce and stir until blended.
6. Place the oysters on the buttered toast, pour the sauce over them, and garnish with the chopped parsley.

SHRIMP COCKTAIL

◆

SERVES 6

SHRIMP

1 teaspoon pickling spice

1 stalk celery, coarsely chopped

3 to 4 black peppercorns

1 pound large shrimp, shelled and deveined

COCKTAIL SAUCE

1 cup chili sauce or ketchup

3 to 4 tablespoons drained white horseradish

2 tablespoons fresh lemon juice

1 teaspoon Worcestershire sauce

Salt and black pepper to taste

A splash of Tabasco red pepper sauce

1. *To prepare the shrimp:* Bring a large pot of water to a boil and add a pinch or two of salt. Add the pickling spice, celery, and peppercorns to the water and let simmer for about 5 minutes. (If you have a tea infuser, put the pickling spice in it and place it in the pot.)
2. Bring the water to a vigorous boil and add the shrimp all at once, stirring to keep them from clumping.
3. Once the water returns to a second boil, turn off the heat and drain the shrimp in a colander.
4. Cool the cooked shrimp under cold running water. To cool them more quickly, place them in a bowl with ice and cold water, cover the bowl, and place in the refrigerator. Pat them dry before serving.
5. *To prepare the sauce:* Combine the chili sauce, horseradish, lemon juice, Worcestershire sauce, salt and pepper, and Tabasco sauce. Mix well and refrigerate.
6. Serve with the chilled shrimp.

✦ Pickling spice is a packaged mixture of cinnamon, allspice, mustard seeds, coriander, bay leaves, ginger, and other spices. You can find it in the spice section of your supermarket.

✦ Prepared horseradish is available in two varieties: red and white. The red owes its color to the addition of beets, which also slightly affects its flavor.

TARTE AU FROMAGE
(Cheese Pie)

◆

SERVES 8 TO 10

One 17-ounce package frozen puff pastry sheets or a 16-ounce
  package of frozen phyllo dough, thawed according to
  package directions
1 pound grated or shredded cheese, preferably a mixture of
  Gruyère, Swiss, and Parmigiano-Reggiano
2 eggs
2 cups half-and-half
Salt and pepper to taste
A pinch of ground nutmeg

1. Preheat the oven to 375°F.
2. Butter well a rectangular baking pan about 15 × 10 × 1 inch, preferably nonstick.
3. Cover the baking pan with enough pastry sheets to form a thin, even layer.
4. Spread the grated cheese evenly over the dough, covering it completely.
5. Using a whisk, beat the eggs with the half-and-half, salt and pepper, and nutmeg until foamy.

Continued

6. Drizzle the egg-and-cream mixture over the cheese.
7. Bake for about 30 minutes, or until the edges are golden and crisp and the cheese mixture is a deep golden color as well.
8. Serve warm.

TIPS AND TIDBITS

+ This is a typical dish from the Jura region of France. It makes a wonderful appetizer or lunch dish.

ONION AND TOMATO TART
(Pissaladière)
◆

MAKES TWO 14-INCH TARTS

½ cup olive oil, plus more as needed
1 clove garlic, crushed
6 onions, minced
1 tablespoon sugar, plus more to taste
One half of a 35-ounce can crushed tomatoes
A pinch of herbes de Provence, plus more as needed
Salt and pepper to taste
2 frozen pizza shells, unthawed, or a 32-ounce package of frozen pizza dough, thawed
Pitted olives, preferably black Niçoise or Kalamata

1. Preheat the oven to 425°F.
2. Heat the olive oil in a sauté pan and add the garlic and onions.
3. Sauté the onions and garlic in the olive oil until the onions are soft.
4. Add the sugar to caramelize the onions, and continue cooking until the onions turn a deep golden color, about 30 minutes.
5. Add the crushed tomatoes, the herbes de Provence, salt and pepper, and, if necessary, additional sugar. Simmer for 20 minutes and allow to cool.

6. While the sauce is cooling, oil two 14-inch round pizza pans with olive oil.
7. Place the frozen pizza shells on the pans and oil the top of the dough.
8. Spread the onion and tomato mixture completely over the pizza shells.
9. Sprinkle with herbes de Provence and drizzle with olive oil. The oil keeps the tarts from drying out.
10. Decorate with the olives and bake for about 30 minutes, or until the edges are golden and crisp.

TIPS AND TIDBITS

✦ This pizzalike tart is a typical dish from Nice and Monaco, often served for lunch or as an appetizer. Although the authentic version is made with pizza dough, you can also use puff pastry or phyllo dough.

✦ If they are available, Vidalia onions are particularly delicious in this recipe.

✦ Herbes de Provence is a combination of dried herbs, usually basil, fennel seeds, lavender, marjoram, rosemary, sage, summer savory, and thyme. You can purchase this blend in a small jar or crock in the spice section of your supermarket.

MUSHROOM-SPINACH SOUFFLÉ ROLL

◆

SERVES 10

FILLING

2 tablespoons butter

4 shallots, finely chopped

1¹/₂ to 2 cups chopped mushrooms

Continued

1 cup frozen chopped spinach, thawed and well drained

1 tablespoon Dijon mustard

Two 3-ounce packages cream cheese, at room temperature

Salt and pepper to taste

SOUFFLÉ LAYER

4 tablespoons ($^1/_2$ stick) butter

$^1/_2$ cup flour

$^1/_2$ teaspoon salt

$^1/_8$ teaspoon white pepper

2 cups milk

5 eggs, separated

1. Preheat the oven to 400°F.
2. Grease a 15$^1/_2$ × 10 × 1-inch jelly-roll pan. Line with waxed paper, grease again, and dust lightly with flour.
3. *To prepare the filling:* Melt the butter in a skillet and sauté the shallots until tender.
4. Add the mushrooms and cook until they give up their moisture and it evaporates, about 5 minutes.
5. Add the spinach, mustard, and cream cheese and stir. Add salt and pepper to taste.
6. *To prepare the soufflé layer:* Melt the butter in a saucepan and blend in the flour, salt, white pepper, and milk.
7. Bring to a boil, stirring, and cook for 1 minute.
8. Lightly beat the egg yolks, adding a little of the hot milk mixture while beating.
9. Pour the egg yolks into the saucepan with the milk mixture, and cook, stirring, on medium heat for about 1 minute. Do not let it boil.
10. Remove from the heat and allow to cool to room temperature. Stir occasionally.
11. Beat the egg whites until stiff but not dry, and fold into the cooled sauce.
12. Pour into the prepared jelly-roll pan and spread evenly.
13. Bake for 25 to 30 minutes, until well puffed and browned.

14. *To assemble:* As soon as the soufflé layer is done, turn it onto a clean kitchen towel and spread the filling over it. (The filling should still be warm, but if not, reheat it slightly.)
15. Using the towel, roll up the filled soufflé layer to form a jelly roll. Don't worry if it cracks a little.
16. Slide the roll onto a serving platter, seam side down, and cut into 1-inch slices. Serve at room temperature.

TIPS AND TIDBITS

✦ Although this recipe is somewhat complicated, it is really worth the effort. It is particularly attractive and delicious and also makes an impressive lunch or brunch dish.

SUMMER ROLLS

from **NICOLE MILLER**
Fashion Designer; President, Nicole Miller, Ltd.

◆

"It takes a few tries to get these right, but after a while, you get the hang of it. Then you can work on making them look pretty by arranging the leaves as you make the rolls."

MAKES 20 ROLLS

ROLLS

20 rice papers
1 head Boston lettuce
1 package rice stick noodles, cooked according to
package directions
½ cup hoisin sauce, or to taste
1 pound shrimp, shelled, deveined, and cooked, each shrimp cut
in half lengthwise

Continued

1 bunch fresh mint leaves

1 bunch fresh cilantro

1 bunch fresh chives, at least 40 stems (optional)

NUOC CHAM

$^1/_2$ cup fish sauce

$^1/_2$ cup rice wine vinegar

$^1/_2$ cup water

$^1/_4$ cup fresh lime juice

$^1/_4$ cup sugar

1 jalapeño or other chili pepper, finely chopped

2 teaspoons finely chopped garlic

1. *To prepare the rolls:* Lay out a clean kitchen towel on the counter and have all of the ingredients ready.
2. Dip a rice paper in a large bowl of lukewarm water until partially soft but not soggy. This requires a little experimentation to see what works the best.
3. Remove the rice paper from the bowl and lay it out on the kitchen towel.
4. Pat dry with a paper towel.
5. Place half a leaf of lettuce (with the core removed) in the center of the rice paper.
6. Put a handful of rice stick noodles on top and spread out lengthwise.
7. Spread a small amount of hoisin sauce on top.
8. Arrange 3 shrimp halves lengthwise on top of the noodles.
9. Place 2 mint leaves and some cilantro on top.
10. Fold over the top of the rice paper tightly and start forming the roll. Fold in the sides and finish the roll. You may add 2 chives for decoration just before you are finished rolling. If you are not serving the rolls right away, cover them with wet kitchen towels.
11. Just before serving, cut the rolls in half or into quarters with a scissors.
12. *To prepare the nuoc cham:* Combine all of the ingredients in a jar and shake well. Let marinate for at least 2 hours before serving.

13. Serve the spring rolls with the nuoc cham or your favorite peanut sauce.

MEATY COCKTAIL SANDWICHES

MAKES ABOUT 30 SMALL OPEN-FACED SANDWICHES

1 pound hot sausage
1 pound ground beef
1 medium onion, chopped
1 teaspoon dried oregano
1 teaspoon Worcestershire sauce
1 pound Velveeta cheese
2 loaves sliced cocktail rye bread

1. Remove the casing from the sausage and chop the meat.
2. Cook the sausage meat and the ground beef together in a heavy skillet, breaking up the beef with a wooden spoon, until the meat is no longer pink.
3. Add the onion and cook until it is soft and translucent.
4. Add the oregano, Worcestershire sauce, and Velveeta, stirring until the cheese is melted.
5. Place the rye bread slices on a cookie sheet and spoon 1 tablespoon of the mixture on top of each slice.
6. When ready to serve, place under the broiler for about 5 minutes, or until bubbly. Serve hot.

TIPS AND TIDBITS

+ To reduce the fat but keep most of the flavor, use chicken or turkey sausage.
+ It's a good idea to double the recipe and freeze half. You can place the cookie sheet directly in the freezer. Once the sandwiches are frozen, place them in a plastic bag and store in the freezer until ready to use. Don't defrost before broiling.

CHEESE WAFERS

from **LADY BIRD JOHNSON**
Former First Lady; Founder, the Lady Bird Johnson
Wildflower Center

◆

"Cheese wafers are a 'ranch staple' that is served on all occasions: with salads, with cocktails, etc., or just when one of the grandchildren gets the munchies!"

MAKES ABOUT 60 WAFERS

2 cups flour
$^1/_2$ pound (2 sticks) butter or margarine, at room temperature, cut into small pieces
8 ounces sharp Cheddar cheese, grated
1 teaspoon cayenne pepper
$^1/_2$ teaspoon salt
2 cups Rice Krispies cereal

1. Preheat the oven to 350°F.
2. Place the flour in a large bowl and stir in the pieces of butter. Using a fork or your fingers, crumble the pieces until the mixture resembles coarse bread crumbs.
3. Add the grated cheese, cayenne, and salt, and mix well. Fold in the Rice Krispies.
4. Drop by small spoonfuls onto an ungreased cookie sheet and flatten each mound with the back of a spoon.
5. Bake for about 15 minutes. Don't let them get too brown.

TEXAS-STYLE GUACAMOLE

from **DIANE RAVITCH**

Historian, Author

♦

"This is a great dish to serve with cocktails, and easily whipped up at the last minute. When you buy the avocados, make sure they are tender to the touch but not too soft. The dark green Hass avocados are best. If they are hard when you buy them, leave them in a brown paper bag until they ripen (it may take a day or two)."

SERVES 6

2 or more ripe avocados, peeled and pitted
Lemon juice to taste
Salt and pepper to taste
1 tablespoon diced sweet onion, or more
2 to 3 tablespoons finely diced ripe fresh tomato

1. Slice and mash the avocados with a knife and fork, crushing until all the lumps are gone.
2. As you mash, sprinkle abundantly with lemon juice and salt and pepper.
3. Stir in the diced onion and tomato.
4. Sprinkle with more lemon juice to keep the guacamole from darkening. Serve with corn chips.

BLACK BEAN HUMMUS

◆

2 cups canned black beans, rinsed and drained
1 cup canned chickpeas, rinsed and drained
1 tablespoon minced garlic
1 teaspoon ground cumin
2 tablespoons tahini, or more to taste
1 tablespoon lemon juice, preferably fresh
¹/₄ cup olive oil

1. Process all of the ingredients in a blender or food processor until fairly smooth and creamy.
2. Adjust the seasoning and add a little more lemon juice or some water if the hummus is too thick. Store in the refrigerator.

TIPS AND TIDBITS

✦ This hummus is a wonderful spread for pita bread or dip for raw vegetables.

✦ Tahini is a sesame seed paste that can be found in almost every supermarket, sometimes near the peanut butter. It comes in cans and jars and lasts for months in the refrigerator but has to be well stirred every time you use it because the oil separates out.

INDIAN PEANUT DIP

◆

MAKES ABOUT 1 CUP

¹/₂ cup crunchy peanut butter
¹/₄ cup minced onion
¹/₄ cup fresh lemon juice
1 tablespoon soy sauce
2 teaspoons minced garlic
2 teaspoons ground coriander
¹/₄ cup minced fresh parsley

1. Combine all of the ingredients in the bowl of a food processor. Mix for about 1 minute or until they are well blended.
2. Serve at room temperature with crisp vegetables.

GRAMMA'S LOW-FAT SALMON MOUSSE

from **EUGENIA ZUKERMAN**
Flutist; Author; Arts Correspondent, CBS News' Sunday Morning;
Artistic Director, Vail Valley Music Festival

◆

MAKES ABOUT 3 CUPS

1 packet plain gelatin
Juice of ¹/₂ lemon
1 slice onion
¹/₄ cup boiling water
One 16-ounce can salmon (Rubinstein's is best)
¹/₂ cup low-fat mayonnaise

Continued

1 cup plain yogurt
1 teaspoon drained white horseradish
Dill to taste
Salt and pepper to taste
¹/₂ teaspoon curry powder (optional)

1. Combine and process in a blender the gelatin, lemon juice, onion, and water.
2. Add the salmon and blend.
3. Pour the mixture into a bowl and mix in the mayonnaise, yogurt, horseradish, dill, salt and pepper, and curry, if desired. Transfer to an attractive bowl and refrigerate.
4. Serve as a dip, or spread on black bread or crackers.

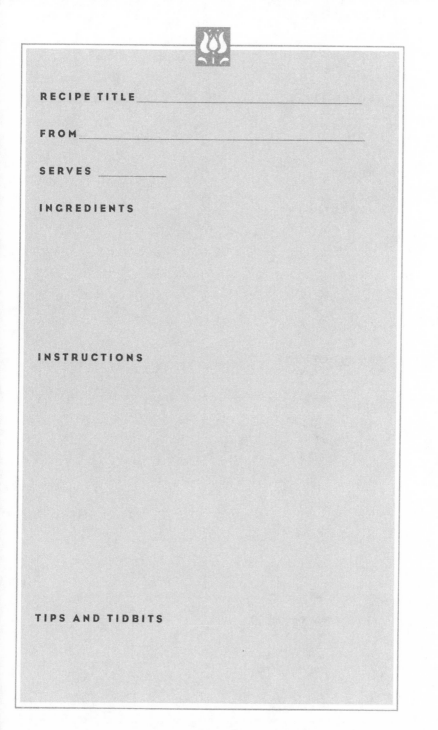

RECIPE TITLE

FROM

SERVES

INGREDIENTS

INSTRUCTIONS

TIPS AND TIDBITS

RECIPE TITLE_____

FROM_____

SERVES _____

INGREDIENTS

INSTRUCTIONS

TIPS AND TIDBITS

SOUPS

MAKING SOUP

✦ Always start with cold water. Hot tap water sometimes contains minerals that may affect the soup's flavor.

✦ Use a large pot with a heavy bottom, such as good-quality stainless steel or enameled cast iron.

✦ A covered pot requires less heat than one that is uncovered or only partially covered. A cover also prevents evaporation and keeps the soup from getting too thick.

+ A handheld electric blender, also called an immersion blender, is wonderful for pureeing soup right in the pot. It saves transferring the hot soup to a food processor or blender.

+ To reheat soup, bring it to a gentle simmer on the stove, being careful not to overcook it. You can also reheat it in a microwave oven, but be sure to stir it so it heats evenly thoughout.

+ Leftover soup, especially if it contains beans, tends to thicken in the refrigerator. If this happens, add some water or broth when reheating it.

REMOVING THE FAT FROM SOUP

+ The easiest way to remove fat from soup is to place the pot, once it has cooled, in the freezer or refrigerator for several hours. Once the fat has risen to the top and hardened, you can lift it off with a spoon or spatula.

+ A quicker way to remove the fat is to skim it off the hot soup with a large spoon or a special ladle designed for this purpose. This method is much faster than refrigerating the soup but is not as effective.

+ If the hot soup has only a small amount of fat on the surface, you should be able to remove most of it by "wiping" the surface with a paper towel.

DRIED BEANS VERSUS CANNED BEANS

+ Many soups are made with beans and it is a good idea to keep a supply of canned beans on hand. Be sure to rinse them well and drain them before using.

+ If you are using dried beans, which tend to be firmer and more flavorful than canned beans, be sure to follow the package directions for soaking them.

+ Soaking the beans overnight is generally considered the best way to prepare dried beans.

+ A quicker soaking method calls for boiling the dried beans for a minute or two, removing the pot from the heat, and letting it stand, covered, for an hour.

+ Another quick method calls for covering the dried beans with 2 inches of boiling water, covering the pot, and letting it stand for an hour or more, until the beans have plumped to twice their original size.

SERVING SIZES

+ If you are serving soup as a first course, count on 1 cup per person.

+ If the soup is a main course, served with bread and a salad, you'll need 1 1/2 to 2 cups per person.

ASPARAGUS SOUP

from **JUDITH VIORST**
Author, Poet, Winner of One Emmy Award

◆

"This recipe was invented by Leslie Oberdorfer."

S E R V E S   1 2

2 onions, chopped
2 cloves garlic, minced
3 tablespoons butter
Six 15-ounce cans asparagus, drained (do not use
  fresh asparagus)
Salt to taste
Lemon pepper to taste
Six 14-ounce cans chicken broth (College Inn is best)
1 to 1¹/₂ tablespoons fresh lemon juice, or to taste
1¹/₂ teaspoons ground cumin, or to taste
Sour cream, for garnish
Red caviar, for garnish

1. Sauté the onions and garlic in the butter until the onions are soft.
2. Transfer to a large, heavy pot and add the asparagus, salt, lemon pepper, and chicken broth. Simmer for 20 to 30 minutes.
3. Add the lemon juice and blend with a handheld electric blender or in a blender or food processor until smooth.
4. Stir in the cumin.
5. Serve hot, cold, or at room temperature, topped with a dab of sour cream and red caviar.

BLUEBERRY SOUP

◆

SERVES 3 TO 4

¹/₃ cup frozen pineapple juice concentrate, thawed
¹/₂ cup water
1 teaspoon lemon juice, preferably fresh
2¹/₂ cups fresh or unsweetened frozen blueberries, washed
    and stemmed
¹/₂ teaspoon vanilla extract

1. Combine the pineapple juice concentrate, water, and lemon juice in a blender. *Do not use a food processor.*
2. Add 1¹/₂ cups of the blueberries and blend until smooth.
3. Add the remaining 1 cup blueberries and the vanilla extract. Stir well (do not blend) and serve immediately.

TIPS AND TIDBITS

✦ If you are not serving the soup immediately, refrigerate it before adding the remaining whole berries. If it thickens or separates in the refrigerator, put it back in the blender for a minute and then add the whole berries.

✦ If the blueberries are too tart or you would like to serve this as a dessert, add a bit of sugar or artificial sweetener.

✦ If you like chunkier soup, add more whole blueberries or pieces of other fruits, such as sliced strawberries or small melon balls.

CREAM OF BROCCOLI SOUP—
WITH NO CREAM

from **ROSALYNN CARTER**

Former First Lady;
Vice Chair, the Carter Center

◆

SERVES 4

1 medium onion, chopped
1 clove garlic, crushed
1 bay leaf
1 tablespoon sunflower or other vegetable oil (or spray the pan
    with Pam)
1 pound broccoli, stalks and florets, chopped
1 small potato, peeled and chopped
2¹/₂ cups vegetable or chicken broth
Salt and pepper to taste
Juice of ¹/₂ lemon (about 1 to 1¹/₂ tablespoons)
Plain low-fat yogurt or sour cream, for garnish

1. Sauté the onion, garlic, and bay leaf in the sunflower oil until the
   onion is soft, 3 to 4 minutes.
2. Add the broccoli, potato, and broth and simmer gently, covered,
   until the broccoli is tender but still bright green, about 10 minutes.
3. Remove the bay leaf and allow the mixture to cool a little.
4. Puree in a blender until nearly smooth. Season with salt and pepper and add the lemon juice.
5. Serve hot—you may need to reheat the soup just before serving—
   and garnish with a dollop of yogurt or sour cream.

CHICKEN SOUP

◆

One 3 to 4-pound chicken, cut up
8 cups low-sodium chicken broth, preferably College Inn
2 to 3 carrots, peeled and cut into pennies
1/2 cup chopped leeks, white and green parts
1 stalk celery with its leaves, coarsely chopped
1/2 bunch fresh dill
Salt and pepper to taste

1. Combine the chicken and the broth in a large pot and bring to a boil. Reduce the heat, partially cover, and simmer until the chicken is cooked, about 20 minutes. Periodically skim off any foamy material that rises to the surface.
2. Remove the chicken from the pot, allow to cool, and remove the meat from the bones. Cut the meat into bite-sized pieces.
3. While the chicken is cooling, use a paper towel or spoon to skim the fat from the surface of the soup.
4. Add the vegetables and the dill to the soup and simmer for about 10 minutes. Remove the dill with a slotted spoon or tongs.
5. Return the chicken to the soup, add salt and pepper, and serve.

TIPS AND TIDBITS

✦ This soup is very rich and becomes even heartier if you add cooked noodles or rice just before serving.

✦ Or, if you prefer a clear broth, strain the soup and discard the vegetables before returning the chicken to the soup.

✦ If you tie the dill together with kitchen string, it is easier to remove.

MY FAVORITE CHICKEN-
MUSHROOM SOUP

from **SHIRLEY MacLAINE**
*Actress, Singer, Dancer, Author, Winner of One
Academy Award and Three Emmy Awards*

◆

SERVES 4

1 chicken, about 3 pounds (set aside the liver)
1 clove garlic, crushed
1 teaspoon ground coriander
1 teaspoon crushed black peppercorns
4 ounces mushrooms, sliced
1 teaspoon soy sauce

1. Cook the chicken in water—just enough to cover—until tender.
2. Remove the meat from the bones and cut into small pieces.
3. Place the chicken bones back in the water and boil gently for about 2 hours. Strain and set the stock aside.
4. In a large skillet, sauté the garlic, coriander, and peppercorns in a small amount of oil.
5. Add the mushrooms, chicken meat, chicken liver, soy sauce, and 4 cups of the chicken stock. Simmer for 10 to 15 minutes, stir well, and serve.

CLAM CHOWDER FOR A PARTY

◆

SERVES 15 TO 20

8 ounces fresh mushrooms, chopped
2 tablespoons butter or margarine

Two 10-ounce cans New England clam chowder
One 10-ounce can cream of asparagus soup
One 10-ounce can cream of celery soup
One 10-ounce can cream of mushroom soup
Two 14-ounce cans stewed tomatoes
One 16-ounce can green beans, drained
One 16-ounce can creamed corn
One 6-ounce can clams, drained and chopped
2 cups milk
²/₃ cup sherry
2 tablespoons chopped fresh parsley
³/₄ teaspoon curry powder
¹/₂ teaspoon pepper

1. In a very large, heavy pot, sauté the mushrooms in the butter until they start to brown.
2. Add all of the other ingredients, stir well to combine, and bring to a simmer.
3. Cook until thoroughly heated and serve hot.

TIPS AND TIDBITS
✦ This is a quick and easy party dish everyone will love. Serve with crusty bread or rolls.

EASY HEARTY CORN CHOWDER

from **KAY BAILEY HUTCHISON**
U.S. Senator from Texas

◆

SERVES 6

One 14-ounce can creamed corn
One 15-ounce can whole kernel corn
One 10-ounce can cream of chicken soup
1 potato, peeled and chopped into small pieces
³/₄ cup chopped celery
¹/₂ cup chopped cooked bacon, sausage, or ham
Salt and pepper to taste

1. Combine all of the ingredients in a large pot and cook over low heat until the potatoes and celery are tender, about 15 to 20 minutes.
2. Add water for the desired thickness.

COLD CUCUMBER SOUP

from **AGNES GUND**
Former President, Museum of Modern Art;
Recipient, National Medal of Arts

◆

SERVES 4

1 cucumber, peeled, seeded, and cut into pieces
1 scallion (green onion), white and some of green,
    or 1 shallot, minced
One 10-ounce can cream of chicken soup
One 10-ounce soup can measure of milk
1 cup plain yogurt or sour cream or a combination of both
1 tablespoon minced fresh dill
¹/₄ teaspoon dried basil
Salt to taste
¹/₂ cup small raisins (optional)

1. Place the cucumber and scallion in a blender with some of the cream of chicken soup. Blend until the desired consistency is reached, but do not puree.

2. Pour the mixture into a large bowl. With a wire whisk, stir in the rest of the soup along with the milk, yogurt, dill, and basil.
3. Add salt, and stir in the raisins, if desired.
4. Chill several hours or overnight. Serve cold.

GAZPACHO

◆

SERVES 4 TO 6

¹/₂ cup canned tomato juice, preferably Sacramento, plus more as needed

1 small onion, cut into chunks

1 medium green bell pepper, seeded and cut into chunks

1 medium cucumber, peeled and cut into chunks

1 clove garlic, minced

A few sprigs of fresh dill (optional)

¹/₂ teaspoon salt

2 tablespoons olive oil

1 tablespoon cider vinegar or white vinegar

5 large ripe tomatoes, peeled, or 8 to 10 canned peeled tomatoes or a combination of both fresh and canned tomatoes

A few drops of Tabasco red pepper sauce

A dash of cayenne pepper

1. Place the tomato juice, onion, bell pepper, cucumber, garlic, dill, if desired, salt, olive oil, and vinegar in a blender or food processor and process until the vegetables are finely chopped. (If you like a chunkier soup, chop more coarsely.) Pour the mixture into a large bowl and set aside.
2. Place the peeled tomatoes in the blender or processor and process until smooth.

Continued

3. Add the tomatoes to the chopped vegetables and stir in the Tabasco sauce and cayenne. Adjust the seasoning if necessary.

4. Place in the refrigerator for several hours and serve well chilled. If the soup becomes too thick, stir in some additional tomato juice before serving.

TIPS AND TIDBITS

✦ An easy way to peel fresh tomatoes is to drop them into a pot of boiling water until their skins start to crack, about a minute. Remove and allow the tomatoes to cool for a few minutes before peeling.

✦ Unless fresh tomatoes are in season, it's better to use canned tomatoes, which are harvested at their peak.

EASY LOW-FAT GAZPACHO

◆

SERVES 4 TO 6

4 cups canned tomato juice, preferably Sacramento
1 clove garlic, minced
1 red bell pepper, seeded and cut into chunks
2 tablespoons dried onion flakes
1¹/₂ medium cucumbers, peeled and cut into chunks
1 tablespoon white vinegar
2 to 3 dashes Tabasco red pepper sauce
1 teaspoon salt, or to taste
Several shakes of pepper

1. Place 1 cup of the tomato juice in a blender along with the garlic, half the bell pepper chunks, the onion flakes, and two-thirds of the cucumber chunks. Process until smooth.

2. Add 2 more cups of the tomato juice, the vinegar, Tabasco sauce, salt, and pepper, and blend for a few seconds.

3. Pour into a large bowl, add the remaining 1 cup of tomato juice, stir well, and chill in the refrigerator for several hours.
4. Just before serving, return the soup to the blender and mix for a few seconds. You may have to do this in two batches.
5. Pour into bowls and serve well chilled with the remaining cucumber and bell pepper chunks as a garnish.

LENTIL SOUP

◆

SERVES 8

1 tablespoon olive oil
²/₃ cup diced celery
¹/₃ cup diced onion
¹/₂ cup diced leeks, the white and some of the green
¹/₄ cup diced shallot
2 medium garlic cloves, minced
One 48-ounce can chicken broth, preferably College Inn
2 cups water
1¹/₄ cups dried brown lentils, rinsed
2 teaspoons grainy mustard
2 teaspoons red wine vinegar
Salt and pepper to taste

1. Heat the olive oil in a large, heavy pot.
2. Sauté the celery, onion, leeks, shallot, and garlic over low heat until they soften, about 5 minutes.
3. Add the chicken broth, water, and lentils and bring to a boil.
4. Lower the heat, partially cover the pot, and simmer until the lentils are soft, about 30 to 40 minutes.

Continued

5. When the lentils are done, stir in the mustard, vinegar, and salt and pepper.
6. If you prefer a thicker, more porridgelike consistency, puree the soup in a blender or food processor or with a handheld electric blender.

TIPS AND TIDBITS
✦ You can easily make this a vegetarian soup by using vegetable stock instead of chicken broth.

LENTIL SOUP WITH GINGER
◆

SERVES 6 TO 8

2 tablespoons olive oil
1 large onion, chopped
3 to 4 large cloves garlic, minced
3 to 4 tablespoons diced or grated fresh ginger (about 3 to 4
*   inches of a peeled fresh gingerroot)*
3 to 4 carrots, peeled and diced
3²/₃ cups water
1 pound dried brown lentils, rinsed
Four 14-ounce cans chicken broth, preferably College Inn
Salt and pepper to taste
A few dashes of balsamic vinegar

1. In a large, heavy pot, heat the olive oil and cook the onion, garlic, and ginger over low heat for several minutes, until soft.
2. Add the carrots and ²/₃ cup of the water, raise the heat, and simmer for a minute or two.
3. Stir in the lentils, the chicken broth, and the remaining 3 cups water.
4. Partly cover the pot and simmer, stirring often, over low heat for 30 to 40 minutes, until the lentils are tender.

5. Remove the pot from the heat, allow the soup to cool for a few minutes, and add salt, pepper, and the balsamic vinegar. Serve immediately.

TIPS AND TIDBITS

✦ Fresh gingerroot is available in the produce section of most supermarkets.

✦ For a thicker consistency, puree all or some of the soup in a blender or food processor. Or use a handheld electric blender directly in the soup pot.

SPLIT PEA SOUP

SERVES 8

1 cup dried green split peas, rinsed
6 cups canned chicken broth, preferably College Inn
4 cups water
1 medium onion, chopped
1 stalk celery with its leaves, chopped
2 to 3 carrots, peeled and coarsely chopped
½ teaspoon curry powder
Salt and pepper to taste

1. Place the split peas in a large pot with the chicken broth and water and bring to a boil. Skim off the white foam that forms on the surface.

2. Add the rest of the ingredients, lower the heat, and simmer, covered, for about 3 hours.

3. If you like a thicker soup, you can put all or some of it in a blender or food processor and process until smooth. If you have a handheld electric blender, you can puree the soup directly in the pot.

✦ For a change, try adding a smoked ham hock to the soup while the soup is cooking. You can then either discard the ham hock or cut off the meat and add it to the soup.

✦ Whenever you use a blender to process hot soup, make sure the soup has cooled a bit; piping hot liquids may shoot up when you turn the blender on.

TOMATO-DILL BISQUE

◆

SERVES 3 TO 4

2 tablespoons butter

1 to 2 medium onions, chopped

2 cloves garlic, thinly sliced

4 large tomatoes, about 2 pounds, peeled, seeded, and cubed

½ cup water

1 chicken bouillon cube

2 to 3 teaspoons chopped fresh dill, or ¾ teaspoon dried dill

¼ teaspoon salt

⅛ teaspoon pepper

½ cup mayonnaise or plain yogurt

1. Over medium heat, melt the butter in a saucepan and cook the onions and garlic for 3 minutes.
2. Add the tomatoes, water, bouillon cube, dill, salt, and pepper and simmer for 10 minutes.
3. Remove from the heat and allow to cool. Place half the soup at a time in a blender and process until smooth.
4. Stir in the mayonnaise and refrigerate overnight.
5. Serve either cold or hot.

GRANDMA PEARL'S HEALTHFUL
VEGETABLE SOUP

◆

SERVES 3

One 10-ounce can tomato soup
Milk as needed
³/₄ cup cooked white rice (leftover rice from your last Chinese
    meal is fine)
1 cup cooked cabbage, cut into pieces, not shredded
³/₄ cup chopped cooked potato
¹/₂ cup chopped cooked zucchini
¹/₂ cup cooked sliced carrots or peas or a combination of both
Salt and pepper to taste
Soy sauce to taste (optional)
A few sprigs of fresh dill, chopped (optional)

1. Heat the tomato soup with water and/or milk as per the directions
   on the can. Use at least a little milk.
2. Stir in the rice and all of the cooked vegetables.
3. Season with salt and pepper and the soy sauce and dill, if desired.
   Serve hot.

TIPS AND TIDBITS

+ Making the soup a day ahead and refrigerating it overnight will blend
  the flavors and make the soup thicker.
+ If you would like the soup to taste more like stuffed cabbage, double the
  amounts of cabbage and rice.

RECIPE TITLE_____

FROM_____

SERVES _____

INGREDIENTS

INSTRUCTIONS

TIPS AND TIDBITS

RECIPE TITLE _____

FROM _____

SERVES _____

INGREDIENTS

INSTRUCTIONS

TIPS AND TIDBITS

VEGETABLES, SALADS, AND VEGETARIAN DISHES

Also check out:

The chapters **NOODLES, POTATOES, RICE, AND GRAINS** and **PASTA** also have many vegetarian recipes.

STORING FRESH FRUITS AND VEGETABLES

✦ Most fresh fruits keep well in the refrigerator. However, make sure they are ripe before you refrigerate them.

✦ Even ripe bananas, contrary to Chiquita's admonition, can be put in the refrigerator. Although their skins will turn black, their flesh will remain white. (Some people enjoy frozen bananas as a snack.)

✦ Most fresh vegetables can be stored in the refrigerator. If you keep them in a plastic bag, make sure the bag is perforated or kept open so that air can circulate.

✦ A few fresh vegetables do not need to be refrigerated but do better stored in a cool, dry place:

—**Eggplants**   —**Tomatoes** (stem side up)
—**Sweet potatoes**   —**Winter squash** (acorn, butternut)
—**White potatoes** (in a dark place)

✦ Fruits should always be washed to remove pesticide residues and dirt, but wash them just before eating.

✦ A few vegetables should be washed and dried before refrigerating:

—**Lettuce**   —**Swiss chard**
—**Spinach**   —**Watercress**

While washing and drying greens can be time-consuming, a salad spinner is very helpful. After spinning, the greens are practically dry. If necessary, you can finish the drying process by spreading the greens on paper towels.

HOW TO RIPEN FRUITS AND VEGETABLES

✦ You can often ripen bananas, pears, tomatoes, avocados, and other fresh produce at home by placing them in a brown paper bag at room temperature for a few days. Keep the bag away from sunlight, and turn the fruit every day or two so it ripens evenly.

✦ You can hasten the process by adding an apple or a banana to the bag; they both give off ethylene, a gas that speeds ripening.

MAKING GREAT SALADS

✦ Carefully wash all salad greens and then dry them, either on paper towels or in a salad spinner.

✦ Try combining different kinds of greens: romaine lettuce, Boston lettuce, radicchio, arugula, baby spinach, cabbage, endive.

✦ In addition to the usual salad vegetables (tomatoes, cucumbers, carrots, scallions, green bell peppers), try adding chunks of apple or other fruit, crumbled feta or blue cheese, bean sprouts, chickpeas, sunflower seeds, or tofu.

✦ Basic salad dressings generally have a three-to-one oil-to-vinegar ratio.

✦ A good-quality extra-virgin olive oil is much more flavorful than canola or other light oils.

✦ Try experimenting with flavored vinegars: balsamic, sherry, cider, raspberry, tarragon, rice wine. Sometimes, lemon juice or lime juice can substitute for vinegar, especially if the salad contains fruit.

✦ Dijon mustard—dry or prepared—adds a nice flavor and also acts as an emulsifier to keep the oil and vinegar combined.

✦ Other popular additions to dressings include minced shallots or scallions, and fresh or dried herbs, such as tarragon, basil, and thyme.

USING CANNED AND FROZEN FRUITS
AND VEGETABLES

Canned and frozen fruits and vegetables are often just as nutritious as fresh produce, and it is a good idea to keep a supply on hand. Because the fruits and vegetables used for canning and freezing are harvested when they are ripest, they sometimes contain even more vitamins and minerals than some fresh produce, which is often picked before it is ripe and may lose some nutrients while in transit or sitting on the store shelf.

Frozen Packages

+ Frozen fruits and vegetables should be kept in the freezer until you are ready to use them. Follow the package directions for thawing and cooking.

+ If a recipe calls for thawed fruits or vegetables, defrost them in the refrigerator or in a microwave oven.

+ Once you have thawed a frozen food, do not refreeze it.

Cans and Bottles

+ Before buying or using a canned food, check the can for bulges, dents, and leaks. A bottle lid should never bulge. These are all signs that the bacteria that cause botulism may be present. Because the poison produced by the bacteria is colorless and odorless, *if you have even the slightest doubt that a canned or bottled food is contaminated, don't taste it—throw it out!*

+ Other signs of spoilage include cloudiness, discoloration, mold, bubbles, and a spurting of liquid when the can is opened. *If a canned or bottled food looks peculiar or smells "off," don't take a chance—throw it out!*

+ All canned and bottled foods, including fruits, vegetables, juices, sauces, and soups, should be stored in a cool place, such as a pantry closet or a kitchen cabinet that is not close to the oven.

+ Once a can has been opened, transfer its contents to a glass or plastic container with a lid, cover, and store it in the refrigerator. This is especially true for canned tomatoes, tomato juice, and other acidic foods. And don't forget to label the container with the date and contents.

+ Try to use canned goods within a year after purchasing them; they do lose some flavor and nutritional value over time.

THREE-BEAN SALAD

◆

Two 15-ounce cans chickpeas, preferably S&W
Two 15-ounce cans red kidney beans, preferably S&W
8 ounces fresh green beans, ends trimmed
1/2 medium green bell pepper, seeded and chopped
1/2 medium red onion, chopped or sliced into thin rings
1/2 cup cider vinegar
2 tablespoons sugar, or more to taste
1/2 teaspoon salt
A dash of pepper
1/2 cup canola or other light vegetable oil

1. Rinse and drain the chickpeas and kidney beans, and place in a large bowl.
2. Bring a pot of water to a boil and drop in the green beans. When the water returns to a boil, drain the beans and cut them into inch-long sections. They should still be somewhat firm and fairly crunchy.
3. Add the green bell pepper, onion, and green beans to the bowl.
4. In a small bowl, whisk together the vinegar, sugar, salt, and pepper, stirring until the sugar and salt are dissolved. Slowly stir in the canola oil.
5. Pour the dressing over the bean mixture, toss well, and refrigerate for several hours, preferably overnight. Stir well before serving.

TIPS AND TIDBITS

+ If the onion is too strong, soak the chopped pieces or the slices in a bowl of cold water for about 20 minutes. Be sure to dry them on a paper towel before adding them to the salad.

BLACK BEAN SALAD

♦

Two 15-ounce cans black beans, rinsed and drained
¹/₂ cup diced green bell peppers
¹/₂ cup diced red bell peppers
¹/₂ cup fresh (1 ear), canned, or frozen corn
3 to 4 scallions (green onions), the white part and some of the
*   green, diced*
1 medium or large tomato, diced
1 large clove garlic, minced
3 tablespoons lime juice, preferably fresh
5 tablespoons canola or other light vegetable oil
¹/₂ teaspoon salt
Pepper to taste
A dash of Tabasco red pepper sauce

1. In a large bowl, combine the black beans, green and red bell peppers, corn, scallions, diced tomato, and garlic.
2. In a small bowl, whisk together the lime juice, canola oil, salt, pepper, and Tabasco sauce.
3. Pour the dressing over the vegetables and mix well. Add more salt and pepper, if necessary.
4. Store in the refrigerator, but serve at room temperature. Stir well before serving.

TIPS AND TIDBITS

+ Whenever you are whisking together a vinaigrette, add the salt to the acid (vinegar, lemon juice, lime juice) before adding the oil. It will dissolve much faster in the acid than in the oil.

BLACK BEAN, CORN, AND FETA SALAD WITH PITA

♦

SERVES 4

One 15-ounce can black beans, rinsed and drained
One 15-ounce can corn, or cooked kernels from 2 ears of
    fresh corn
$^1/_2$ cup chopped red onions
$^1/_2$ cup chopped celery or red bell peppers
2 ounces feta cheese (or more to taste), crumbled
3 tablespoons balsamic vinegar
2 tablespoons olive oil plus another tablespoon for browning
    the pita
Salt and pepper to taste
One 6-inch pita, cut into $^1/_2$-inch squares

1. Combine the beans, corn, red onions, celery, and feta cheese in a large bowl.
2. In a small bowl, whisk together the vinegar and 2 tablespoons of the olive oil. Pour the dressing over the bean mixture and toss to coat. Season with salt and pepper if necessary.
3. In a skillet, heat the remaining 1 tablespoon olive oil and cook the pita squares, stirring occasionally, until golden. Drain on paper towels and season with salt and pepper.
4. Just before serving, add the pita squares to the salad and toss.

TIPS AND TIDBITS

✦ If you have leftovers and want to serve this dish the next day, remove the soggy pita squares and prepare a fresh batch.

CHEF'S SALAD

♦

SERVES 4

1 large head romaine lettuce or an equivalent amount of your
   favorite salad greens
1 small cucumber, peeled and sliced
$^1/_2$ cup sliced scallions (green onions)
$^1/_2$ cup thin strips of cooked chicken or turkey
$^1/_2$ cup thin strips of cooked ham, roast beef, or other meat
$^1/_2$ cup thin strips of Swiss cheese
$^1/_3$ cup red wine vinegar
1 shallot, minced
1 teaspoon Dijon mustard
Salt and pepper to taste
1 cup olive oil
2 hard-boiled eggs, cut into wedges or slices
2 large tomatoes, cut into wedges or slices

1. Wash and dry the lettuce leaves and cut or tear into bite-sized
   pieces. Place in a large bowl.
2. Add the cucumber, scallions, chicken, ham, and cheese, and toss
   gently.
3. In a small bowl, whisk together the vinegar, minced shallot, mustard, and salt and pepper.
4. Slowly whisk in the olive oil.
5. Pour about $^3/_4$ cup of the dressing on the salad and mix until everything is lightly coated. Add more if needed.
6. Place the egg and tomato wedges around the edge of the bowl,
   cover, and refrigerate until ready to serve.

TIPS AND TIDBITS

✦ An attractive way to prepare cucumber is to score the surface by running
   a fork down its length. When you slice the cucumber, each round will
   have a ridged edge.

✦ Although packaged salad greens are very convenient, whole heads of lettuce are fresher.

CHOPPED SALAD WITH PITA CRISPS

SERVES 4 (OR 2 AS AN ENTRÉE)

1 small head romaine lettuce, shredded or chopped
¹/₂ cup canned chickpeas, rinsed and drained (or substitute fresh, canned, or frozen corn)
¹/₂ cup diced tomatoes
¹/₂ red bell pepper, seeded and diced
¹/₂ yellow bell pepper, seeded and diced
¹/₂ red onion, diced
1 small cucumber, peeled and diced
¹/₄ cup pitted black olives, chopped
4 ounces feta cheese, or more to taste
3 tablespoons olive oil
1 tablespoon balsamic vinegar
Salt and pepper to taste
One 6-inch pita, cut into ¹/₂-inch pieces

1. Combine the lettuce, chickpeas, tomatoes, red bell pepper, yellow bell pepper, red onion, cucumber, and olives in a large bowl.
2. Crumble the feta cheese into the mixture.
3. In a small bowl, whisk together 2 tablespoons of the olive oil and the vinegar and pour the dressing over the salad, mixing to combine well. Add salt and pepper. Store in the refrigerator.
4. To make the pita crisps, heat the remaining 1 tablespoon olive oil in a skillet until very hot and sauté the pita pieces, stirring often, until they are crisp and golden.
5. Drain the pita crisps on a paper towel and season with salt and pepper. Add them to the salad just before serving.

+ If you want to serve leftover salad the next day, remove the soggy pita crisps and sauté fresh ones.
+ If your tomatoes are very juicy, they may make the salad too watery. You can drain off some of the liquid by placing the diced tomatoes in a sieve or colander. Adding a few sprinkles of salt will draw out more of the juice.

COLESLAW

◆

SERVES 10 TO 12

1 medium or large head of cabbage, grated or thinly sliced
2 carrots, peeled and grated (optional)
1 small onion, thinly sliced
6 tablespoons sugar
1/2 cup canola, corn, or other light vegetable oil
3/4 cup cider vinegar
1/2 teaspoon salt
1/2 teaspoon dry mustard
1 teaspoon celery seeds or caraway seeds

1. Place the grated cabbage in a large bowl. Add the grated carrots, if desired, and the sliced onion and toss to combine.
2. Sprinkle the mixture with 4 tablespoons of the sugar, mix well, cover, and place in the refrigerator for a few hours.
3. In a small saucepan, heat the canola oil, vinegar, salt, dry mustard, and the remaining 2 tablespoons sugar. When the mixture starts to boil, stir well to combine all of the ingredients and break up any clumps of dry mustard. (You can also combine the sauce ingredients in a heat-proof glass bowl or measuring cup and bring the mixture to a boil in a microwave oven.)

4. Remove from the heat and pour the hot dressing over the chilled cabbage mixture. Sprinkle with the celery seeds, stir well, and return the bowl to the refrigerator for another few hours. Serve cold.

TIPS AND TIDBITS
✦ You can keep this coleslaw in the refrigerator for a few days, but it should be drained if it starts to taste too vinegary.

HEALTH SLAW

◆

SERVES 10

8 cups shredded cabbage
2 cups shredded carrots
2 cups diced cucumbers (scrape the seeds out first)
1/2 cup chopped red onions
1 green bell pepper, seeded and cut into slivers
1/4 cup sugar
1 cup white vinegar
1/2 cup canola or safflower oil
1/4 teaspoon celery seeds
Salt and pepper to taste

1. Toss the cabbage, carrots, cucumbers, red onions, and bell pepper in a very large bowl.
2. Combine the sugar, vinegar, oil, celery seeds, and salt and pepper and pour over the vegetables. Mix well.
3. Serve immediately or the next day—it gets better with age!

TIPS AND TIDBITS
✦ It's easiest to grate the cabbage and carrots using the medium grating disk of a food processor. Otherwise, use the largest holes of a square hand grater.

CRUNCHY CHINESE SALAD

1 small head Napa cabbage, chopped or shredded

4 scallions (green onions), the white part and some of the green, thinly sliced

One 3-ounce package ramen noodle soup, any flavor (discard the flavor packet)

2 tablespoons butter or margarine

$1/4$ cup sesame seeds

$1/2$ cup sliced or slivered almonds

$1/2$ cup canola, safflower, or other light vegetable oil

$1/2$ teaspoon soy sauce

$1/4$ cup white vinegar

6 tablespoons sugar

1. Combine the cabbage and scallions in a large bowl. Set aside.
2. Before opening the noodle package, crunch it with your hands to break the noodles into pieces.
3. Melt the butter in a heavy skillet and add the broken noodles, the sesame seeds, and the almonds. Cook, stirring occasionally, over medium heat until everything is lightly browned, about 5 minutes.
4. When the noodle mixture is done, pour it onto paper towels to cool and drain.
5. To make the salad dressing, combine the canola oil, soy sauce, vinegar, and sugar in a Pyrex or other microwave-proof bowl and microwave for about 1 minute, or until the sugar is dissolved.
6. When the dressing is done, allow it to cool completely, about 15 to 20 minutes.
7. Just before serving, combine the noodle mixture with the greens and toss with the dressing.

✦ If you do not have a microwave oven, place the dressing ingredients in a small, heavy sauté pan and cook, stirring, over a low flame until the sugar is dissolved.

SPICY CUCUMBER SALAD

◆

SERVES 3 TO 4

2 medium cucumbers
1 teaspoon soy sauce
1 tablespoon white vinegar
1 tablespoon sugar
2 teaspoons sesame oil
$^1/_4$ teaspoon Tabasco red pepper sauce, or to taste
$^1/_2$ teaspoon salt, or to taste

1. Peel the cucumbers and cut them in half lengthwise. Scrape out the seeds and cut the cucumber halves into $^1/_4$-inch-thick C-shaped slices. Place them in a bowl.
2. In a small bowl, combine the soy sauce, vinegar, sugar, sesame oil, Tabasco sauce, and salt. Stir well to dissolve the sugar.
3. Pour the dressing over the cucumber slices and mix thoroughly. Chill slightly before serving. If you keep this in the refrigerator for more than 1 hour, stir well before serving. If you store it in a covered container, turn the container over periodically to keep the cucumber slices marinated.

ARTICHOKE AND SPINACH CASSEROLE

◆

*Two 13-ounce cans artichoke hearts (not the marinated ones),
    drained and cut in half*
*Three 10-ounce packages frozen chopped spinach, thawed and
    well drained*
8 ounces regular or low-fat cream cheese
6 tablespoons regular, low-fat, or skim milk
2 tablespoons regular or low-fat mayonnaise
A dash of pepper
Grated Parmesan cheese, for sprinkling

1. Preheat the oven to 375°F.
2. Spread a very thin layer of oil on the bottom of a 13 × 9-inch casserole dish. Or spray the dish with Pam.
3. Place the artichoke chunks evenly over the bottom of the casserole dish and cover them with the drained spinach.
4. In a blender or food processor, combine the cream cheese, milk, mayonnaise, and pepper until smooth.
5. Pour the mixture over the spinach and sprinkle liberally with the grated cheese.
6. Bake for 40 minutes. Serve hot.

TIPS AND TIDBITS

✦ Draining thawed spinach can be quite tedious; it's best to squeeze it with your hands.

BROCCOLI-RICE CASSEROLE

from **DIANA WILLIAMS**
Television News Anchor

◆

"This is my kids' favorite. Very easy, but *not* low-fat."

SERVES 5 TO 6

1 cup rice
One 10-ounce can cream of chicken soup
One 8-ounce jar Cheez Whiz
4 tablespoons (¹/₂ stick) margarine
One 10-ounce package frozen chopped broccoli or spinach,
*   thawed and well drained*
Crushed Ritz crackers, for topping (optional)

1. Preheat the oven to 375°F.
2. Grease a large casserole dish.
3. In a heavy saucepan, bring 2 cups of water to a boil. Add the rice, stir, cover the pan, and reduce the heat to very low.
4. While the rice is cooking, which should take about 20 minutes, combine the soup, Cheez Whiz, and margarine in a large saucepan and cook over low to medium heat until blended.
5. When the rice is cooked, add it—along with the broccoli—to the soup mixture. Stir to combine.
6. Pour the mixture into the prepared casserole dish and top with the crushed Ritz crackers, if desired.
7. Bake for 25 to 30 minutes.

GLAZED CARROTS

◆

1 tablespoon butter
1 pound carrots, peeled and cut into 1-inch-thick rounds
¹/₂ cup apple juice
¹/₂ teaspoon honey
Salt and pepper to taste

1. Melt the butter in a heavy pan and cook the carrots over medium heat until they start to brown, about 8 to 10 minutes. Stir occasionally.
2. Add the apple juice and honey, stir, and simmer the carrots over low heat until the carrots soften and the sauce thickens into a glaze, about 15 to 20 minutes. Stir often.
3. Season with salt and pepper.

TIPS AND TIDBITS

◆ For a change, try using a combination of orange juice and brown sugar instead of the apple juice and honey.

CARROT RING

◆

4 cups grated carrots (about 1¹/₂ pounds)
¹/₄ cup packed brown sugar
3 tablespoons unsalted butter or margarine, at
   room temperature
2 eggs, or 3 egg whites
1 cup flour

¹/₂ teaspoon salt

¹/₂ teaspoon baking powder

1 tablespoon lemon juice, preferably fresh

1. Preheat the oven to 350°F.
2. Butter a 4- to 6-cup baking mold or Bundt pan.
3. Place the grated carrots in a large bowl. Set aside.
4. In a separate bowl (or food processor), combine the brown sugar with the butter.
5. Beat in the eggs.
6. Stir in the flour and salt.
7. In a small bowl, combine the baking powder and lemon juice. Add to the flour mixture.
8. Stir the flour mixture into the carrots and combine well. You may want to use your hands.
9. Pour the carrot mixture into the buttered mold and bake for about 1¹/₄ to 1¹/₂ hours, until the surface is golden and crisp.

CORN PUDDING

SERVES 6 TO 8

Two 10-ounce packages frozen corn, thawed

¹/₄ cup sugar

1 teaspoon salt

2 cups regular or low-fat milk

4 eggs

¹/₂ teaspoon vanilla extract

4 tablespoons (¹/₂ stick) unsalted butter, melted and allowed to cool to room temperature

3 tablespoons flour

¹/₄ cup chopped fresh chives, plus more for garnish

Grated nutmeg, for sprinkling

1. Preheat the oven to 350°F.
2. Butter a 1½-quart casserole dish.
3. In the bowl of a food processor, pulse half the corn until it is coarsely chopped.
4. In a bowl, combine the chopped corn, the remaining unchopped corn, the sugar, and the salt. Set aside.
5. In another bowl, whisk together the milk, eggs, vanilla extract, butter, flour, and chives. Stir the mixture into the corn.
6. Pour the corn mixture into the prepared casserole dish and sprinkle with nutmeg.
7. Bake for about 45 minutes, or until the center is nearly set. Garnish with the extra chives.

EGGPLANT CASSEROLE

from DEBBIE REYNOLDS

Actress, Singer

SERVES 6 TO 8

1 large eggplant
3 medium tomatoes, sliced
Salt and pepper to taste
1 cup grated Swiss cheese
1 cup grated Parmesan cheese
1 tablespoon butter
½ cup tomato sauce
¼ cup seasoned bread crumbs

1. Preheat the oven to 350°F.
2. Grease the bottom and sides of a 12 × 9-inch baking dish.
3. Peel the eggplant, slice into rounds, and soak in cold salted water for 30 minutes. Drain and pat dry.

4. Combine the eggplant with the tomato slices and season with salt and pepper. Place a layer (about a third of the mixture) in the bottom of the prepared baking dish.
5. Combine the grated cheeses, and sprinkle about a third of the mixture on the eggplant-tomato layer.
6. Repeat the procedure, and place a third layer of the eggplant-tomato mixture on top. (You should have about a third of the grated cheese mixture left over.)
7. Dot the surface with the butter and spoon the tomato sauce on top.
8. Cover with the bread crumbs and the remaining grated cheese.
9. Bake for 1 hour. Serve hot.

CURRIED LENTILS

◆

SERVES 4

1 cup dried brown lentils, rinsed
3 cups chicken broth or water
2 large onions, finely chopped
1 tablespoon olive oil
1 clove garlic, minced
1 teaspoon curry powder

1. In a medium pot, combine the lentils, broth, and half the onions. Bring to a boil, lower the heat, cover, and simmer until the lentils are tender, about 20 to 30 minutes. Drain.
2. While the lentils are cooking, heat the olive oil in a heavy pan, add the remaining onions, and sauté until they soften and start to brown.
3. Add the garlic, stir, and cook for another minute or two.
4. When the lentils are done and drained, add them to the onion and garlic mixture along with the curry powder. Combine well, cover, and heat for a few more minutes.

✦ Lentils can be stored in their original bag, tightly sealed, or in an airtight container. They should be kept at room temperature and last about a year.

OKRA STEW

from **COKIE ROBERTS**

Journalist, Author, Television and Radio News Analyst,
Winner of the Edward R. Murrow Award
and Two Emmys

◆

"As a Louisianian, I like to cook dishes from the Southern and Creole traditions. Okra stew can be made as a pure vegetarian dish without the sausage, but it's not as good. Also, and this is the beauty, it's really fine to substitute already chopped frozen or canned okra for the fresh. It's also okay to substitute fresh tomatoes for the canned. At the time of year when both tomatoes and okra are in the garden, I do use fresh of each, but I also serve this more as a sautéed dish, cooked briefly, without meat, than as a stew."

SERVES 6 TO 8

8 ounces andouille or other smoked sausage (such as
  kielbasa), chopped
Oil, butter, or lard, for browning
1 large onion, chopped
1 green bell pepper, seeded and chopped (optional)
1 pound okra, sliced crosswise
One 28-ounce can tomatoes
Tabasco red pepper sauce to taste
Salt and pepper to taste

1. Brown the sausage in a little oil, butter, or lard on medium-high heat.
2. Add the onion and bell pepper, if desired, cook for a couple of minutes, and then add the okra. Cook for a couple of minutes more.
3. Add the tomatoes, juice and all.
4. Add Tabasco sauce, salt, and pepper. Turn the heat to low and simmer until the sauce is thick and the okra is very tender, about 15 minutes.
5. Okra stew is especially good with rice or cheese grits. Have more Tabasco sauce on the table.

SPINACH-PHYLLO-LAYERED SOUFFLÉ

SERVES 10 TO 12

One 16-ounce package frozen phyllo dough
12 tablespoons (1½ sticks) butter
Two 10-ounce packages frozen spinach
3 leeks, white part only, well washed and cut into ½-inch-thick rounds
1 medium onion, chopped
8 ounces fresh mushrooms, sliced into narrow strips
Salt and pepper to taste
Grated nutmeg to taste
8 ounces feta cheese, crumbled
4 ounces goat cheese
1 egg
A few sprigs of parsley, chopped

1. Thaw the phyllo dough according to the directions on the package. (This may take several hours.)
2. Preheat the oven to 350°F.

Continued

3. Butter a 13 × 9-inch baking dish.
4. When the phyllo is thawed, unfold the sheets and place them between damp kitchen towels to prevent them from drying out.
5. Melt 8 tablespoons of the butter to use with the phyllo.
6. Microwave the spinach for 6 to 7 minutes and drain all of the water. Set aside.
7. Sauté the leeks and onion in 2 tablespoons of the remaining butter until translucent.
8. In a separate pan, sauté the mushrooms in the remaining 2 tablespoons butter until limp. Season with salt, pepper, and nutmeg. Set aside.
9. In a medium bowl, whip together the feta cheese, goat cheese, egg, and parsley. Set aside.
10. To assemble the soufflé, place a layer of 2 to 3 phyllo sheets on the bottom of the baking dish. Brush with the melted butter and cover with the onion-leek mixture.
11. Add another layer of phyllo sheets, brush with butter, and cover with the sautéed mushrooms.
12. Add a third layer of phyllo sheets, brush with butter, and cover with the cooked spinach.
13. Cover with the final layer of phyllo sheets, brush with butter, and cover with the cheese mixture.
14. Bake for 35 to 45 minutes, loosely covering the pan with aluminum foil after 20 minutes to keep the soufflé from burning. When done, the top will be golden brown.

BAKED SQUASH

from **JOAN BAEZ**

Folksinger, Songwriter, Social Activist, Author

◆

"You can use any winter squash—this one is the easiest for me."

SERVES 2

1 acorn squash
1 tablespoon honey
¹/₄ teaspoon ground cinnamon
A pinch of salt

1. Preheat the oven to 350°F.
2. Cut the squash in half and scoop out the seeds. Place the halves, cut side up, in a baking pan.
3. Pour the honey in the hollow of each half.
4. Sprinkle the squash with the cinnamon and salt.
5. Bake for 30 to 45 minutes, depending on the size of the squash. The flesh should be soft when you insert a fork.

ROASTED VEGETABLE MEDLEY

SERVES 6 TO 8

12 medium red potatoes, well washed and cut into quarters
   or chunks
4 carrots, peeled and cut into thick slices
2 medium onions, cut into quarters or thick slices
1 to 2 green or red bell peppers, seeded and cut into chunks
Olive oil for drizzling
Salt and pepper to taste

1. Preheat the oven to 375°F.
2. Spread or spray a layer of oil on the bottom of a large roasting pan.
3. Scatter the vegetables, cut side down, in one layer over the bottom of the pan. (The pieces should all be similar in size.)
4. Drizzle a small amount of olive oil over the vegetables, stirring to coat, and sprinkle with salt and pepper.

Continued

5. Roast for about 1 hour, or until the vegetables are tender. (After half an hour, check occasionally to scrape off any vegetables sticking to the bottom of the pan.)
6. Add more salt and pepper, if necessary, and serve.

TIPS AND TIDBITS

+ Try substituting any of your own favorite vegetables, keeping in mind that firm vegetables like sweet potatoes and parsnips are better than soft ones. If you add garlic cloves, do not peel them.

+ For an easy cleanup, before you start peeling the vegetables, line your sink with a few sheets of newspaper or paper towels and do your peeling over the paper. When done, simply roll up the paper and throw it away.

VEGETABLE RAGOUT
◆

SERVES 6

1 medium onion, diced
3 to 4 tablespoons olive oil
3 cloves garlic, minced
2 medium zucchini, diced
1 medium yellow squash, diced
1 medium red bell pepper, seeded and chopped
1 cup fresh (2 ears) or canned corn
2 medium or large tomatoes, chopped
$1/2$ teaspoon dried oregano
Salt and pepper to taste
$1/2$ cup coarsely chopped or shredded fresh basil

1. In a large, heavy pan, sauté the onion in the olive oil until soft.
2. Add the garlic and cook another minute or two.

3. Add the zucchini, squash, bell pepper, and corn, and cook, stirring, for 4 to 5 minutes.
4. Stir in the tomatoes, oregano, and salt and pepper. Simmer, covered, for 10 minutes.
5. Uncover and simmer for another 5 minutes.
6. Add the basil and stir to combine.
7. Serve hot or at room temperature. This dish is good to make a day ahead; it will be even better the next day.

TIPS AND TIDBITS

✦ Squash comes in two basic varieties: Summer squash, such as zucchini and yellow (crookneck), have thin edible skins, soft seeds, and tender flesh. Winter squash, such as acorn, butternut, and spaghetti, have thick skins, hard seeds, and firm flesh.

✦ When buying squash, look for smaller ones. Larger squash have a soft spongy center and more seeds.

VEGETABLE "PIE"

◆

SERVES 2 TO 4

25 Triscuit crackers, crushed

3 tablespoons unsalted butter or margarine, melted

1 cup chopped onions

3 tablespoons olive oil

1 medium red bell pepper, seeded and chopped

1 medium green bell pepper, seeded and chopped

2 medium zucchini, trimmed and chopped

2 teaspoons minced garlic

Salt and pepper to taste

2 ounces fontina cheese, coarsely grated

2 to 3 tablespoons chopped fresh basil

1. Preheat the oven to 350°F.
2. Combine the Triscuit crumbs and melted butter. Press half the mixture onto the bottom of an 8-inch pie pan or baking dish. Set aside.
3. In a large pan, cook the onions in the olive oil, stirring often, until they are soft. Add the red and green bell peppers and continue cooking for about 2 minutes, stirring often.
4. Add the zucchini to the pan and cook, stirring occasionally, for another 5 minutes. Add the garlic and salt and pepper. Cook the mixture, still stirring, until the vegetables are tender, 2 to 3 minutes more.
5. Remove the pan from the heat and stir in the fontina cheese and chopped basil.
6. Spread the vegetable mixture over the layer of crumbs in the pie pan and sprinkle the remaining crumbs over the top.
7. Bake for about 10 minutes. Serve hot.

TIPS AND TIDBITS

✦ Here's an easy way to chop fresh basil: Stack 5 or 6 leaves on top of one another and roll up the stack lengthwise to make a tiny "cigar." With a sharp knife, cut the "cigar" crosswise, making very thin strips.

VEGETABLE PITA PIZZAS
◆

SERVES 2

Two 6-inch whole wheat pitas
3 tablespoons olive oil, plus more as needed
Salt to taste
1¹/₃ cups grated mozzarella cheese
1 small red onion, thinly sliced
2 cloves garlic, minced
1 small red bell pepper, seeded and thinly sliced

1 small green bell pepper, seeded and thinly sliced
1 small zucchini, thinly sliced
4 mushrooms, sliced
1 teaspoon dried oregano
Pepper to taste
1 small fresh tomato, seeded and chopped
3 tablespoons coarsely chopped fresh basil
3 tablespoons grated Parmesan cheese

1. Preheat the oven to 350°F.
2. Cut the two pita breads horizontally in half, forming 4 rounds.
3. Arrange the rounds on a baking sheet, cut side up, and brush them lightly with some olive oil. Sprinkle them with salt to taste and toast in the oven for 5 minutes, or until they are pale gold and crisp.
4. Sprinkle about half the mozzarella cheese (²/₃ cup) on the toasted pita rounds and return them to the oven to bake for about 1 minute, or until the cheese is melted.
5. In a large pan, cook the onion and garlic in the 3 tablespoons of olive oil, stirring until the onion is soft. Add the bell peppers and continue cooking and stirring until the peppers are soft, about 4 minutes.
6. Add the zucchini, mushrooms, oregano, and salt and pepper to taste and continue cooking and stirring for another 2 minutes.
7. Stir in half of the remaining mozzarella (¹/₃ cup) and spoon the mixture on top of the 4 pita rounds.
8. Top the rounds with the rest of the mozzarella, the chopped tomato, the basil, and the grated Parmesan cheese.
9. Broil for about 3 minutes, or until the cheese is melted.

TIPS AND TIDBITS

✦ If the pita breads are hard to cut, use a scissors to trim the edges and the halves will separate.

VEGETABLE-CHEESE QUESADILLAS

◆

SERVES 2

¹/₂ cup chopped onions
1 tablespoon olive oil, plus more as needed
1 yellow squash, halved lengthwise and thinly sliced crosswise
3 cups firmly packed coarsely chopped fresh spinach
1 large tomato, seeded and chopped (about 1 cup)
1¹/₂ teaspoons white wine vinegar
¹/₈ teaspoon dried oregano
Salt and pepper to taste
6 Kalamata or other cured olives, pitted and chopped
Four 6-inch flour tortillas
4 ounces mozzarella cheese, coarsely grated

1. In a large pan, cook the onions in the olive oil, stirring, for 5 minutes. Add the squash and spinach and cook, stirring, until the spinach is wilted.
2. Add the tomato, vinegar, oregano, and salt and pepper and cook, stirring, until the squash has softened and the liquid is almost gone.
3. Remove the pan from the heat and stir in the olives and any additional salt and pepper.
4. Place 2 of the tortillas on a jelly-roll pan and place half the vegetable mixture on each one. Sprinkle them with the mozzarella cheese and cover with the remaining 2 tortillas. Brush the tops lightly with olive oil.
5. Broil for about 2 minutes, or until the tops are golden. Turn the quesadillas over with a large spatula, brush the tops with more oil, and broil for 2 minutes more.

TIPS AND TIDBITS

✦ The easiest way to seed a tomato is to cut it in half crosswise (not through the stem) and gently squeeze each half.

HOW TO USE THOSE EXTRA ZUCCHINI

from **BEVERLY CLEARY**

Author, Winner of the American Library Association's John Newberry Medal and Laura Ingalls Wilder Award

◆

"This recipe serves two for a luncheon dish, more as a vegetable, and it may easily be doubled. The next time you plant a vegetable garden, remember that three seeds will provide enough zucchini for a family of four and the neighbors."

SERVES 2 OR MORE

2 medium zucchini, washed but unpeeled
1 egg
¹/₄ cup Bisquick
2 to 3 tablespoons grated onion, or more to taste (optional)
Butter, for frying

1. Grate the zucchini onto paper towels to drain off the moisture.
2. Beat the egg and Bisquick together thoroughly in a blender or with an eggbeater or electric mixer.
3. Stir in the grated zucchini and grated onion, if desired.
4. Melt some butter in a frying pan, and drop in large spoonfuls of the zucchini mixture, much like making pancakes. Brown on both sides, drain on paper towels, and serve.

RECIPE TITLE_____

FROM_____

SERVES _____

INGREDIENTS

INSTRUCTIONS

TIPS AND TIDBITS

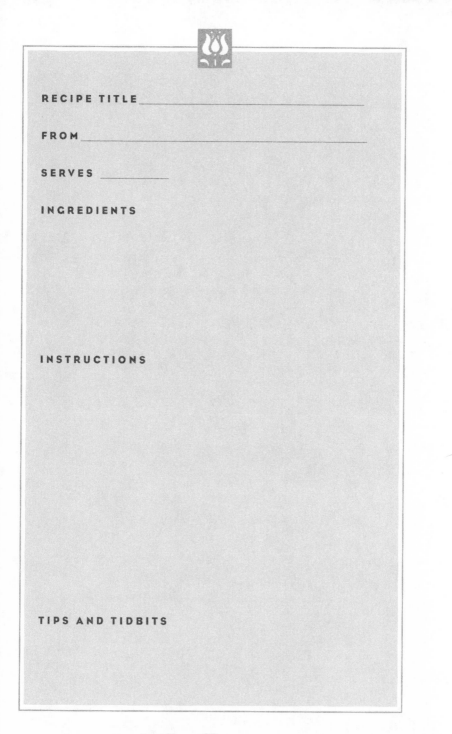

RECIPE TITLE

FROM

SERVES

INGREDIENTS

INSTRUCTIONS

TIPS AND TIDBITS

NOODLES,
POTATOES,
RICE,
AND GRAINS

Also check out:

Broccoli-Rice Casserole • p. 79

The chapter **PASTA** also has many related recipes.

TIPS AND HINTS ON...
BUYING AND STORING POTATOES

✦ One potato weighing 6 to 8 ounces is a single portion.
✦ Choose potatoes that are smooth, firm, and have very few eyes.

+ Avoid potatoes with sprouts, dark spots, cuts, mold, or greenish areas, which will be bitter and possibly toxic.
+ Try to get potatoes best suited for your particular purpose:

> + Starchy potatoes, such as *Idaho* and *russet,* are best for baking and making French fries and mashed potatoes; their flesh will be fluffy.
> + Waxy potatoes, such as *round red* and *round white,* are best for boiling as well as for recipes calling for sliced or diced potatoes, such as potato salad.
> + *New potatoes* are recently harvested small or large potatoes with red or white skins that can be rubbed off easily with your fingers. Their flesh is usually firm. They are best for steaming and roasting.

+ There are also many interesting but less well known varieties you might want to try: *All Blue, Purple Peruvian, Yukon Gold, Yellow Finn,* and *Red Pontiac.*
+ *Sweet potatoes* are not related to white potatoes, nor are they yams, with which they are often confused. (True *yams* are the starchy white tuberous roots of an African vine and they are not widely available in the United States.) Whether their skins are yellowish or orange, they may be used interchangeably.
+ If you buy canned, frozen, or instant potatoes, keep in mind that they often have a great deal of added sodium, fat, or sugar.
+ Store potatoes—unwashed—in a cool, dark place. They can be unwrapped or kept in a brown paper bag or perforated plastic bag. Storing potatoes in the refrigerator or any other very cold place will affect their flavor.
+ Potatoes can be stored for about two months, except for *new potatoes,* which are more perishable and should be used within a week of purchase.
+ Do not store potatoes together with onions; each can cause the other to spoil.
+ Check stored potatoes periodically. One spoiled potato can cause the others to decay. Throw out any potatoes that show signs of spoilage. If you need to use a spoiled potato, cut away all of the affected areas.

◆ By the way, potatoes themselves are not fattening—the fat comes from the butter and sour cream we like to put on them. Next time, try one of these low-fat toppings:

—**Salsa** (prepared or homemade)   —**Low-fat cottage cheese**
—**Diced vegetables**   —**Grated cheese**
—**A spoonful or two of soup**   —**Your favorite herbs or spices**

PREPARING POTATOES

◆ It is best to keep potato skins on, since they are rich in nutrients. But be sure to scrub them well.

◆ If you must peel them, try to remove the thinnest possible layer. The flesh directly under the skin also contains many nutrients.

◆ Peeled raw potatoes will start to discolor if they are not cooked immediately. If you cannot cook them right away, put them in a bowl and add enough cold water to cover.

◆ Certain metals also discolor potatoes. It is best to use stainless-steel pots and utensils.

◆ If your potatoes do become discolored, don't worry about it. They may look unappetizing, but the discoloration in no way affects their flavor or quality.

◆ Baking and boiling are the best ways to cook whole potatoes. Microwaving is generally not recommended, although in a pinch it is certainly quick (about five minutes for one large potato).

Baking Potatoes

◆ Bake potatoes by simply placing them on a shelf in a preheated oven. Do not wrap them in aluminum foil; the skins will not get crisp.

◆ Before baking, prick the skin with a fork in several places to allow steam to escape as the potato heats up. Otherwise, the potato might explode.

◆ An average-sized white potato bakes in forty-five to sixty minutes at 400°F. Sweet potatoes cook somewhat faster. You can speed up the baking process by inserting a metal nail or skewer into the potato's center.

However, the nail or skewer will be extremely hot when the potato is done, so be very careful when removing it.

✦ Sweet potatoes often exude a sticky juice while baking. If it drips onto the oven floor, it can be hard to clean off. It's best to catch the drips on a sheet of aluminum foil placed on the shelf directly under the potatoes.

Boiling Potatoes

✦ To boil potatoes, place them in a large pot and add enough cold water to cover them completely. Salt the water after it comes to a boil.

✦ When boiling potatoes, cooking time depends on potato size:

Small	10 to 15 minutes
Medium	20 to 25 minutes
Large	35 to 45 minutes

✦ If you add whole garlic cloves to the water, the garlic will become soft and sweet and will be delicious when mashed with the potatoes.

BUYING AND STORING RICE

✦ White or brown? *White rice,* sometimes called milled rice, has had the husk, bran, and most of the germ removed. Thus, it has lost most of its nutrients. *Brown rice* has had only its husk removed, making it more nutritious and somewhat more flavorful. However, it takes longer to cook than white rice and is more perishable.

✦ Rice grains are available in different lengths, but the one most commonly used is *long-grain.* When cooked, these grains are fluffy and will separate easily. However, *short-grain* rice (also known as sticky rice) is preferable for some recipes, including many Asian dishes, because it is very starchy and has a tendency to clump. *Converted rice* has been parboiled and is somewhat harder—but more nutritious—than regular rice. It takes a little longer to cook.

✦ There are also a number of special rices available, which are best suited to certain types of dishes: *Arborio* for risotto, *basmati* for Indian dishes, *glutinous* (sweet) for Japanese dishes.

+ *Wild rice* is not exactly rice and not exactly wild. It is, in fact, a long-grained marsh grass. It has a rich, nutty flavor and is nice as a side dish or mixed with regular rice, which helps deflect its high cost. It is important to rinse wild rice very well before cooking.

+ *Instant* and *quick-cooking* rice are convenient time-savers but do not have the same flavor and texture as long-grain rice that has been boiled or steamed.

+ *Flavored rice mixes* containing packets of seasoning or sauce are easy to use. Keep in mind, though, that they are often high in fat and sodium, and you might want to use only half the flavoring packet.

+ All rice should be stored in an airtight container. White rice may be kept in a cabinet for as long as a year, but brown rice should be refrigerated and used within a month.

+ Cooked rice keeps well for about a week in the refrigerator. Add some liquid, such as chicken broth or water, before reheating.

PREPARING RICE

+ Since rice is available in so many forms, it is important to read the package label for specific cooking directions.

+ White and brown rice should *not* be rinsed before cooking. On the other hand, imported and wild rice should always be carefully rinsed to remove any dirt and debris.

+ A foolproof method of cooking long-grain white rice:

    + Bring the liquid to a boil in a fairly heavy pot with a tight-fitting lid, using twice as much liquid as rice.

    + Once the liquid boils, add the rice and stir it a few times.

    + Quickly cover the pot and cook over *very low heat.* (If your lid doesn't fit tightly, place a damp paper towel over the pot and place the lid on top of it. This will help keep the steam from escaping.)

    + Check after fifteen minutes. Once the liquid has been completely absorbed, the rice is done. If the rice is still wet, remove the cover and continue cooking over very low heat for a few more minutes.

    + Once the rice is done, remove from the heat and let stand, covered, for five to ten minutes before serving.

- Brown rice is cooked the same way but takes somewhat longer, about forty-five minutes.
- Another method for boiling rice is to drop it into a large pot of boiling water the same way you cook pasta. After twenty minutes, taste it to see if it is tender. When the rice is done, drain it thoroughly in a sieve or colander.
- All types of rice can be cooked in liquids other than water. Chicken broth is a flavorful alternative, as is a mixture of half fruit juice and half water.
- To enhance the flavor of rice, add some salt to the cooking liquid before adding the rice. If you want to avoid salt, try seasoning the liquid with some herbs and spices. A few drops of lemon juice added just before the rice is done will help keep white rice white as well as add some flavor.
- Although you can cook rice in a microwave oven, it really isn't any faster than boiling. If you do use a microwave, be sure to check the directions on the package.
- Always fluff cooked rice with a fork before serving.

For tips and hints on cooking noodles, see the chapter "Pasta."

NOODLE PUDDING

from **MERYL POSTER**

Copresident of Production, Miramax Films

◆

SERVES 20

One 16-ounce package medium noodles
$^1/_2$ pound (2 sticks) butter
2 cups sour cream
$1^1/_2$ cups sugar
6 eggs, beaten
$^1/_2$ teaspoon vanilla extract
$^1/_4$ cup milk
1 apple, cored and chopped
$^1/_2$ cup raisins
Ground cinnamon, for sprinkling
Crushed cornflakes, for topping
Apricot jam, for dabbing

1. Preheat the oven to 350°F.
2. Cook the noodles in salted boiling water for 6 minutes. Drain.
3. Add the butter to the drained noodles and stir well to coat
4. In a large bowl, combine the sour cream, sugar, eggs, vanilla extract, milk, apple, and raisins. Add the noodles and mix well.
5. Pour the mixture into two ungreased baking pans (14 × 8 × 2$^1/_2$ inches or of similar size).
6. Sprinkle with cinnamon and top with crushed cornflakes, then dab with apricot jam.
7. Bake for 1 hour.

LOW-FAT NOODLE PUDDING
(Kugel)

◆

SERVES 6 TO 8

8 ounces medium or broad noodles, preferably the no-yolk kind

*1 tablespoon margarine or butter, plus some extra for dotting
the surface*

³/₄ cup low-fat or nonfat cottage cheese

¹/₂ cup low-fat sour cream or plain nonfat yogurt

2 cups skim or low-fat milk

*2 apples (preferably 1 red and 1 yellow), cored (but not
peeled) and cut into bite-sized pieces*

1 cup golden raisins

3 egg whites, or 1 egg and 1 egg white

Scant ¹/₂ cup sugar

1 teaspoon vanilla extract

Ground cinnamon, for sprinkling

¹/₄ cup cornflake crumbs, plus more as needed

1. Preheat the oven to 350°F.
2. Lightly grease a 13 × 9-inch glass, Pyrex, or other baking dish.
3. Bring a large pot of salted water to a boil and add the noodles. Cook for about 10 minutes and drain. (The noodles should be fairly firm, not mushy.) While the noodles are in the colander, stir in the margarine until they are fairly well coated. Set aside.
4. In a large bowl, combine the cottage cheese, sour cream, milk, apples, raisins, egg whites, sugar, and vanilla extract. Stir until well blended and the sugar is dissolved.
5. Add the cooled noodles to the mixture, stirring well, and pour into the prepared baking dish.
6. Sprinkle the surface liberally with cinnamon and then with the cornflake crumbs.
7. Dot the surface with dabs of margarine and bake until the surface is light brown and some of the noodles are crisp, about 1¹/₄ hours.

✦ You can buy cornflake crumbs in the supermarket, usually in the bread department, or make them yourself.

✦ Add ¼ cup dried cherries along with the raisins for extra color and flavor.

NOODLE-RICE CASSEROLE

SERVES 12

12 tablespoons (1½ sticks) margarine or butter
One 16-ounce package fine noodles
2 cups white rice
Two 10-ounce cans onion or French onion soup
Two 14-ounce cans chicken broth, preferably College Inn
1 tablespoon soy sauce
1 cup water
One 8-ounce can water chestnuts, drained and sliced (optional)

1. Preheat the oven to 350°F.
2. Melt the margarine in a very large pan. Add the uncooked noodles and cook, stirring frequently and turning with a spatula, until they are lightly browned.
3. Add the uncooked rice, onion soup, chicken broth, soy sauce, water, and water chestnuts. Mix well.
4. Pour into a large (4-quart) casserole dish and bake for 45 minutes.

TIPS AND TIDBITS

✦ This is one of our all-time favorites—easy and delicious, great for dinner parties.

THE BEST CHINESE NOODLES

SERVES 8 TO 10

1 pound regular or thin spaghetti

4 to 5 cloves garlic, finely minced

¹/₄ cup finely chopped or grated fresh ginger (about 4 inches of a peeled gingerroot)

¹/₂ cup canola or other light vegetable oil

²/₃ cup tahini

¹/₂ cup creamy peanut butter

¹/₂ cup soy sauce

¹/₄ cup dry sherry

¹/₄ cup sherry vinegar

¹/₄ cup honey

2 tablespoons sesame oil, preferably dark

A pinch of cayenne pepper, or more to taste

1 red bell pepper, seeded and sliced into very thin strips

1 yellow bell pepper, seeded and sliced into very thin strips

3 to 4 scallions (green onions), the white part and some of the green, thinly sliced on the diagonal

1. Bring a large pot of water to a boil and add some salt and a few drops of oil. Drop in the spaghetti, stir, and bring the water to a second boil. Cook until the spaghetti is firm yet tender, about 10 minutes. While the spaghetti is boiling, prepare the sauce.
2. Place the minced garlic and the ginger in a food processor or blender and process for a few seconds to combine them.
3. Add the vegetable oil, tahini, peanut butter, soy sauce, sherry, vinegar, honey, sesame oil, and cayenne and process until smooth.
4. When the spaghetti is done, drain it in a colander and place in a large bowl. While still warm, toss the spaghetti with about two-thirds of the sauce. Make sure the individual noodles are well coated.

5. Serve warm or at room temperature, garnished with the sliced red and yellow bell peppers and scallions. Serve the remaining sauce on the side.

TIPS AND TIDBITS

✦ Tahini, or sesame paste, comes in cans or jars and can be purchased in most supermarkets.

COLD NOODLES IN SPICY PEANUT SAUCE

◆

SERVES 4

8 ounces thin spaghetti
3 tablespoons canola, corn, or other light vegetable oil
2 tablespoons creamy peanut butter
2 tablespoons soy sauce
1 tablespoon water
1 teaspoon sugar
¹/₄ cup minced onion
¹/₂ teaspoon ground ginger
A dash of Tabasco red pepper sauce
1 small cucumber, peeled, seeded, and cut into 1-inch slivers

1. Bring a pot of salted water to a boil and cook the spaghetti according to package directions.
2. When the spaghetti is done, drain it and toss with 1 tablespoon of the oil, coating the noodles well. Place in the refrigerator to cool.
3. In a large bowl, combine the remaining 2 tablespoons oil, the peanut butter, soy sauce, water, sugar, onion, ginger, and Tabasco sauce. Stir until well blended and creamy.
4. Add the spaghetti, toss to coat the noodles well, and top with the cucumber slivers. Chill in the refrigerator until ready to serve.

GUILT-FREE FRENCH FRIES

◆

SERVES 6

6 large baking potatoes, well washed
2 egg whites
¹/₄ teaspoon paprika
Salt and pepper to taste
Garlic powder to taste

1. Preheat the oven to 400°F.
2. Spray a large baking pan or cookie sheet with vegetable oil.
3. Slice each potato (unpeeled) lengthwise into ¹/₄-inch-thick ovals and then slice each oval into thin strips.
4. Combine the egg whites, the paprika, salt, pepper, and garlic powder in a large bowl.
5. Add the potatoes to the bowl and mix to coat.
6. Pour the potatoes onto the prepared baking pan and spread them into a single layer, leaving a little space between them.
7. Bake for about 40 to 45 minutes, turning the fries over 5 or 6 times, until crisp. Serve immediately.

TIPS AND TIDBITS

+ You might also want to try Guilt-Free Potato Chips: Using a knife, food processor, or even a cheese plane, thinly slice two large white or sweet potatoes (unpeeled), drain the slices on paper towels, and place them on a well-greased baking sheet. Bake at 450°F for about twenty minutes, but watch them carefully to make sure they don't burn. (Sweet potato slices will cook faster than white potatoes.) Remove the chips with a spatula and season with salt and pepper to taste.

OPRAH'S POTATOES

from **OPRAH WINFREY**
Actress, Producer, Author, Creator and Host of The
Oprah Winfrey Show, *Creator of* O, the Oprah Magazine,
Winner of Seven Emmy Awards

SERVES 12

2¹/₂ *pounds red potatoes*
2¹/₂ *pounds Idaho potatoes*
¹/₂ *cup Butter Buds powder*
1 *cup chicken stock*
2 *cups skim milk*
¹/₈ *teaspoon cayenne powder (optional)*
4 *tablespoons creamy pureed horseradish*
1¹/₂ *tablespoons ground black pepper*

1. Wash potatoes well; leave the skin on; cut potatoes in half.
2. Place potatoes in kettle and fill with water to cover. Bring to a boil; reduce heat to low. Cover and simmer until potatoes are very tender.
3. Drain all water; add Butter Buds and begin to mash. Add chicken stock, skim milk, cayenne powder, horseradish, black pepper, and mash until creamy, but still slightly lumpy.

Copyright © 1994 Harpo, Inc. All rights reserved.

BLUE MASHED POTATOES

from **JANE SMILEY**
*Author, Essayist, Winner of the 1992 Pulitzer Prize for
Fiction and Four O. Henry Awards*

SERVES 4 TO 6

2 pounds blue potatoes
5 tablespoons butter
1 cup cream, warmed but not brought to a boil
Salt and pepper to taste
Chopped chives, for garnish

1. Quarter the potatoes and boil them in salted water until soft. Drain the water and briefly place the pot back on the burner to steam off the remaining water.
2. Remove from the heat and take off the peels quickly, being careful to keep the cooked potatoes warm. Drop in 4 tablespoons of the butter. As it melts, mash the potatoes by hand until there are no more chunks.
3. Add 1/2 cup of the cream and salt and pepper.
4. Whip with an electric mixer, continuing to add cream until the potatoes are creamy.
5. Stir in the remaining 1 tablespoon butter and additional salt and pepper to taste.
6. Garnish with the chives and serve.

ROASTED POTATOES

SERVES 3 TO 4

1 1/2 to 2 pounds small red potatoes, each about 2 inches
in diameter
2 to 3 tablespoons olive oil
1 tablespoon dried oregano or rosemary, whichever you
like better
1 to 2 cloves garlic, crushed
1/2 teaspoon salt, preferably kosher or sea salt
Pepper or paprika to taste

1. Preheat the oven to 400°F.
2. Line a large, shallow baking dish or a jelly-roll pan with aluminum foil.
3. Wash the potatoes well, cut them into quarters, and place in a bowl.
4. Drizzle the olive oil over the potatoes and toss them with the oregano, garlic, salt, and pepper. Make sure they are well coated.
5. Spread the potatoes on the prepared pan, skin side up. Try not to let them touch.
6. Roast for about 1¼ hours. When done, adjust the seasoning—more salt may be needed—and serve hot.

TIPS AND TIDBITS

✦ Try using chunks of sweet potatoes to make a delicious variation of this dish. Use canola or another light vegetable oil instead of the olive oil and omit the garlic and herbs, but sprinkle with a combination of ¹/₂ teaspoon curry powder, ¹/₄ teaspoon salt, ¹/₄ teaspoon cumin, a pinch of ground cloves, and a pinch of cayenne pepper. Because sweet potatoes cook faster than white potatoes, check them after forty-five minutes.

POTATO PANCAKES
(Latkes)

◆

SERVES 6

2 medium onions, cut into chunks

4 to 5 medium baking potatoes, peeled and cut into chunks (if you want to peel and cut them beforehand, keep them in a bowl of cold water so they won't turn brown)

2 eggs, lightly beaten

1 teaspoon salt

Continued

¹/₄ teaspoon pepper, preferably white

3 to 6 tablespoons flour or matzo meal, or more or less
  as needed

Peanut, canola, or other light vegetable oil, for frying

1. Grate the onions or place them in the bowl of a food processor and process until fairly small.
2. Grate the potatoes and add them to the grated onions or add to the processor and continue processing until finely chopped.
3. Drain the onion-potato mixture in a sieve or colander to remove the excess liquid. (Place the sieve or colander in a large bowl so that when you pour off the liquid, you can save the starch that settles to the bottom.)
4. Put the mixture in a large bowl and stir in the eggs, salt, and pepper.
5. Add the reserved potato starch and enough of the flour to thicken the batter. Keep the rest on hand in case you need to add more (i.e., if the latkes start to fall apart as you cook them).
6. Pour about ¹/₄ inch of oil into a large, heavy pan and heat it until a drop of water sizzles vigorously. The oil should be so hot that it spatters. (Be careful not to get burned.)
7. Using a large spoon, drop about ¹/₄ cup of the potato mixture into the pan. If necessary, flatten the latke with the back of the spoon. Continue adding spoonfuls to the pan, but don't crowd the latkes.
8. Cook the latkes for about 6 to 8 minutes a side, depending on how crisp you like them.
9. When the latkes are done, drain them on paper towels, sprinkle with salt to taste, and serve immediately.

TIPS AND TIDBITS

+ It is a good idea to taste the first latke right away in case you need to add more salt or grated onion to the batter.
+ Applesauce is the traditional accompaniment for latkes, although some people prefer sour cream or sprinkle them with sugar.
+ If you can't serve the latkes right away, you can keep them warm and fairly crisp by placing them on wire cookie racks placed directly on your

oven rack in a 250°F oven. Be sure to place a sheet of aluminum foil on the shelf below the latkes or on the oven floor to catch any oil drips.

POTATO PUDDING
(Kugel)

◆

¹/₄ cup peanut, canola, or other light vegetable oil, plus more
  as needed
6 medium baking potatoes, peeled
6 medium red or sweet white onions
3 eggs, lightly beaten
¹/₂ cup matzo meal
1¹/₂ teaspoons salt
³/₄ teaspoon pepper

1. Preheat the oven to 350°F.
2. Prepare a 13 × 9-inch baking pan by spreading a thin layer of oil on the bottom.
3. Cut the potatoes and onions into chunks and grate or process together in a food processor until the mixture becomes a slightly coarse puree. You will have to do this several times to process all of the onions and potatoes. After each batch is done, pour it into a sieve or colander to drain off the excess liquid.
4. Pour the potato mixture into a large bowl and add the eggs, matzo meal, salt, and pepper. Mix well.
5. Place the prepared baking pan in the oven for 10 minutes.
6. Pour the potato mixture into the heated pan, pour the ¹/₄ cup oil over the top, and bake until the top is dark brown and crisp, 1 to 1¹/₂ hours.

TIPS AND TIDBITS
✦ This mixture can also be used to make potato pancakes.

DILLED POTATO SALAD

◆

SERVES 4

1 pound small red potatoes (about 8 or 9 potatoes), well
  washed and cut into quarters
Salt and pepper to taste
1 cup regular or low-fat sour cream, plus more as needed
1/3 to 1/2 cup chopped red onions
1/2 cup chopped fresh dill

1. Put the potatoes into a pot of cold water. Add salt and bring to a boil. After the water starts to boil, cook the potatoes until they are tender, about 10 minutes.
2. When the potatoes are done, drain them, place in a bowl, and season with salt and pepper.
3. While the potatoes are still hot, add the sour cream and toss gently.
4. Add the onions and dill, mix, and allow to cool to room temperature before placing in the refrigerator.
5. Refrigerate for several hours or overnight. Just before serving, mix again, adjust the seasoning, and add more sour cream if needed.

TIPS AND TIDBITS

✦ To reduce the fat even more, try using a combination of 1/2 cup low-fat sour cream and 1/2 cup plain nonfat yogurt.

POTATO SALAD WITH FETA CHEESE

SERVES 4

1¹/₂ pounds red potatoes, well washed, quartered, and cut into
    ³/₄-inch-thick slices
¹/₄ cup fresh lemon juice
Salt to taste
¹/₂ cup diced pimientos
¹/₂ cup pitted black olives
3 scallions (green onions), the white part and some of the
    green, minced
8 ounces feta cheese, crumbled
³/₄ teaspoon dried oregano
¹/₂ cup olive oil
Pepper to taste

1. Boil the potatoes until they are tender, 8 to 10 minutes. Drain them and place in a large bowl.
2. Toss the potatoes with 2 tablespoons of the lemon juice and salt to taste. Set aside to cool to room temperature.
3. When cool, add the pimientos, olives, scallions, and feta cheese to the potatoes and mix.
4. In a small bowl, whisk together the remaining 2 tablespoons lemon juice and the oregano and slowly add the olive oil.
5. Pour the dressing over the potato mixture and gently toss to coat. Adjust the seasoning with salt and pepper, and refrigerate. Serve cold or at room temperature.

TIPS AND TIDBITS

✦ Although canned black olives are fine for this recipe, you will get a tastier dish using fresh cured olives. Two good choices are Kalamata (medium-sized, purplish-black olives with a tangy flavor) and Gaeta (smaller, purplish-brown olives with a milder flavor).

TARRAGON POTATO SALAD

◆

1 pound small or medium red potatoes, unpeeled
3 tablespoons sour cream
2 tablespoons plain yogurt
2 teaspoons tarragon vinegar
A dash of cayenne pepper
1 tablespoon chopped fresh dill
1 tablespoon chopped fresh parsley
2 teaspoons capers, rinsed and chopped
Salt and pepper to taste

1. Wash the potatoes well and cook in boiling salted water until they are tender, about 20 minutes.
2. In a large bowl, combine the sour cream, yogurt, vinegar, and cayenne pepper. Stir in the dill, parsley, and capers.
3. When the potatoes are done, drain them, cut them into slices or quarters, and add to the dressing. Mix well.
4. Season with salt and pepper, and refrigerate until ready to serve.

SWEET POTATO AND SCALLION SALAD

◆

SERVES 8

4 large sweet potatoes (preferably long skinny ones),
*   well washed*
1 bunch scallions (green onions), the white part and 3 inches of
*   the green*
¹/₂ cup olive oil, plus some extra for drizzling

Salt and pepper to taste
1 tablespoon Dijon mustard
¹/₄ cup cider vinegar
¹/₄ cup balsamic vinegar
1 tablespoon honey
A few tablespoons chopped fresh parsley, for garnish

1. Preheat the oven to 375°F.
2. Cut the (unpeeled) potatoes into 1-inch cubes.
3. Place the potatoes and scallions in a large roasting pan, drizzle with some olive oil, and stir to coat. Sprinkle with salt and pepper.
4. Roast the potatoes and scallions for about 45 minutes, or until tender. (If the scallions are getting very soft, remove them from the pan and set aside.)
5. Drain the potatoes and scallions on paper towels and allow them to cool.
6. While they are cooling, whisk together the mustard, vinegars, and honey. Slowly whisk in the ¹/₄ cup olive oil.
7. When the scallions are cool, chop them into small pieces.
8. Place the potatoes and scallions in a large bowl and slowly add the dressing, tossing to coat. (You may not need all of the dressing.)
9. Adjust the seasoning, if necessary, garnish with the chopped parsley, and store in the refrigerator.
10. Serve cold or at room temperature. When served cold, this makes a very refreshing summer salad.

TIPS AND TIDBITS

+ Balsamic vinegar is available at a wide range of prices. The one we like best is Fini; it's a bit pricey but worth it. By the way, just a splash of balsamic vinegar on a salad is a tasty low-calorie, nonfat alternative to regular salad dressing.

SWEET POTATO CASSEROLE

♦

4 to 5 medium sweet potatoes, peeled and cut into chunks
About 2 cups pineapple or orange juice
4 tablespoons ($^{1}/_{2}$ stick) margarine or butter
1 egg, lightly beaten
$^{1}/_{2}$ teaspoon salt
$^{1}/_{4}$ teaspoon ground cinnamon
8 regular-sized marshmallows (or more!)

1. Preheat the oven to 350°F.
2. Place the potato chunks in a large pot and add enough pineapple juice to cover. Bring to a boil, cover, and simmer until soft, about 20 minutes.
3. When the potatoes are done, drain them but *save the juice.*
4. Place the potatoes in a bowl and mash them into coarse chunks. Add the margarine, egg, salt, cinnamon, and about 6 tablespoons of the drained juice.
5. Beat with an electric mixer until fairly creamy. Add more of the drained juice if necessary.
6. Spoon the mixture into an 8-inch round or square baking dish and lightly press the marshmallows into the top, spacing them evenly. Bake for 30 minutes.

TIPS AND TIDBITS

+ If you're partial to marshmallows, or have lots of kids in the house, you might want to cover the *entire* surface of the casserole with marshmallows!
+ If you are making this dish a day ahead, bake the potato mixture *without* the marshmallows and refrigerate overnight. Before serving, top with the marshmallows and bake the dish for twenty minutes or so to reheat it and melt the marshmallows.

WILD RICE

from JANET GUTHRIE

Professional Race Car Driver, the First Woman to Compete
in the Indianapolis 500 and the Daytona 500

◆

SERVES 10 TO 12

8 ounces carrots, peeled
8 ounces onions
8 ounces mushrooms
⅓ cup olive oil
Four 14-ounce cans low-sodium, nonfat chicken broth
1 pound wild rice (preferably Brule River), rinsed well
2 bay leaves
1¼ teaspoons salt
1¼ teaspoons sesame oil (fragrant Japanese style)

1. Coarsely chop the carrots, onions, and mushrooms. Be sure to keep them separate.
2. Put each vegetable, separately, into a food processor and finely chop until each piece is about two to five times the size of a grain of wild rice.
3. Put the olive oil into a 4½-quart pot over medium-high heat. Sauté the carrots and onions until the onions are tender but not brown, stirring as needed, then add the mushrooms and sauté until they have yielded most of their moisture.
4. Add 3 cans of the chicken broth and the wild rice, bay leaves, and salt. Simmer very gently until the wild rice begins to pop open. Depending on the rice, this may take an hour or two. Check after 45 minutes to make sure the rice isn't getting dry; add the remaining 1 can chicken broth as needed.
5. When done, remove the bay leaves, stir in the sesame oil, and adjust the seasoning.

WILD RICE AND CRANBERRY SALAD

◆

SERVES 12

6½ cups water
½ cup chicken broth, preferably College Inn
2½ cups wild rice, rinsed well
1 cup dried cranberries
1 cup golden raisins
1 cup chopped scallions (green onions), the white part and
    some of the green
¾ cup toasted pine nuts
½ cup chopped fresh parsley
2 tablespoons grated orange peel
½ cup orange juice, preferably fresh
¼ cup cider vinegar
½ cup olive oil
Salt and pepper to taste

1. Bring the water and chicken broth to a boil in a large saucepan.
2. Add the wild rice and bring to a boil. Reduce the heat and simmer,
   stirring occasionally, until the rice is tender, about 40 minutes.
3. Drain the rice and place in a large bowl to cool.
4. Add the cranberries, raisins, scallions, pine nuts, parsley, and orange
   peel.
5. In a small bowl, whisk together the orange juice and vinegar.
6. Gradually, whisk in the olive oil.
7. Slowly add the dressing to the rice mixture, using just enough to
   coat.
8. Season with salt and pepper, cover, and refrigerate. It's a good idea
   to make this a day ahead, just be sure to serve at room temperature.

TIPS AND TIDBITS

✦ To toast pine nuts (or any other nut, spice, or seed), spread them evenly
  on a small metal tray and bake them in a toaster oven at 300°F for just

a few minutes. You can also toast them in a dry skillet over medium heat. Watch them very carefully to make sure they don't burn. When you start to smell them, they're done.

+ For a slightly different flavor, instead of 1 cup dried cranberries, use 1/2 cup dried cranberries and 1/2 cup dried cherries.

WILD RICE SALAD WITH PECANS

◆

SERVES 6 TO 8

4 cups chicken broth, preferably College Inn
2 cups water
1 cup (about 1/2 pound) wild rice, rinsed well
1 1/2 cups pecan halves
1 cup golden raisins
4 scallions (green onions), the white part and some of the
green, minced
Grated peel of 1 orange (optional)
Salt and pepper to taste
3 tablespoons olive oil
6 tablespoons orange juice

1. Pour the chicken broth and water into a large pot and bring to a boil.
2. Add the rice and bring to a boil. Lower the heat, and simmer, uncovered, for 35 to 40 minutes. After 35 minutes, start checking to see if it is done; it should be tender, not mushy.
3. Drain the rice, put it in a bowl, and add the pecans, raisins, scallions, and grated orange peel, if desired. Mix thoroughly and season with salt and pepper.
4. In a separate bowl, combine the olive oil and orange juice. Pour over the rice mixture, stir to combine, and allow the salad to stand for several hours before serving.

+ If you are making this dish a day ahead, add the pecans just before serving. Otherwise, they'll become soggy.
+ It's important to properly cook the wild rice. If overcooked, it becomes gluey, and if undercooked, it is too tough and hard to chew.

COUSCOUS SALAD

SERVES 2

1 cup chicken broth, preferably College Inn
$^2/_3$ to $^3/_4$ cup couscous
$^1/_2$ teaspoon Dijon mustard
2 tablespoons balsamic vinegar
1 teaspoon sugar
$^1/_2$ medium red bell pepper, seeded and cut into thin strips
$^1/_2$ medium yellow bell pepper, seeded and cut into thin strips
2 scallions (green onions), the white part and some of the
   green, thinly sliced

1. Bring the chicken broth to a boil and stir in the couscous. Cover the pot and remove from the heat. After 5 minutes, remove the cover, stir, and set the pot aside to cool.
2. In a serving bowl, combine the mustard, vinegar, and sugar. Mix well to dissolve the sugar.
3. Stir the bell peppers and scallions into the dressing and add the couscous, stirring to combine.
4. Serve warm or at room temperature.

COUSCOUS WITH RAISINS AND ALMONDS

♦

SERVES 4

1¹/₂ cups chicken broth
¹/₃ cup raisins
2 scallions (green onions), the white part and some of the
green, thinly sliced
1 teaspoon unsalted butter
1 cinnamon stick
Salt to taste
1 cup couscous
¹/₃ cup slivered or sliced almonds, preferably toasted

1. In a medium pot, bring to a boil the chicken broth, raisins, scallions, butter, cinnamon stick, and salt.
2. Stir in the couscous, cover the pot, and remove from the heat.
3. Allow the pot to stand for about 5 minutes, then fluff up the couscous with a fork and remove the cinnamon stick.
4. Stir in the almonds.
5. Serve at room temperature.

TABBOULEH

from **DONNA E. SHALALA**
President, University of Miami;
Former Secretary of Health and Human Services

♦

"Tabbouleh is nutritious as well as delicious. The preparation and eating of tabbouleh was always a family affair when I was growing up in Cleveland. My mother, grandmother, and aunts would sit together and talk while chopping the parsley and mint. Now, when I have time, I make tabbouleh with my friends and, in a new way, re-create the socializing of my family."

SERVES 4 TO 6

½ cup cracked wheat (fine or medium bulgur)
1 cup fresh lemon juice, plus more to taste
3 bunches parsley
2 bunches mint
1 small bunch scallions (green onions), thinly sliced
2 cups chopped ripe tomatoes
Salt and pepper to taste
¼ cup virgin olive oil

1. Place the cracked wheat in a small bowl and add the lemon juice. Add water to cover and allow to stand for 3 hours.
2. Meanwhile, wash and dry the parsley and mint leaves, and chop them separately—preferably by hand, not in a food processor. You should have about 3 cups of finely chopped parsley and 2 cups of finely chopped mint.
3. When it is ready, drain the cracked wheat, squeezing out the liquid, and combine it with the parsley, mint, scallions, and tomatoes. Mix well.
4. Season with salt and pepper. Add the olive oil and additional lemon juice to taste.
5. Try to wait before eating so the flavors can meld. Serve with lettuce leaves, young grape leaves, or thin Lebanese bread.

TABBOULEH WITH CURRANTS AND PINE NUTS

SERVES 4

1 cup bulgur (cracked wheat)

3 scallions (green onions), the white part and some of the
green, minced

1/4 cup chopped fresh parsley

1/2 cup dried currants

1/4 cup pine nuts

2 tablespoons canola or other light vegetable oil

2 tablespoons lime juice, preferably fresh (about 1 small lime)

1. Place the bulgur in a medium bowl and cover with boiling water. Let it stand until all the water is absorbed. The wheat should be firm, not hard. If necessary, add some more boiling water and allow it to stand for a few more minutes.
2. When the bulgur is ready, stir in the scallions, parsley, currants, and pine nuts.
3. In a separate bowl, combine the oil and lime juice. Pour it over the wheat mixture and mix well.
4. Store in the refrigerator and serve cold or at room temperature.

RECIPE TITLE_____

FROM_____

SERVES _____

INGREDIENTS

INSTRUCTIONS

TIPS AND TIDBITS

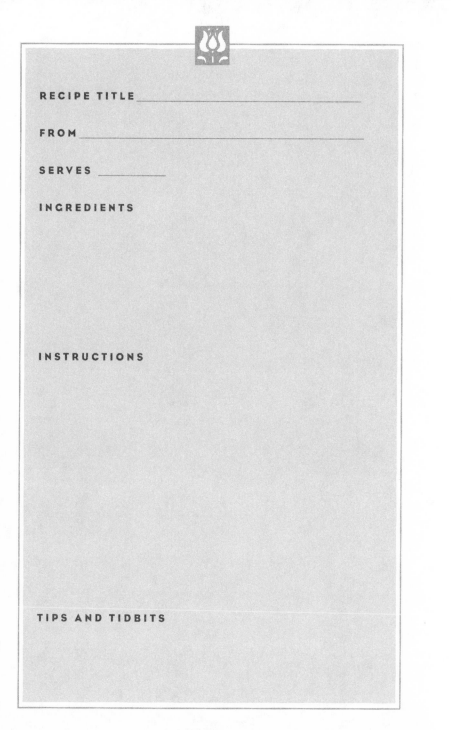

RECIPE TITLE

FROM

SERVES

INGREDIENTS

INSTRUCTIONS

TIPS AND TIDBITS

PASTA

TIPS AND HINTS ON...
HOW TO COOK PASTA

✦ Pasta should always be cooked in a pot of vigorously boiling water, using 4 quarts of water per pound of pasta. (Covering the pot will make the water boil faster.) Adding a few drops of oil to the boiling water helps prevent the pasta from sticking together, although the coated pasta may absorb less sauce. Salt is also often added to the boiling water as a flavoring, usually about 1 or 2 teaspoons per pound of pasta.

+ Drop the pasta into the boiling water all at once and stir it with a long-handled spoon to separate the strands or pieces. Do not cover the pot after adding the pasta.

+ Once the water returns to a boil, stir the pasta and start your timer. The cooking time, usually ranging from eight to ten minutes, depends on the size and shape of the pasta. It's always a good idea to check the directions on the package.

+ The best way to see if your pasta is done is to remove a piece and taste it; if it's too hard, continue boiling another few minutes. The Italian expression *al dente* means that the pasta is cooked to the point of being tender yet still firm when you bite into it. If you are using the pasta to make lasagna, or any other dish that requires further cooking, it is better to keep it fairly firm so it won't get mushy when it cooks later on.

+ When the pasta is ready, drain it immediately in a colander or large sieve. Do not rinse with water, but toss it with whatever sauce or dressing you are using. This will keep the pieces from sticking together and allow the pasta to absorb more of the flavor. If you can't add the sauce right away, toss the pasta with some butter or oil.

+ It's a good idea to save about 1/4 cup of the drained pasta water. It's handy in case you want to thin your pasta sauce.

PASTA SAUCES AND DRESSINGS

+ Every supermarket has a wide variety of pasta sauces, and it is a good idea to keep some on hand for quick last-minute meals. You can use them directly from the jar or improvise by adding your favorite seasonings and any leftover vegetables.

+ Canned lentil or other bean soups as well as some bottled salad dressings make tasty pasta sauces.

+ It is also very easy to make a fresh sauce, and you can often do it while the pasta is boiling. Olive oil and sautéed minced garlic make a delicious sauce you can serve alone or with the addition of one or more of the following:

—Sun-dried or fresh tomatoes

—Olives or capers

—Sautéed or raw mushrooms

—Chunks of canned tuna

—Cubed or shredded mozzarella cheese

—Crumbled feta cheese

—Roasted peppers

—Cut-up broccoli, carrots, snow peas, cauliflower, or other vegetable, raw or steamed

—Fresh or dried herbs, such as oregano, marjoram, and basil

HOW MUCH TO MAKE

✦ When serving pasta as a main course, count on approximately 4 ounces of pasta and 1 cup of sauce per person. Obviously, these amounts will vary depending on what other ingredients you add to the dish and what else you are serving along with the pasta.

FRESH TOMATO-BASIL SAUCE

from **BOBBI BROWN**
Professional Makeup Artist;
Founder and CEO, Bobbi Brown Cosmetics

◆

MAKES ABOUT 3 CUPS, ENOUGH FOR
8 TO 12 OUNCES OF PASTA

3 tablespoons olive oil
2 cloves garlic, chopped
Salt (preferably sea salt or kosher salt) and pepper to taste
5 large ripe yellow tomatoes, chopped
¹/₄ cup chopped fresh basil, or to taste
Freshly grated Romano cheese, for sprinkling

1. In a heavy skillet, heat the olive oil and sauté the chopped garlic. Add salt and pepper.
2. Add the tomatoes and simmer for a couple of minutes.
3. Add the basil and cook for another 10 to 15 minutes.
4. Serve over pasta and sprinkle with the freshly grated Romano cheese.

PESTO

MAKES ABOUT 1 CUP,
ENOUGH FOR 1 POUND OF PASTA

2 cups fresh basil leaves
1/2 cup olive oil
2 tablespoons pine nuts
2 cloves garlic, minced
1 teaspoon salt
1/2 cup grated Parmesan cheese
2 tablespoons grated Romano cheese

1. In a blender or food processor, combine the basil leaves, olive oil, pine nuts, garlic, and salt. Process until smooth.
2. Pour into a bowl and stir in the grated cheeses.
3. Serve over pasta.

TIPS AND TIDBITS

✦ To make a lower-fat pesto, process 2 cups fresh basil leaves, 1/3 cup pine nuts, 2 to 3 cloves garlic, and 1/3 cup grated Parmesan cheese until the mixture forms a smooth paste. Continue blending while drizzling in 1/4 cup or more fresh lemon juice.

✦ You can easily divide the sauce into small portions, about 1/4 cup each, and freeze for future use.

EASY PASTA SALAD

◆

8 ounces penne, fusilli, or other small pasta
2 to 4 cups assorted raw or lightly steamed vegetables (sugar
*   snap peas, cherry tomatoes, broccoli or cauliflower florets,*
*   baby carrots)*
Olive oil, for drizzling
¹/₂ cup grated Parmesan cheese, or to taste
Salt and pepper to taste
Garlic powder to taste (optional)

1. In a large pot of salted boiling water, cook the pasta according to package directions. Drain and place in a large bowl.
2. Add the prepared vegetables and toss with the olive oil, Parmesan cheese, salt and pepper, and garlic powder, if desired.
3. Serve warm or at room temperature.

TIPS AND TIDBITS

✦ When measuring grated or shredded cheese—Parmesan or any other—pack it gently, not firmly, in the measuring cup to eliminate any air pockets.

OBERLIN PERFECTIONIST PASTA

from **NANCY S. DYE**
President, Oberlin College

♦

SERVES 4 TO 6

14 ounces small shell pasta
2 teaspoons minced garlic
1 tablespoon black pepper
2 teaspoons salt
½ cup balsamic vinegar
¼ cup olive oil
Cayenne pepper or Tabasco red pepper sauce to taste
One 16-ounce bag frozen corn, thawed
One 15-ounce can black beans, rinsed and drained
1 red bell pepper, seeded and diced
1 green bell pepper, seeded and diced
1 red onion, diced
1 cup packed cilantro leaves, chopped

1. Drop the pasta into a large pot of salted boiling water. Once the water returns to a boil, stir the pasta and cook about 8 to 10 minutes, until the shells are al dente, tender yet still firm.
2. While the pasta is cooking, whisk together the garlic, black pepper, salt, balsamic vinegar, olive oil, and cayenne.
3. Once the shells are done, drain immediately and place in a large bowl.
4. Add the corn, black beans, red bell pepper, green bell pepper, red onion, and cilantro to the shells, stirring well to combine.
5. Add the dressing and toss thoroughly.
6. Refrigerate for 2 hours to allow the flavors to blend. Serve at room temperature.

ORIENTAL PASTA WITH CHICKEN

◆

SERVES 4

8 ounces fusilli, penne, or other small pasta
1 pound boneless, skinless chicken breasts, cut into chunks
¹/₂ cup ginger teriyaki marinade (enough to coat the chicken)
1 to 2 cups assorted vegetables (such as sugar snap peas, sliced
*   carrots, broccoli or cauliflower florets, cut-up green, yellow,*
*   or red bell peppers)*
Honey mustard salad dressing, preferably Ken's Steakhouse

1. Preheat the oven to 350°F.
2. In a pot of salted boiling water, cook the pasta according to package directions. Drain and set aside to cool.
3. Place the chicken chunks in a baking dish and coat them with the ginger teriyaki marinade.
4. Bake the chicken for 5 to 10 minutes, depending on the size of the chunks, until tender.
5. Steam the vegetables until they start to soften, about 5 minutes. If you like your vegetables crisp and crunchy, use them raw without steaming them at all.
6. Place the pasta, chicken (including the juices from the pan), and vegetables in a large bowl and toss with just enough honey mustard salad dressing to lightly coat them.
7. Serve at room temperature, but store in the refrigerator.

TIPS AND TIDBITS

+ If the salad seems too dry before you serve it, add more honey mustard salad dressing.
+ You can steam the vegetables in a steamer over boiling water or put them in a glass bowl with a little water in the bottom and soften them in a microwave oven.
+ When you are tired of chicken, shrimp makes a nice substitute.

PASTA WITH GARLIC AND OIL
(Aglio e Olio)

from **ADRIENNE VITTADINI**

Fashion Designer; Former Chairwoman,
Adrienne Vittadini Enterprises, Inc.

◆

SERVES 4

1 pound spaghetti or linguini
¹/₂ cup extra-virgin olive oil
1 teaspoon finely chopped garlic
1 tablespoon finely chopped fresh Italian (flat-leaf) parsley
¹/₄ teaspoon red pepper flakes, plus more to taste
1 tablespoon salt, plus more to taste

1. Bring 4 quarts of water to a boil in a large pot. Add 1 tablespoon of salt and the pasta, stirring until the strands are submerged. Bring to a second boil and cook until the pasta is al dente, tender yet still firm.
2. While the pasta is cooking, put the olive oil and garlic in a large skillet and cook over medium-high heat until the garlic begins to change color.
3. Add the parsley, red pepper flakes, and salt to taste. Stir well and remove from the heat.
4. When the pasta is done, pour into a colander and drain.
5. Return the skillet to the stove and warm the sauce over low heat.
6. Add the drained pasta to the sauce, and toss until the noodles are well coated.
7. Adjust the seasoning, adding more salt or red pepper flakes if needed, and serve at once.

PASTA GENOVESE

◆

SERVES 4

1 pound fusilli, penne, shells, or other small pasta
2 tablespoons olive oil
1¹/₂ cups diced fresh tomatoes
Salt and pepper to taste
¹/₄ cup pesto sauce
Grated Parmesan cheese, for sprinkling

1. Bring a large pot of water to a boil, add some salt, and drop in the pasta. Bring to a second boil, stir, and cook the pasta until al dente, tender yet still firm, about 8 to 10 minutes. Drain in a colander.
2. While the pasta is cooking, heat the olive oil in a large, heavy pan and cook the tomatoes for a few minutes.
3. Add salt and pepper, the cooked pasta, and the pesto. Mix well and sprinkle with Parmesan cheese. Serve hot.

PASTA PUTTANESCA

from **KAITY TONG**
Television News Anchor, Winner of the
Edward R. Murrow Award

◆

"This is a quick and easy dish, but very tasty, especially if you like a zesty, spicy sauce. Serve with a hearty red wine and salad. Voilà!"

SERVES 4

1 pound linguini
Two 35-ounce cans whole peeled plum tomatoes
¹/₄ cup olive oil (best quality)
1 teaspoon dried oregano

^{1}/$_2$ cup pitted Niçoise olives
^{1}/$_4$ cup capers, drained
4 to 6 cloves garlic, finely chopped
8 anchovy fillets, coarsely chopped
^{1}/$_2$ cup chopped fresh Italian (flat-leaf) parsley, plus extra
   for garnish
2 teaspoons salt
^{1}/$_8$ teaspoon red pepper flakes, or to taste

1. In a large pot of salted boiling water, cook the linguini according to package directions.
2. While the pasta is cooking, drain the canned tomatoes, cut each tomato in half, and squeeze out and eliminate as much of the juice as possible.
3. Combine the tomatoes and olive oil in a skillet and bring to a boil.
4. Keeping the sauce at full boil, stir in—one at a time—the oregano, olives, capers, garlic, anchovy fillets, parsley, salt, and red pepper flakes. Stir frequently.
5. Reduce the heat and cook for a few more minutes, until the sauce has thickened. Serve at once over the hot drained pasta, and garnish with some chopped parsley on top.

PENNE WITH CABBAGE AND SAUSAGE

from **NORA EPHRON**

Author, Essayist, Director, Producer, Screenwriter

SERVES 6 TO 8

1 pound penne or spaghetti
6 hot sausages, skin removed
^{1}/$_2$ large onion, sliced the long way

Continued

¹/₃ head cabbage, cut into pieces and little chunks
2 cups Rao's marinara sauce
Salt to taste
Grated cheese to taste

1. Drop the pasta into a large pot of salted boiling water. Bring to a second boil, stir, and continue cooking until the pasta is tender yet still firm, about 10 to 12 minutes.
2. While the pasta is boiling, break the sausage meat into small pieces, and sauté with the onion in oil until almost cooked.
3. Add the cabbage and cook, covered, until the cabbage is wilted, about 7 to 8 minutes.
4. Add the marinara sauce, stir, and simmer for 10 minutes more. Add salt.
5. Toss with the drained cooked pasta and serve with grated cheese.

PENNE WITH LENTILS AND SPINACH

SERVES 4

One 10-ounce package frozen chopped or whole spinach
8 ounces penne
1 to 2 tablespoons olive oil
1 medium onion, finely chopped
1 large clove garlic, finely minced
One 19-ounce can Progresso lentil soup
Salt and pepper to taste
Grated Parmesan cheese to taste

1. Bring a large pot of water to a boil; add some salt and the frozen spinach. Allow it to simmer for 8 to 10 minutes, occasionally stirring to break up the frozen block. When the spinach is done, remove it with a slotted spoon and place in a colander to drain.

2. Bring the water back to a boil and add the penne. When it comes to a second boil, stir the pasta to keep it from sticking, and boil until it is al dente, tender yet still firm, about 10 minutes. When the penne is done, drain it in a colander, but save a little of the pasta water.

3. While the pasta is cooking, heat the olive oil in a large skillet and cook the onion over low heat until it softens, about 5 minutes.

4. Stir in the garlic and cook for another minute or two.

5. Add the lentil soup and cook for another few minutes to heat thoroughly.

6. Squeeze as much water as you can out of the cooked spinach and add the spinach to the pan.

7. Add the drained penne and stir to combine. If the sauce seems a little dry, stir in a few tablespoons of the reserved pasta water.

8. Add salt and pepper and serve with grated Parmesan cheese.

TIPS AND TIDBITS

✦ This makes a wonderful one-dish dinner that you can prepare without running to the store—you can easily keep all of the ingredients on hand and always be ready to make an impromptu meal.

PENNE PROVENÇAL

◆

SERVES 2 TO 3

1 pound cherry tomatoes, cut in half
About ¹/₄ cup olive oil
¹/₄ cup freshly grated Pecorino Romano cheese
¹/₄ cup seasoned bread crumbs
8 ounces penne
Salt and pepper to taste

1. Preheat the oven to 425°F.
2. Place a layer of the cherry tomato halves, cut side up, on the bottom of a 13 × 9-inch baking dish.
3. Drizzle 3 tablespoons of the olive oil over the tomatoes, then sprinkle with the grated cheese and the bread crumbs.
4. Place the dish in the oven and bake for about 20 to 25 minutes, until the tomatoes are wilted.
5. While the tomatoes are roasting, bring a pot of water to a boil, add some salt, and cook the penne until done, about 10 minutes. Drain.
6. When the tomatoes are done, add the penne to the baking dish and stir carefully to combine.
7. Add the remaining 1 tablespoon olive oil if the mixture seems too dry. Season with salt and pepper.
8. Serve hot, sprinkled with extra cheese, if desired.

PENNE WITH SWISS CHARD

SERVES 2 TO 4

1 pound Swiss chard, well washed
A pinch of red pepper flakes, or more to taste
3 cloves garlic, thinly sliced
2 tablespoons olive oil
$^1/_4$ cup water
Salt and pepper to taste
1 cup canned crushed tomatoes
8 ounces penne or other tubular pasta
$^1/_4$ cup grated Parmesan cheese

1. Tear the leaves off the Swiss chard and chop them coarsely.
2. In a large, heavy pan, cook the red pepper flakes and the garlic in the olive oil, stirring, until the garlic is slightly colored.

3. Add the Swiss chard leaves, the water, and salt and pepper, cover the pan, and cook for 5 minutes.
4. Stir in the tomatoes and continue cooking, covered, until the leaves are tender, about 3 more minutes.
5. While the chard is cooking, boil the penne in salted water according to package directions.
6. When the pasta is done, drain it and toss with the Swiss chard mixture and the Parmesan cheese.

TIPS AND TIDBITS

✦ If you like a crunchy texture, chop the stems and add them along with the leaves in step 3.

SPAGHETTI WITH MARINARA SAUCE

♦

SERVES 4

1 pound spaghetti or similar pasta
1 cup fresh parsley leaves
4 cloves garlic, crushed
3 to 4 tablespoons olive oil
One 28-ounce can crushed tomatoes
³/₄ teaspoon dried oregano
¹/₂ teaspoon dried thyme
1 teaspoon salt
A pinch of red pepper flakes, more if you like a spicy sauce

1. Drop the spaghetti into salted boiling water and while it is cooking, prepare the sauce.
2. Place the parsley and garlic in the bowl of a food processor and process until finely chopped.

Continued

3. Heat the olive oil in a saucepan and cook the parsley and garlic over low heat until the garlic is soft, about 3 to 5 minutes.

4. Add the tomatoes, oregano, thyme, salt, and red pepper flakes, bring to a boil, and then lower the heat until the sauce just simmers. Cook for about 5 minutes more.

5. Adjust the seasoning, if necessary, and pour the sauce over the drained spaghetti.

TIPS AND TIDBITS

+ If you don't mind some extra fat, this sauce is even better if you add a pound of sweet Italian sausage (or turkey sausage) cut into 1-inch rounds and well browned and drained.

+ A half pound of mushrooms, sliced and sautéed, is another nice variation.

SPAGHETTI WITH WHITE CLAM SAUCE

SERVES 2

8 ounces spaghetti, linguine, or fettuccine

3 tablespoons olive oil

1 tablespoon minced onion or shallot

1 medium clove garlic, minced

2 tablespoons chopped fresh parsley

¹/₈ teaspoon red pepper flakes

¹/₄ cup white wine

One 10-ounce can whole baby clams (preferably Roland),
*   liquid reserved (if you use another brand, discard the liquid*
*   and use a small bottle of clam juice instead)*

1 tablespoon butter or margarine

2 tablespoons grated Parmesan cheese

Salt to taste

1. Bring a large pot of water to a boil, add some salt and a few drops of oil, and cook the spaghetti for about 10 minutes. The pasta should be al dente, tender yet still firm. Drain and set aside.
2. Heat the olive oil in a large pan and cook the onion over a low flame for several minutes, until it softens.
3. Add the garlic and cook, stirring, for another minute or two.
4. Stir in the parsley and red pepper flakes.
5. Pour in the wine, raise the heat, and let the mixture boil for a few minutes, until it has reduced a bit.
6. Add the clam juice and simmer for several minutes more.
7. Add the clams and cook just long enough for them to be thoroughly heated.
8. Turn off the heat, add the butter and grated cheese, and mix until thoroughly combined. Add salt.
9. Pour the sauce over the drained pasta and serve.

TORTELLINI WITH POTATOES AND TOMATOES

SERVES 3

1 tablespoon olive oil
1 large red onion, finely chopped
2 medium to large potatoes (about 1 pound), peeled and diced
1 clove garlic, minced
2 ripe medium tomatoes, diced
Red pepper flakes to taste
Salt and freshly ground black pepper to taste
1 pound tortellini

1. Heat the olive oil in a nonstick pan and sauté the onion until soft and beginning to brown.
2. Add the potatoes and garlic and cook until the potatoes are nearly tender, about 15 minutes.
3. Add the tomatoes, red pepper flakes, and salt and pepper, and continue cooking for another 5 minutes.
4. Bring a pot of water to a boil, add some salt, and cook the tortellini according to package directions. Drain and add to the potatoes. Mix well and serve.

TIPS AND TIDBITS

✦ While cheese tortellini are the most popular, many other interesting types are available. Try using one of the vegetable- or meat-filled varieties to add a different flavor.

BROCCOLI WITH ZITI

from **DR. JOY BROWNE**
Psychologist, Author, Radio Talk-Show Host

"Basically, I just love both broccoli and the word *ziti.* This is good for you, easy to make, and as good the next day as it is originally, and kids love it even if they don't love broccoli. Leftovers can be reheated or served cold the next day. I always make a double recipe. Add a salad and some French or Italian bread (drizzling a head of garlic with olive oil and cooking at 350°F for an hour makes a wonderful spread), and you can run a marathon!"

SERVES 4

12 ounces ziti
1¹/₂ pounds fresh broccoli
8 sprigs fresh parsley
2 large cloves garlic, smashed

¹/₄ cup olive oil
1 tablespoon butter (for flavor)
¹/₄ cup freshly grated Parmesan cheese
¹/₂ teaspoon freshly ground pepper

1. Cook the ziti first, since it will take the longest. Drop it into a large pot of salted boiling water, bring to a second boil, and cook until tender, yet still firm, approximately 10 to 12 minutes.
2. Wash and chop the broccoli and briefly steam or microwave it, but don't overcook it.
3. Chop the parsley and garlic together and sauté over low heat for a couple of minutes in a mixture of the olive oil and butter. Don't overcook.
4. When the ziti is done, drain it and return it to the pot.
5. Add the broccoli to the ziti.
6. Stir in the garlic-and-parsley mixture, followed by the Parmesan cheese and pepper. Serve hot.

LASAGNA

SERVES 8 TO 10

1¹/₂ pounds sweet Italian sausage, or a combination of sweet and hot sausage
1 medium onion, chopped
2 tablespoons olive oil
2 cloves garlic, minced
2 tablespoons sugar
1¹/₂ teaspoons salt
1¹/₂ teaspoons dried basil
¹/₂ teaspoon fennel seeds

Continued

¹/₄ teaspoon pepper

¹/₄ cup chopped fresh parsley

One 35-ounce can tomatoes (about 4 cups)

One 12-ounce can tomato paste

¹/₂ cup water

15 ounces regular or part-skim ricotta cheese

1 egg, lightly beaten

One 8-ounce package oven-ready (no boil) lasagna noodles
    (you'll need 12 noodles)

12 ounces regular or part-skim mozzarella cheese,
    coarsely shredded

³/₄ cup grated Parmesan cheese

1. Remove the casings from the sausage and chop the meat into small bits.
2. Sauté the onion in the olive oil over low heat until soft, about 5 minutes.
3. Add the garlic and continue cooking for another few minutes, until the garlic starts to color.
4. Add the the sausage and cook, stirring occasionally, until the meat is brown, about 10 minutes.
5. Add the sugar, 1 teaspoon of the salt, the basil, the fennel seeds, the pepper, and 2 tablespoons of the chopped parsley. Mix well.
6. Add the tomatoes, tomato paste, and water and bring to a boil. Reduce the heat and simmer the mixture, uncovered, for about 1¹/₂ hours.
7. When the sauce is ready, preheat the oven to 375°F.
8. In a small bowl, combine the ricotta cheese, the egg, the remaining 2 tablespoons parsley, and the remaining ¹/₂ teaspoon salt.
9. Spoon about a cup of the tomato sauce into a 13 × 9-inch baking dish.
10. Place 3 of the lasagna noodles crosswise in the pan, making sure they do not touch one another or the sides of the pan. (They will expand as the lasagna cooks.)
11. Spoon another cup of sauce over the noodles.
12. Spread one-third of the ricotta mixture over the sauce.

13. Sprinkle one-quarter of the shredded mozzarella cheese over the ricotta layer.
14. Repeat steps 10 through 13 twice.
15. Place the final 3 lasagna noodles in the pan and cover with the remaining sauce.
16. Sprinkle with the remaining mozzarella and the Parmesan cheese.
17. Cover the pan with aluminum foil, tenting it so that it doesn't rest on the cheese, and bake for 25 minutes.
18. Remove the foil and bake for another 25 minutes.
19. When done, allow the lasagna to cool for 15 minutes before serving.

TIPS AND TIDBITS

✦ To save cooking time, eliminate steps 5 and 6 and add 4 to 5 cups of your favorite bottled spaghetti sauce to the sausage-onion mixture.

✦ Turkey sausage also works in this recipe.

✦ This makes a wonderful dish for company because it is actually better if you make it a day or two ahead. It also freezes well.

✦ When reheating this or any casserole-type dish, an easy way to judge the interior temperature is to insert a knife into the center for about 30 seconds, remove it, and then carefully touch the blade.

LOW-FAT SPINACH LASAGNA

from **JODY WILLIAMS**
Coordinator, International Campaign to Ban Landmines;
Winner of the 1997 Nobel Peace Prize

◆

"This lasagna is really good. It doesn't taste like a boring low-fat item at all. I've served it quite a few times to dinner guests, and everyone then seems to want to make it themselves.

"Instead of the canned diced tomatoes, you may substitute a 29-ounce can of tomato sauce, although the diced tomatoes make the sauce more interesting. For the cottage cheese–ricotta mixture, you could substitute 1½ cups of either cheese, and for the mozzarella-Cheddar combination, you can use 6 ounces of grated mozzarella."

SERVES 8

1 medium onion, diced
3 cloves garlic, chopped
2 carrots, peeled and chopped or shredded
One 26-ounce jar Classico roasted garlic pasta sauce
One 14-ounce can diced tomatoes
1 teaspoon dried thyme
1 teaspoon dried oregano
1 teaspoon dried basil
A dash of black pepper
½ medium green, red, or yellow bell pepper, diced
Red pepper flakes to taste
1 cup nonfat cottage cheese
½ cup nonfat ricotta cheese
One 10-ounce package frozen chopped spinach, thawed and
    well drained
¼ teaspoon white pepper
⅛ teaspoon ground nutmeg
2 tablespoons grated nonfat Parmesan cheese
¼ cup nonfat half-and-half, or more or less as needed
One 8-ounce package oven-ready (no boil) lasagna noodles
4 ounces low-fat mozzarella cheese, grated
2 ounces low-fat Cheddar cheese, grated

1. Preheat the oven to 350°F.
2. In a nonstick skillet sprayed with nonfat cooking spray, sauté the onion, garlic, and carrots until the onion starts to soften.
3. Stir in the pasta sauce, tomatoes, thyme, oregano, basil, black pepper, and diced bell pepper. Add the red pepper flakes.
4. Bring the sauce to a boil, reduce the heat, and simmer until the vegetables are partially cooked, about 10 minutes.

5. In a bowl, blend the cottage cheese, ricotta cheese, spinach, white pepper, nutmeg, and grated Parmesan cheese.
6. Add enough of the half-and-half to give the mixture an easy spreading consistency.
7. Spread a thin layer of the cooked sauce on the bottom of a 13 × 9-inch baking dish.
8. Arrange a layer of noodles on top of the sauce, and cover with a layer of the cheese-spinach mixture. Sprinkle with some of the grated mozzarella and Cheddar cheeses, and top with more of the sauce.
9. Repeat this procedure until all of the noodles, sauce, cheese-spinach mixture, and grated cheeses are used up.
10. Cover the baking dish with aluminum foil and bake for 30 minutes. Remove the foil and continue baking until the noodles are tender, about another 25 minutes. Allow to stand for 5 minutes before serving.

MANICOTTI

from **GERALDINE A. FERRARO**
*Vice Presidential Candidate, 1984, the First Woman
to Run as a Major Party Nominee for National Office;
Former Congresswoman from New York*

◆

"The pancakes may be made the day before and refrigerated. On the day you serve, just fill and bake. If you make the pancakes the day before, put waxed paper between them to prevent sticking."

MAKES 12 TO 14 MANICOTTI (SERVES 4 TO 6)

1 cup flour
1 cup water
³/₄ teaspoon salt

Continued

7 *eggs*

2 *pounds ricotta cheese*

1/4 *cup grated Parmesan cheese, plus extra for sprinkling*

Pepper to taste

1 *pound mozzarella cheese, cut into thin strips*

1 *cup tomato sauce*

1. Preheat the oven to 350°F.
2. *To prepare the pancakes:* Combine the flour, the water, and 1/4 teaspoon of the salt, and beat until smooth. Beat in 4 of the eggs, one at a time.
3. Heat a 5- or 6-inch skillet and grease with a few drops of oil.
4. Scoop up about 3 tablespoons of batter and pour it into the hot skillet. Roll the pan to distribute it evenly. Cook over low heat until firm. *Do not brown.* Turn and cook lightly on the other side. Continue making pancakes until all of the batter is used up. (Do not grease the pan a second time.)
5. *To prepare the filling:* Mix together the remaining 3 eggs, the ricotta cheese, the 1/4 cup grated cheese, the remaining 1/2 teaspoon salt, and pepper to taste.
6. *To assemble the manicotti:* Place about 2 tablespoons of the filling along with a strip of mozzarella on each pancake and roll up.
7. Spoon tomato sauce onto the bottom of a large shallow baking dish, using just enough to cover.
8. Place the rolled pancakes in the dish, seam side down. Cover with more tomato sauce and sprinkle with some grated cheese.
9. Bake for 45 minutes. Serve hot accompanied with additional tomato sauce and grated cheese.

RECIPE TITLE_____

FROM_____

SERVES _____

INGREDIENTS

INSTRUCTIONS

TIPS AND TIDBITS

RECIPE TITLE

FROM

SERVES

INGREDIENTS

INSTRUCTIONS

TIPS AND TIDBITS

POULTRY

◆

Also check out:

Oriental Pasta with Chicken • p. 136

TIPS AND HINTS ON...

BUYING AND STORING POULTRY

✦ When selecting a package of fresh chicken or turkey, always check the "sell by" date on the label to get the freshest meat.

✦ In general, try to get fresh poultry; it will often be tastier and juicier than frozen.

- Be sure that the package is not leaking, since any juice that leaks out may contain harmful bacteria that can contaminate the other foods in your grocery bag. It's a good idea to make sure the package is placed in its own plastic bag.
- At home, refrigerate poultry immediately, keeping it in its original package.
- Fresh poultry is highly perishable and will keep in the refrigerator no longer than two days. If you have to keep it longer, remove it from its original packaging, wrap it in aluminum foil, and freeze it. (Don't forget to label and date it.)
- To defrost frozen poultry, place it on a plate in the refrigerator to thaw, and try to cook it shortly after it has defrosted. Frozen poultry generally takes a long time to defrost, and if you are cooking chicken parts, it's a good idea to take them out of the freezer early in the morning or even the night before you plan to cook them. *If you are defrosting a large bird, a rule of thumb is that it takes one day of defrosting for every 4 pounds. Thus, a 20-pound turkey will take five days!*

HOW MUCH TO BUY

- A boneless, skinless chicken breast half (also called a cutlet), about 6- to 8-ounces, will generally serve one person.
- A 2½- to 3½-pound chicken, either cut into parts or roasted whole, will serve two to three people. These chickens are often called broilers or fryers.
- A 3½- to 6½-pound bird, called a roaster, is good for roasting whole, stewing, or barbecuing, and serves four to six people.
- Capons, generally 7 to 10 pounds, are larger, meatier birds. They are extremely tender and flavorful, and serve eight or more.
- When buying a whole turkey, it is best to get 1 pound per person plus some extra for leftovers. To feed ten people, for example, you should get a 12-pound bird. Remember, the total weight of the turkey includes the neck and giblets, which are usually wrapped in paper inside the bird's cavity—don't forget to remove them before cooking!
- A turkey breast (which generally weighs 4 to 6 pounds) can be roasted the same way you would a whole bird and is ideal for serving a small number of people.

POACHING CHICKEN BREASTS FOR CHICKEN SALAD

+ It's easy to prepare moist, tasty chicken for chicken salad by starting with bone-in chicken breasts and poaching them.

+ Place the breasts in a pot and cover with canned chicken broth (you'll probably need about 4 cups). Bring to a boil, then lower the heat to a simmer for about a minute or two. Cover the pot, turn off the heat, and allow the chicken to cool to room temperature, about 2 hours.

+ After removing the chicken from the pot, save the cooking liquid to use as chicken stock.

SALMONELLA

+ Because some poultry is contaminated with salmonella bacteria when it leaves the processing plant, it is extremely important that you wash up very carefully after handling raw chicken and turkey.

+ Although the bacteria are killed by cooking, *contaminated juices and scraps of raw meat may be left on your cutting board, knives, countertop, even your sponge or dish towel, and then transferred to other foods or your hands.* This is particularly important to keep in mind if you will be using those same surfaces or utensils to cut salad greens, slice bread, or prepare other foods that will not be heated before they are served.

+ Using warm, soapy water, carefully wash your hands as well as every object that came in contact with the raw chicken or turkey.

+ It is also a good idea to use paper towels to wipe off your countertop, since a sponge may absorb and retain the contaminated juices. If you do use a sponge to wipe up, run it through a cycle in the dishwasher or boil it for a few minutes. (In general, it's a good idea to periodically wash your sponge in the dishwasher.)

+ Once the chicken or turkey is cooked, *never* place it on the same platter or cutting board that you used when it was raw. And be sure to use a different fork!

+ For information on food safety, call the Meat and Poultry Hotline of the USDA Food Safety and Inspection Service at (800) 535-4555.

BARBECUED CHICKEN

SERVES 2 TO 3

One 2¹/₂- to 3-pound chicken, cut up (you may also want to
remove the skin)
¹/₂ cup chopped celery
¹/₂ cup chopped onions
2 tablespoons brown sugar
¹/₄ cup lemon juice, preferably fresh
1 cup ketchup
3 tablespoons Worcestershire sauce
1 scant cup water
1 tablespoon salt
A few sprinkles of cayenne pepper

1. Preheat the oven to 350°F.
2. Place the chicken pieces in a baking dish.
3. Combine the remaining ingredients and pour over the chicken.
4. Bake, covered, for 1¹/₂ hours.

TIPS AND TIDBITS

✦ Mushrooms—canned or fresh—make a nice addition to this dish.

CHICKEN CACCIATORE

SERVES 4 TO 6

2 tablespoons olive oil, plus more as needed
One 3- to 4-pound chicken, cut up, with skin and fat removed
1 large or 2 medium onions, chopped
3 cloves garlic, minced

8 ounces white mushrooms, sliced
¹/₄ cup white wine
One 16-ounce can whole or crushed tomatoes
One 6-ounce can tomato paste
¹/₂ teaspoon salt
Pepper to taste
1¹/₂ tablespoons dried oregano
1¹/₂ tablespoons dried marjoram
1 bay leaf
Grated Parmesan cheese, for sprinkling

1. Heat a large, heavy pan and add the olive oil. Brown the chicken parts in two batches and remove from the pan. Set aside.
2. Add the onions (with more oil if needed) and cook until soft, about 5 to 8 minutes.
3. Add the garlic and cook for another 2 minutes or so. Don't let the garlic brown.
4. Push the onions and garlic to one side of the pan and add the sliced mushrooms. Sauté the mushrooms, stirring, until they start to brown, about 4 or 5 minutes.
5. Pour in the wine and scrape up any brown bits on the bottom of the pan.
6. Add the tomatoes, tomato paste, salt, pepper, oregano, marjoram, and bay leaf. Stir to combine and bring the mixture to a simmer.
7. Add the browned chicken, cover, and simmer over low heat for about 1 hour.
8. When done, remove the bay leaf and serve over hot spaghetti noodles sprinkled with grated Parmesan cheese.

TIPS AND TIDBITS

+ This dish is tastier the next day, so if you are making it for company, prepare it a day in advance.
+ When chopping garlic, sprinkle it with salt. The salt will make it easier to chop and also help keep it from sticking to the knife.

CHICKEN CHILI

2 tablespoons olive oil, plus more as needed

1 pound boneless, skinless chicken cutlets, cut into
bite-sized pieces

1 cup chopped onions

2 cloves garlic, minced

2 cups chicken broth, preferably College Inn

Two 19-ounce cans white kidney beans, rinsed and drained

1 pound tomatillos, preferably fresh, hulled, rinsed, and
coarsely chopped

1/2 teaspoon dried oregano

1/2 teaspoon ground coriander

1/2 teaspoon ground cumin

Chopped onion, for garnish

Chopped tomato, for garnish

Sour cream, for garnish (optional)

1. Heat the olive oil in a large pan and brown the chicken pieces, stirring frequently. Remove from the pan and set aside.
2. Add the onions to the pan, along with some more oil if necessary, and cook over low heat until soft, about 5 minutes.
3. Add the garlic, stir, and cook for another few minutes.
4. Add the chicken broth, bring to a simmer, and cook for a few minutes.
5. Add the beans, chopped tomatillos, oregano, coriander, cumin, and browned chicken pieces.
6. Simmer, uncovered, until the sauce thickens, at least 30 minutes.
7. Serve garnished with chopped onion and tomato and a dollop of sour cream, if desired.

✦ If you cannot find tomatillos (either fresh or canned), you can substitute three green bell peppers.

✦ Yellow rice is a nice accompaniment for this dish.

LEMONY GRILLED CHICKEN

◆

SERVES 4

*4 boneless, skinless chicken cutlets (about 1¹/₂ to
2 pounds total)*
³/₄ cup fresh lemon juice, about 3 large lemons
2 teaspoons kosher salt
1 teaspoon freshly ground pepper
¹/₂ teaspoon dried thyme
³/₄ cup olive oil

1. Trim the fat from the cutlets and place the chicken in a glass bowl or a Ziploc bag. Set aside.
2. In a small bowl or a measuring cup, whisk together the lemon juice, salt, pepper, and thyme.
3. Add the olive oil and mix well.
4. Pour the marinade over the chicken, cover, and refrigerate for several hours.
5. Before cooking, pat the chicken dry.
6. Cook the chicken on a charcoal grill or in a grill pan. Cook just until done—the chicken should still be very moist inside—about 6 to 8 minutes per side. Don't overcook.
7. After removing from the heat, allow the chicken to stand for a few minutes before serving.

✦ Squeeze lemons before you buy them. The softer ones are juicier.

✦ A good way to serve any leftover chicken is to cut it into thin slices and add it to a salad or sandwich. Or, cut it into chunks and turn canned chicken broth into a hearty soup, especially if you also add rice, noodles, or canned corn.

MUSTARD CHICKEN

SERVES 4

¹/₄ cup Dijon mustard
¹/₄ cup grainy mustard
¹/₄ cup your choice of another mustard
¹/₄ cup white vinegar
¹/₃ cup apple juice
1¹/₂ tablespoons fresh or frozen lemon juice
1 shallot, peeled and thinly sliced
1 clove garlic, minced
Freshly ground pepper, to taste
4 boneless, skinless chicken cutlets (about 1 to 2 pounds total)

1. In a non-aluminum bowl or a Ziploc bag, combine the mustards, vinegar, apple juice, lemon juice, shallot, garlic, and pepper.
2. Add the chicken and coat with the sauce. Cover the bowl (or seal the bag) and refrigerate for 2 to 4 hours, turning occasionally.
3. When ready to cook, preheat the broiler or a grill pan.
4. Remove the chicken from the marinade and broil or grill for 3 to 4 minutes per side, until the chicken is no longer pink inside.

6. Ladle ¼ cup of the sauce on a serving platter and arrange the chicken on top. Spoon additional sauce over the chicken and serve.

TIPS AND TIDBITS

✦ Be very careful whenever you place a hot liquid in the blender. It tends to shoot up when you turn the blender on.

✦ You will probably have leftover sauce—it is delicious over rice, noodles, or couscous.

EASY CHICKEN PROVENCE

from **JOSIE NATORI**
Fashion Designer; Founder and CEO,
The Natori Company

◆

SERVES 4

One medium 2- to 2½-pound chicken, cut up
2 teaspoons salt
2 teaspoons pepper
½ cup flour
½ cup olive oil
1 clove garlic, chopped
1 green bell pepper, seeded and coarsely chopped
2 onions, coarsely chopped
1 stalk celery, coarsely chopped
½ teaspoon dried tarragon
½ teaspoon dried basil
One 2-ounce can pitted black olives, chopped
One 2-ounce can pitted green olives, chopped
12 fresh mushrooms, chopped

Continued

One 7-ounce can pimientos, chopped
One 8-ounce can tomato sauce
$^1/_2$ cup canned chicken broth
4 teaspoons dry sherry
$^1/_2$ cup chopped fresh parsley

1. Season the chicken with the salt and pepper and dredge in the flour.
2. Heat the olive oil in a large, heavy skillet and brown the chicken.
3. Remove the chicken from the pan and add the garlic, bell pepper, onions, celery, tarragon, and basil. Sauté approximately 5 minutes.
4. Add the olives, mushrooms, and pimentos to the pan and cook for an additional 5 minutes.
5. Add the tomato sauce, chicken, and chicken broth and continue cooking slowly over low heat for 45 minutes.
6. Add the sherry and parsley and cook for 5 minutes more.
7. Serve over rice or noodles or with mashed potatoes.

CHICKEN WITH RICE

from **MADELEINE L'ENGLE**

*Author, Winner of the American Library
Association's John Newberry Medal and Margaret A. Edwards
Award for Lifetime Achievement*

◆

"This chicken dish can be served either hot or cold."

SERVES 4 TO 6

*2 to 3 boneless, skinless chicken breasts (about
    1$^1/_2$ pounds total)*
1 cup rice
1 tablespoon dried tarragon
4 teaspoons mustard

2 to 3 *large cloves garlic, chopped*
Chopped chives to taste
$1/4$ cup lemon juice
1 tablespoon olive oil, or more to taste
Salt and pepper to taste
One 10-ounce can cream of celery soup
One 14-ounce can artichoke hearts, drained and chopped
One 8-ounce can water chestnuts, drained and sliced
$1/4$ cup Hellmann's mayonnaise, or light sour cream or
  plain yogurt

1. Simmer the chicken breasts in a pot of salted water for about 15 minutes or cook them in a microwave oven. When the chicken is done, allow to cool and cut into medium-sized pieces. Set aside.
2. Bring 2 cups of salted water to a boil in a heavy saucepan. Add the rice, stir, cover, and reduce the heat. Simmer gently for 20 minutes.
3. While the rice is cooking, make the sauce by combining the tarragon, 3 teaspoons of the mustard, the garlic, chopped chives, 2 tablespoons of the lemon juice, the olive oil, and salt and pepper.
4. When the rice is done, fluff it with a fork and add it to the sauce, mixing well.
5. Make a circle of the rice on a large platter and spoon the cooked chicken into the middle of the circle.
6. In a medium-sized saucepan, heat the cream of celery soup, artichoke hearts, water chestnuts, the remaining 2 tablespoons lemon juice, and the remaining 1 teaspoon mustard. Mix well.
7. Stir in the mayonnaise and pour the sauce over the chicken.

SESAME CHICKEN AND SNOW PEAS IN APRICOT SAUCE

from JANE FONDA

Actress; Author; Social Activist; Winner of Two
Academy Awards, One Emmy, and Five Golden Globe Awards

◆

"Apricots are an excellent source of beta carotene, one of the antioxidants I encourage you to consume regularly for overall good health. Keep dried apricots on hand for snacks, especially in winter when the fresh ones are out of season. This sauce is so delicious that you'll want to try it without the chicken, spooned over steamed vegetables or rice."

SERVES 4

2 teaspoons dark sesame oil
3 cloves garlic, minced
1 pound boneless, skinless chicken breasts, cut into thin strips
1 tablespoon sesame seeds
$^1\!/_3$ cup sliced dried apricots
$^1\!/_2$ cup water
$^1\!/_2$ cup apricot preserves
1 tablespoon reduced-sodium soy sauce
1 tablespoon Dijon mustard
$^1\!/_2$ teaspoon grated fresh ginger
8 ounces snow peas, ends trimmed

1. In a large nonstick frying pan, heat the sesame oil over medium heat and sauté the garlic for 1 minute.
2. Add the chicken to the pan and sauté until browned on the outside and no longer pink in the center, about 5 minutes.
3. Add the sesame seeds to the pan and sauté, stirring frequently, until browned, about 2 minutes.
4. Add the apricots, water, apricot preserves, soy sauce, mustard, and

ginger and bring to a boil. Reduce the heat to low, and simmer for 5 minutes.

5. Add the snow peas and simmer until tender but still somewhat crisp, about 5 minutes. Divide into 4 portions and serve.

SESAME PASTE CHICKEN

♦

SERVES 4

1 pound bone-in chicken breasts
2 tablespoons creamy peanut butter
1 tablespoon soy sauce
1 tablespoon white vinegar
¹/₄ teaspoon cayenne pepper
¹/₄ teaspoon red pepper flakes, or to taste
1 to 2 teaspoons minced fresh ginger
2 cloves garlic, minced
1 tablespoon minced scallion
2 teaspoons hot sesame oil or peppercorn oil
¹/₄ cup chopped, roasted peanuts as garnish (optional)

1. Place the chicken breasts in a large pot, cover with salted water, and simmer for about 10 to 15 minutes. When the chicken is done, it should be moist inside, with no trace of pink. Remove from the pot and allow to cool.
2. Shred the chicken with your fingers and place in a large bowl.
3. In a separate bowl, combine the remaining ingredients except for the peanuts, if using.
4. Pour the dressing over the chicken and toss. If the mixture seems too thick, add some more oil.
5. Sprinkle with chopped roasted peanuts, if desired, and serve cold or at room temperature, with rice.

✦ To make peppercorn oil, heat a tablespoon of black peppercorns in 1/4 cup peanut oil for 10 minutes. Strain before using.

✦ This also makes a nice appetizer, especially served on a bed of lettuce.

SEVEN-FLAVOR CHICKEN

◆

SERVES 6 TO 8

1/8 teaspoon ground cinnamon
1 clove garlic, finely minced
1/2 teaspoon ground ginger
Salt and pepper to taste
1/2 cup soy sauce
2 tablespoons sugar
Two 3-pound chickens, cut up

1. In a large bowl, whisk together the cinnamon, garlic, ginger, salt and pepper, soy sauce, and sugar.
2. Add the chicken parts, stir to make sure they are well coated, and refrigerate for several hours or overnight.
3. When ready to cook, preheat the oven to 350°F.
4. Place the chicken in an oiled shallow roasting pan and bake for about 40 minutes, basting occasionally and turning once.

TIPS AND TIDBITS

✦ If you prefer to broil the chicken, place it in a well-oiled broiler pan and broil for 20 to 30 minutes, basting occasionally and turning once.

SPICY CHICKEN BREASTS

◆

SERVES 4

1 teaspoon salt
1/2 teaspoon paprika
1 1/2 teaspoons pepper
1 teaspoon granulated or powdered garlic
1 teaspoon granulated or powdered onion
1 teaspoon dried basil
8 small boneless, skinless chicken cutlets (about 3 ounces each)

1. Heat a heavy skillet or grill pan over medium heat for 8 to 10 minutes, until a splash of water bursts into dancing droplets.
2. While the pan is heating, combine the seasonings and sprinkle over both sides of the chicken. Rub to spread evenly.
3. When the pan is ready, cook the chicken for about 3 minutes on each side. You'll know the chicken is ready when it is bronze on the outside and still moist on the inside, with no trace of pink.

TIPS AND TIDBITS

✦ This dish is *very spicy,* but you can easily tone it down by decreasing the amounts of paprika and pepper. You can also add your own touch by eliminating the basil and using any other herbs (or spices) that you like, such as oregano and rosemary, two herbs that go well with chicken.

✦ Applesauce is a wonderful accompaniment for this chicken.

✦ Don't worry if the pan looks very messy; it cleans quite easily. And if you're using a grill pan, it helps to coat it first with a light vegetable oil or cooking spray.

THAI-STYLE CASHEW CHICKEN

from **LOIS B. DeFLEUR**

President, Binghamton University–State University of New York

◆

SERVES 8

6 tablespoons oyster sauce

$^1/_4$ cup packed brown sugar

6 tablespoons soy sauce

3 dried chili peppers (or more or less to taste), cut into
$^1/_2$-inch strips

3 cloves garlic, minced

2$^1/_2$ to 3 pounds boneless chicken breasts or tenders, cut into
$^1/_4$-inch strips

$^3/_4$ cup flour

$^3/_4$ cup peanut or vegetable oil

1 large onion, cut into $^3/_8$-inch strips

1 bunch scallions (green onions), cut into 1$^1/_2$-inch strips

$^1/_2$ cup cashew nuts

$^1/_2$ cup water

1. Make a marinade by combining 2 tablespoons of the oyster sauce, 2 tablespoons of the brown sugar, 2 tablespoons of the soy sauce, 1 of the chili pepper strips, and 1 minced clove of garlic.

2. Marinate the chicken strips for a minimum of 30 minutes, or overnight if possible.

3. When you are ready to cook, place the flour on a plate and roll the chicken strips in it.

4. Heat the oil in a large frying pan or wok over medium-high heat and brown the chicken, a few pieces at a time, until golden brown and crispy on all sides. Remove from the pan and set aside.

5. Pour off all but 2 tablespoons of the oil from the pan. (If the flour has begun to burn, remove it and wash the pan.)

6. Sauté the onion strips and the remaining minced garlic in the pan until crisp-tender.
7. Add the scallions, the cashews, and the remaining chili pepper strips. Toss and lightly sauté.
8. Add the water and the remaining 4 tablespoons oyster sauce, 4 tablespoons soy sauce, and 2 tablespoons brown sugar, stirring well. (If a thicker glaze is desired, increase the water to 1½ cups and thicken with cornstarch.)
9. Add the chicken to the pan and toss with the sauce and vegetables until thoroughly heated. Serve over rice.

CHICKEN-AND-CORN SALAD

SERVES 4

1 pound boneless, skinless chicken cutlets
One 11-ounce can corn, drained
¼ cup thinly sliced scallions (green onions), white part only
1 medium red bell pepper, seeded and diced
Salt to taste
½ cup fat-free honey-Dijon (or your favorite) salad dressing

1. Place the chicken in a large pot, cover with salted water, and simmer for 10 to 12 minutes. When the chicken is done, it should be moist inside, with no trace of pink. (You could also put the chicken in a glass bowl with a little water and cook it in a microwave oven.) Remove from the pot and allow to cool.
2. Cut or tear the chicken into bite-sized pieces and place in a bowl.
3. Stir in the corn, scallions, bell pepper, and salt.
4. Add the dressing and toss to combine. Store in the refrigerator.

CURRIED CHICKEN SALAD

♦

2 to 3 chicken breast halves, bone-in (about 2½ pounds total)
¼ cup regular or low-fat mayonnaise
3 tablespoons regular or low-fat sour cream
2 tablespoons Major Grey's mango chutney, minced
1½ to 2 tablespoons curry powder, or more to taste
½ cup minced scallions (green onions), the white part and
  some of the green
½ cup minced celery (optional)
1 cup seedless red grapes, cut in half
½ cup golden raisins
½ cup unsalted cashew nuts
Cantaloupe and/or honeydew slices, for garnish

1. Bring a large pot of salted water to a boil and add the chicken breasts.
2. Bring to a second boil, lower the heat, and simmer until the chicken is done, about 20 minutes. The meat should be moist on the inside, with no trace of pink.
3. While the chicken is cooking, make the sauce by combining the mayonnaise, sour cream, chutney, curry powder, scallions, celery, if desired, grapes, and raisins in a large serving bowl.
4. When the chicken is done, allow it to cool, and remove the meat from the bones and skin. Cut into bite-sized pieces.
5. Add the chicken to the sauce and mix thoroughly. If not serving immediately, place in the refrigerator.
6. Just before serving, stir in the cashews.
7. Serve cold or at room temperature, garnished with melon slices.

TIPS AND TIDBITS

♦ After cooking the chicken, you can put the bones back in the water and simmer them for another 20 minutes or so to get a nice chicken broth that you can freeze for later use.

✦ You can also use boneless, skinless chicken cutlets, but the meat will not be quite as flavorful.

PINEAPPLE-CHICKEN SALAD

from **CHRIS EVERT**

Tennis Champion; Winner of 18 Grand Slam Singles Titles,
3 Grand Slam Doubles Titles, and 157 Tournaments

◆

SERVES 6 TO 8

4 cups cooked chicken, cut into bite-sized pieces
1 cup pineapple chunks, preferably fresh
1 cup chopped celery
$^{1}/_{2}$ cup minced scallions (green onions)
$^{1}/_{4}$ cup dry-roasted unsalted peanuts
$^{2}/_{3}$ cup mayonnaise, preferably low-fat, low-cholesterol
2 tablespoons chutney
2 tablespoons lemon juice
Grated rind of $^{1}/_{2}$ lemon
$^{1}/_{2}$ teaspoon curry powder
$^{1}/_{2}$ teaspoon salt

1. Combine the chicken, pineapple, celery, scallions, and peanuts in a large bowl.
2. In a small bowl, stir together the mayonnaise, chutney, lemon juice, grated lemon rind, curry powder, and salt.
3. Pour the dressing over the chicken mixture and stir to combine. Refrigerate until ready to serve.

ROAST CHICKEN AND GRAVY

1 large whole chicken, preferably a capon, about 7 to 8 pounds
  (be sure to remove the package of giblets inside the cavity)
2 to 3 tablespoons canola or other light vegetable oil
1/2 teaspoon garlic salt, or more to taste
1 tablespoon dried rosemary
1 large onion, cut into thin slices
1 cup dry white wine

1. Preheat the oven to 350°F.
2. Wash the chicken, pat it dry, and make a few small slits in the skin in the fatty region under the thigh.
3. Rub the entire chicken with the canola oil and then sprinkle it with the garlic salt and rosemary.
4. Place about half the onion slices inside the chicken cavity and the remaining half in the center of a roasting pan.
5. Set the chicken on the onion slices and pour 1/2 cup of the wine over it.
6. Place the pan in the oven and roast for about 2 hours, depending on the size of the chicken (about 20 minutes per pound is a rough estimate). Baste every 20 minutes or so. When you think the chicken is ready, tip it so that some of the juices run out of the cavity. When the juices run clear, not pink, the chicken is done. Also, the skin will be crisp and the drumsticks will be easy to jiggle. (If you are using a meat thermometer, it should register 180°F.)
7. When the chicken is done, remove it to a carving board and allow it to stand for 30 minutes or so before slicing.
8. To make the gravy, add the remaining 1/2 cup wine to the roasting pan and simmer it on top of the stove for several minutes, scraping the brown bits from the bottom of the pan. If there isn't enough liquid, you can add some canned chicken broth. You can also add the neck (cut into pieces) and giblets—but not the liver.

+ To remove the fat from the gravy, pour the gravy into a bowl or measuring cup and place it in the freezer until the fat solidifies on the surface and can be scraped off. Or use a special fat-separating cup.

+ Sometimes a chicken comes with a plastic pop-up timer embedded in the breast meat. Although this type of timer is usually reliable, you can't always depend on it. It may pop up too early or not at all.

+ If you have any questions or problems—and you can't reach Mom—call Butterball Poultry Consumer Information at (800) 288-8372.

ROAST CHICKEN WITH SPICED APPLES AND ONION

SERVES 4

One 3¹/₂-pound chicken
1 medium sweet potato, cut into ¹/₂-inch cubes
1 onion, cut into ¹/₂-inch cubes
2 Granny Smith apples, peeled, cored, and cut into
    ¹/₂-inch cubes
2 shallots, cut into ¹/₂-inch pieces
1 clove garlic, chopped
1 tablespoon olive oil
¹/₂ teaspoon ground cinnamon
¹/₈ teaspoon ground cloves
6 black peppercorns, crushed
Salt to taste

1. Preheat the oven to 350°F.
2. Rinse the chicken and pat it dry.

Continued

3. Boil the sweet potato cubes for about 2 minutes. Drain and rinse with cold water. Put them in a bowl with the onion, apples, shallots, and garlic.

4. In a small bowl, combine the olive oil with 2 tablespoons of water and add it to the sweet potato–apple mixture. Add half the cinnamon, half the cloves, half the crushed peppercorns, and salt to taste. Mix well.

5. Place the chicken on a rack in a roasting pan and place half the sweet potato–apple mixture in the cavity. Scatter the remaining mixture around the chicken.

6. Rub the chicken with the remaining cinnamon, cloves, and crushed peppercorns.

7. Roast the chicken for about 1½ hours, or until the internal temperature reaches 180°F on a meat thermometer. Check occasionally, and add some water if the pan dries out. When the chicken is done, remove from the pan and allow to cool for about 20 minutes before carving.

8. Serve the pan juices with the chicken.

TIPS AND TIDBITS

✦ We prefer to use a V-shaped rack, which helps ensure crisp skin. For easy cleaning, line the rack with a large sheet of aluminum foil. Be sure to poke twenty to thirty holes in it to allow the juices to drip down.

SPICED ROAST CHICKEN

from **TIPPER GORE**
Photographer, Author,
Wife of Former U.S. Vice President Al Gore

◆

SERVES 4

One 3½-pound chicken
2 tablespoons olive oil
1 onion, finely chopped
1 teaspoon garam masala
4 ounces button or brown mushrooms, chopped
1 cup coarsely grated parsnips
1 cup coarsely grated carrots
¼ cup minced walnuts
2 teaspoons chopped fresh thyme
1 cup fresh white bread crumbs
1 egg, beaten
Salt and pepper to taste
1 tablespoon margarine
⅔ cup Marsala wine
Watercress and thyme sprigs, for garnish

1. Preheat the oven to 375°F.
2. Rinse the chicken and pat it dry.
3. Heat the olive oil in a large saucepan, add the onion, and sauté for 2 minutes or until soft. Stir in the garam masala and cook for 1 minute.
4. Add the mushrooms, parsnips, and carrots, and cook, stirring, for 5 minutes. Remove from the heat and stir in the nuts, thyme, bread crumbs, egg, and salt and pepper.
5. Stuff and truss the chicken and place it, breast down, in a roasting pan. Add ¼ cup of water, and roast for 45 minutes. Turn the chicken so that it is breast up and dot with the margarine. Roast for another 45 minutes or until a meat thermometer inserted in the thickest part of the thigh (but not touching the bone) registers 185°F. Transfer to a platter and keep warm.
6. Discard the fat from the roasting pan and add the Marsala to the remaining cooking juices, scraping any browned bits from the bottom of the pan. Boil over high heat for 1 minute to reduce slightly, and adjust the seasoning.
7. Remove the skin and carve the chicken. Garnish with watercress and thyme sprigs, and serve with the stuffing, the pan juices, and seasonal vegetables.

GLAZED TURKEY CUTLETS

3 tablespoons balsamic vinegar
1¹/₂ teaspoons honey
³/₄ pound turkey cutlets, each about ¹/₄ inch thick
¹/₂ cup bread crumbs, seasoned with salt and pepper
¹/₄ cup olive oil
1 tablespoon unsalted butter
2 cloves garlic, minced
¹/₄ cup dry white wine
Minced fresh parsley, for garnish

1. In a small bowl, mix the vinegar with the honey.
2. Dredge the cutlets in the bread crumbs, pressing the crumbs into the surface of the meat.
3. Heat the olive oil in a heavy pan and sauté the cutlets for about a minute or two on each side. Remove from the pan and place on a platter.
4. Drain the pan, melt the butter, and cook the garlic, stirring, for about 1 minute. Stir in the wine and boil until the mixture is reduced to about 2 tablespoons.
5. Stir in the vinegar-honey mixture and boil until syrupy. Spoon it over the turkey cutlets and sprinkle with minced parsley.

ROAST TURKEY AND GRAVY

One 10- to 12-pound fresh turkey with neck and giblets
(usually wrapped in paper inside the cavity)
Butter, for coating the turkey
4 cups chicken broth (preferably College Inn), plus more
as needed
1 onion, coarsely chopped
1 carrot, coarsely chopped
1 stalk celery, coarsely chopped
1 bay leaf
Salt to taste
6 black peppercorns
A pinch of dried thyme
½ cup white wine

1. Take the turkey out of the refrigerator at least 1 hour before cooking so that it warms to room temperature.
2. Preheat the oven to 425°F.
3. Remove the bag containing the neck and giblets and set it aside.
4. Rinse the turkey and pat it dry. If you are stuffing it, this is the time to make the stuffing and place it in the neck and abdominal cavities.
5. Rub the skin with butter and place the bird, breast side up, on a rack in a large roasting pan.
6. Place the pan in the oven and roast the turkey for 30 minutes.
7. Reduce the oven temperature to 350°F and pour about 2 cups of the chicken broth into the pan.
8. Continue roasting for about 2 to 3 hours, basting every 30 minutes or so. (If the breast starts to get too brown, cover it loosely with a "tent" of aluminum foil.) A rule of thumb is that an un-

Continued

stuffed bird takes about 15 minutes per pound, while a stuffed bird takes about 20 minutes per pound.

9. The best way to tell when the turkey is done is to use an instant-read meat thermometer placed in the thigh joint but not touching the bone. A temperature of 170°F to 180°F means the turkey is done. Also, the thigh will move easily when you jiggle it a little, and if you pierce the skin near the thigh, the juices will run clear.

10. When the turkey is done, loosely cover it with foil and set it aside to rest for at least 20 minutes. You can allow it to rest for as long as 1 hour while you finish your gravy and make your side dishes.

11. Start making your gravy stock as soon as you put your turkey in the oven.

12. To make the stock, cut the giblets (*not* the liver) and place them, together with the neck (cut into pieces), in a saucepan.

13. Add the onion, carrot, celery, bay leaf, salt, peppercorns, thyme, and the remaining 2 cups chicken broth.

14. Simmer, partly covered, over low heat for several hours. Remove any scum that appears shortly after heating, and check occasionally to see if more broth is needed. You should end up with about 2 cups of stock.

15. When you are ready to make the gravy, strain the stock and skim off as much fat as you can.

16. After the turkey has been removed from the roasting pan, pour the pan drippings into a bowl or special defatting cup and remove the fat.

17. Return the drippings to the pan, and add the white wine and the gravy stock. Cook over medium heat for about 5 minutes, scraping up the brown bits on the bottom of the pan. Serve warm.

TIPS AND TIDBITS

+ An alternative to coating the turkey with butter is to use mayonnaise, which you slather on generously. This keeps the skin moist and you don't have to baste.

+ It is a good idea to make the gravy stock the day before and refrigerate it overnight. This saves time and also makes it easier to skim off the fat.

◆ If you have any questions or problems—and you can't reach Mom—you can call Butterball Poultry Consumer Information at (800) 288-8372.

RITZ CRACKER STUFFING

from **JOAN HAMBURG**
Radio Talk-Show Host, Consumer Reporter, Author

◆

SERVES 12 TO 14

One 1-pound box Ritz crackers
5 large onions, chopped
3 to 4 tablespoons chicken fat or canola oil, plus more
    as needed
2 to 3 stalks celery, chopped
1 or 2 eggs, lightly beaten
One 14-ounce can chicken broth (optional)

1. Pour the crackers into a large bowl and crumble them into bits. The largest piece should be no larger than a nickel. Set aside.
2. In a large pan, cook the onions in the chicken fat or oil until they are *very brown* but not burned, about 20 minutes.
3. Add the onions and celery to the cracker crumbs and combine well.
4. Stir the egg(s) into the crumb mixture.
5. Spoon the stuffing into a casserole dish and place in the oven about 1½ hours before the turkey is ready.
6. Baste every 20 minutes or so with turkey drippings or the chicken broth. When the stuffing is done, the top and edges will be crisp.

RECIPE TITLE_____

FROM_____

SERVES_____

INGREDIENTS

INSTRUCTIONS

TIPS AND TIDBITS

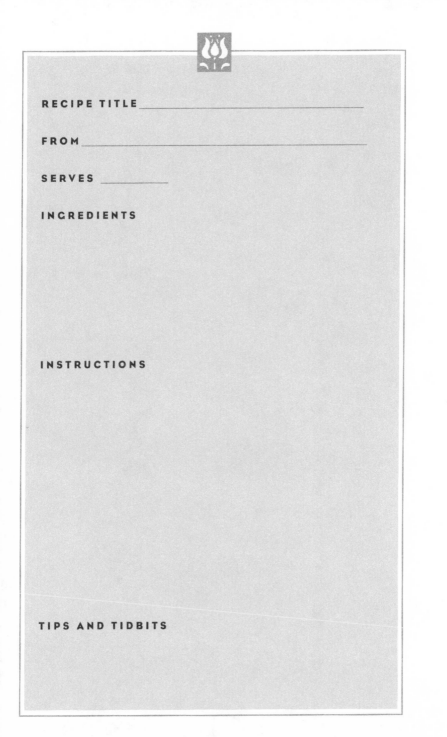

RECIPE TITLE _____

FROM _____

SERVES _____

INGREDIENTS

INSTRUCTIONS

TIPS AND TIDBITS

MEAT

◆

Also check out:

Meaty Cocktail Sandwiches • p. 37
Penne with Cabbage and Sausage • p. 139
Lasagna • p. 147

TIPS AND HINTS ON...

BUYING MEAT

✦ The tenderest, juiciest, and tastiest cuts of meat are those with the most marbling (small flecks or veins of fat). They include the tenderloin, loin, rib, and sirloin.

- The tougher cuts of meat are leaner and more coarsely grained. They include the chuck, brisket, shoulder, breast, and flank.
- Meat from younger animals (veal, lamb) is more tender than that from more mature animals.
- Always buy meat from a refrigerated case and check the label's expiration or "sell by" date to make sure you get the freshest package.
- Don't buy a package that is torn or leaking.
- Never buy meat that is gray or slimy or has an unpleasant "off" odor.
- When buying ground beef, don't be concerned if the meat is brown on the inside and red on the outside. The meat is naturally brown in color but turns red when exposed to the air.

STORING MEAT

- Meat from the butcher should be left in its original paper wrapping. Packaged meat from the supermarket should be rewrapped in aluminum foil or plastic wrap.
- Store meat in the coldest part of the refrigerator and try to use it within three to five days. Ground meat should be used in one to two days.
- Meat freezes very well and can be stored in the freezer for several months. Be sure to label and date the package.
- Always thaw frozen meat in the refrigerator, and make sure it is completely thawed before cooking. Whether you are defrosting a large roast or a pound of chopped meat, you should start defrosting it the evening before you plan to cook it.
- Because raw meat may be contaminated with harmful bacteria, wash your hands, utensils, countertop, and equipment carefully after handling it.
- For information on food safety, call the Meat and Poultry Hotline of the USDA Food Safety and Inspection Service at (800) 535-4555.

HOW MUCH TO BUY

- The number of servings per pound of meat varies according to the cut of meat and how much bone and fat it contains.

CUT OF MEAT (UNCOOKED)	OUNCES PER SERVING
Roast beef, boneless	5 to 8 ounces
Steak, boneless	6 to 8 ounces
Steak, bone-in	12 to 16 ounces
Chopped meat for hamburger	4 to 6 ounces

MARINATING MEAT

+ Tougher cuts of meat can be tenderized as well as seasoned by marinating them or rubbing them with a mixture of herbs and spices. Pricking the surface of the meat with a fork helps speed up the process.

+ Bottled Italian salad dressing makes a handy marinade.

+ To make a fresh marinade, whisk together 1/4 cup of vegetable oil; 1/4 cup of red wine; 2 tablespoons of chopped onion; a clove or two of garlic, crushed; salt and pepper to taste; and some dried herbs, such as thyme and oregano.

+ Small pieces of meat, such as cubes of stew meat, marinate in a few hours; larger pieces take overnight.

COOKING MEAT

+ Remove meat from the refrigerator at least thirty minutes before cooking. It should always be at room temperature before cooking.

+ The best way to tell if your roast or other cut of meat is done is to use a meat thermometer, preferably one of the instant-read kinds. Keep in mind, though, that the internal temperature of the meat continues to rise after you remove it from the heat, so you should take the meat out of the oven when the thermometer still reads 5 to 10 degrees below the temperature you are aiming for.

✦ When cooking a *beef* roast or steak, its final internal temperature should be

  —120°F to 130°F for rare
  —135°F to 145°F for medium-rare
  —150°F to 160°F for medium
  —170°F to 175°F for well done

Ground beef, whether shaped into patties or loaves, should be cooked to an internal temperature of 160°F.

✦ *Pork* should never be eaten rare. It should be cooked to an internal temperature of

  —155°F for medium
  —165°F for well done

✦ *Lamb* roasts and chops should have an internal temperature of

  —120°F to 130°F for rare
  —135°F to 145°F for medium-rare
  —150°F to 160°F for medium
  —170°F to 175°F for well done

✦ Once meat is cooked, let it stand for ten to fifteen minutes before carving or serving it. This allows the juices to be redistributed throughout the meat, making it moister.

✦ When sautéing veal scallops or other thin cuts, you can keep the meat from sticking to the pan by heating the oil until it is very hot, almost smoking, before adding the meat. This is also true for meat that is breaded.

✦ No matter what method you use for cooking meat, be sure you do not overcook it, or it will become dry and tough.

ELEGANT AND EASY FILLET OF BEEF

◆

SERVES 10 TO 12

1 beef fillet (about 5 pounds), preferably the center cut
1 large clove garlic, cut into slivers
Salt and pepper to taste
Horseradish sauce (optional)

1. Preheat the oven to 425°F.
2. Make small slits in the surface of the meat and insert the garlic slivers into them.
3. Sprinkle the beef with salt and pepper and place it in a shallow roasting pan just big enough for the fillet.
4. Place the pan on the center rack of the oven and cook for 10 minutes. Reduce the oven temperature to 350°F and continue cooking. For *rare* meat, cook for another 25 minutes, or until the temperature of the meat reaches 120°F to 130°F on a meat thermometer. For *medium-rare*, cook for about another 35 minutes, or until the thermometer reaches 135°F to 145°F.
5. When the fillet is done, remove the pan from the oven and allow the meat to stand for about 15 to 20 minutes before slicing. Serve hot or at room temperature with horseradish sauce, if desired.

TIPS AND TIDBITS

✦ If possible, ask the butcher to prepare the fillet for roasting. He will wrap it in fat and tie it into a log.

✦ This beef, especially when served cold, is delicious with a creamy **horseradish sauce,** which you can buy in the supermarket or make by combining, either in a blender or by hand, ¹/₂ cup plain nonfat or low-fat yogurt or sour cream, ¹/₂ cup low-fat cottage cheese, 3 tablespoons grated fresh or bottled white horseradish, and 1 teaspoon Dijon mustard.

GLAZED FLANK STEAK

◆

SERVES 4

1¹/₂ pounds flank steak
1¹/₂ teaspoons dried chervil
1¹/₂ teaspoons dried thyme
6 tablespoons maple syrup
3 tablespoons grainy mustard

1. Trim any excess fat from the meat, and with a sharp knife, score the surface on the diagonal, making parallel lines about 2 inches apart. Then cut the meat into strips about 2 inches wide, slicing across (perpendicular to) the diagonal markings.
2. Combine the chervil, thyme, maple syrup, and mustard in a bowl and marinate the strips of meat in the sauce for at least 30 minutes.
3. Just before cooking, preheat the broiler and line a broiler pan with aluminum foil.
4. Place the meat on the broiler pan and broil for 5 to 6 minutes on each side.

GLAZED CORNED BEEF

◆

SERVES 4 TO 6

1 flat-cut corned beef (3 to 4 pounds),
  in vacuum-sealed package
1 onion, quartered
3 to 4 carrots, peeled and cut into 2-inch-long pieces (optional)
4 small potatoes, peeled and cut into chunks (optional)
1 small head cabbage, cut into wedges (optional)

1 tablespoon dry mustard
1 tablespoon brown sugar
1/2 teaspoon white vinegar

1. Place the meat in a deep pot and cover with cold water. Bring to a boil and then reduce the heat to a simmer. Simmer for 3 hours.
2. About 45 minutes to an hour before the meat is done, add the quartered onion and the other vegetables, if desired.
3. When the corned beef is done, remove it from the pot, trim it of all visible fat, and place it in a broiler pan.
4. Preheat the broiler.
5. While the broiler is heating, prepare the glaze: Mix the mustard and brown sugar in a small bowl and add the vinegar by drops, stirring until the mixture reaches a pasty consistency.
6. Spread the glaze on the meat and place under the broiler for about 3 to 6 minutes, until the sugar melts and the glaze browns.
7. To serve, cut slices no more than 1/4 inch thick, and start slicing at the thin corner, slicing across the grain. Serve with the cooked vegetables.

BARBECUED BRISKET

◆

SERVES 6 TO 8

One 3- to 3 1/2-pound brisket (thin or first cut)
2 tablespoons liquid smoke
1 cup ketchup
3/4 cup pineapple juice
1/4 cup Worcestershire sauce
1 teaspoon salt
1 teaspoon celery salt
1/4 teaspoon chili powder

1. Preheat the oven to 400°F.
2. Rub the brisket with the liquid smoke and put it in a roasting pan.
3. Place the pan in the oven and brown the meat on both sides, about 10 to 15 minutes per side.
4. Remove the pan from the oven and reduce the heat to 325°F.
5. Combine the ketchup, pineapple juice, Worcestershire sauce, salt, celery salt, and chili powder in a saucepan and bring to a boil.
6. Pour the sauce over the meat (do not drain off the liquid smoke from the pan), cover, and put back in the oven for 2½ hours, or until tender.
7. Allow the meat to cool before slicing.

TIPS AND TIDBITS

✦ Liquid smoke comes in a small bottle and can be bought at most supermarkets.

✦ Thin or first-cut brisket is relatively lean. If your meat is very fatty, be sure to trim the excess fat.

✦ This dish freezes and reheats very well. If reheating brisket that has been frozen, it is easier to slice while it is still cold.

BRISKET WITH CRANBERRIES

◆

SERVES 8 TO 10

One 4- to 5-pound brisket (thin or first cut)
5 medium onions, cut into slices
A few tablespoons of vegetable oil as needed
2 tablespoons Worcestershire sauce
One 16-ounce can whole berry cranberry sauce
Salt and pepper to taste

1. In the bottom of a Dutch oven or other large, heavy pot that has a cover, sprinkle a thin layer of salt and heat it until it begins to brown. Add the meat and brown it on all sides.
2. Remove the meat and add the onions to the pot, cooking until they are light brown. Add some vegetable oil if the pot is too dry.
3. Add the Worcestershire sauce and cranberry sauce to the pot and mix well with the onions. Add salt and pepper.
4. Place the meat on top of the onion-cranberry mixture. Spoon some of the mixture on top of the meat. Cook, covered, at a low simmer for about 3 hours.
5. When the meat is tender, remove it from the pot and allow it to cool before slicing. Skim the fat off the sauce.
6. Return the sliced meat to the pot to reheat. Serve on a bed of rice, noodles, or couscous.

TIPS AND TIDBITS

✦ If you prefer, you may add the sliced onions raw instead of browning them first.
✦ A good way to defat sauce is to put it in the freezer for an hour or so and simply spoon off the fat that has risen to the surface.

PEPPER STEAK
◆

SERVES 4

*One 1-pound London broil, usually a flank steak or
   shoulder steak*
3 tablespoons teriyaki sauce
2 teaspoons cornstarch
½ teaspoon garlic powder
½ teaspoon dry mustard

Continued

2 tablespoons vegetable oil
2 green bell peppers, seeded and cut into strips
6 scallions (green onions), white part only, cut into thin slices

1. Cut the meat into thin slices holding the knife almost flat and slicing diagonally through to the bottom.
2. Combine the teriyaki sauce, cornstarch, garlic powder, dry mustard, and 1 tablespoon of the vegetable oil in a bowl. Add the meat and stir, making sure each slice is thoroughly coated. Marinate the meat for at least 30 minutes.
3. Heat the remaining 1 tablespoon of oil in a heavy pan and cook the bell peppers and scallions for 2 to 3 minutes.
4. Push the vegetables aside and add the meat, cooking a few minutes on each side. Mix together and serve on a bed of noodles or rice.

TIPS AND TIDBITS
✦ You can vary this dish by adding other vegetables, such as chopped mushrooms, sliced onions, snow peas, or broccoli florets.

BEEF WITH BROCCOLI
◆

SERVES 4

³/₄ pound flank steak
1 tablespoon soy sauce
2 teaspoons cornstarch
6 tablespoons peanut oil, plus extra for drizzling
2 cups broccoli florets with some bite-sized pieces of stem
1 teaspoon sugar
1 teaspoon salt
2 tablespoons sherry or shao-hsing *wine*
2 tablespoons chicken broth, preferably College Inn

1. Cut the flank steak into ¼-inch slices and place it in a shallow bowl.
2. Combine the soy sauce, cornstarch, and a drizzle of peanut oil and pour over the meat. Work the mixture thoroughly with your hands to make sure the meat is well coated. Set aside.
3. Bring a pot of water to a boil, add some salt, and drop in the broccoli stems. Bring to a second boil and add the florets. Cook for 1 minute, drain, and rinse under cold water. Set aside.
4. Heat a wok or heavy skillet and add the 6 tablespoons peanut oil. When the oil is hot, add the slices of beef, stirring to separate them. Continue cooking for a few minutes, until the meat turns grayish. Remove the meat with a slotted spoon, leaving the oil in the pan.
5. Combine the sugar with the salt.
6. Reheat the oil, add the broccoli, and sprinkle with the sugar-and-salt mixture. Cook, stirring, for about 10 seconds.
7. Add the beef, stir to combine, and sprinkle with the sherry.
8. Continue stirring while adding the chicken broth. Cook for a few minutes more, until the broth is incorporated into the sauce. Serve hot.

TIPS AND TIDBITS

✦ If broccoli is not one of your favorites, try substituting other vegetables, such as cauliflower, asparagus, green beans, snow peas, or sugar snap peas.

BEEF PROVENÇAL

◆

SERVES 8 TO 10

A few tablespoons of vegetable oil, or more as needed
One 4-pound lean brisket, cut into large cubes
Salt and pepper to taste

Continued

4 large onions, cut into large chunks
20 cloves garlic (about 2 heads), peeled
1 teaspoon diced orange peel
1 bay leaf
Red wine to cover (about 2 bottles)

1. Heat the vegetable oil in a Dutch oven or other large, heavy pot and brown the meat cubes until golden. Don't add all of the meat at once, just a few cubes at a time.
2. Sprinkle with salt and pepper and add the onions and garlic cloves.
3. Add the orange peel and the bay leaf and enough red wine to just cover all of the ingredients.
4. Cover the pot and simmer over low heat until the meat is tender, about 3 hours.
5. Remove from the heat and allow to cool while covered.
6. Refrigerate; when cold, skim the fat from the surface.
7. Reheat before serving.

TIPS AND TIDBITS

✦ This dish is particularly good when made a day in advance.
✦ A very tasty variation: In step 1, cook 1 pound of bacon in the pot and, after removing it, use the bacon fat (instead of the vegetable oil) to brown the meat. Crumble the bacon and add it along with the onions and garlic in step 2.

BEEF STEW

◆

SERVES 6

3 tablespoons canola or other light vegetable oil
2 pounds beef (stew meat or other cut), trimmed of fat and cut
into cubes
3 tablespoons flour

Salt and pepper to taste
1 large clove garlic, minced
1 large onion, chopped
1 cup beef broth (canned or made from a bouillon cube)
One 8-ounce can tomato sauce
12 black peppercorns
3 whole cloves
1/4 cup chopped fresh parsley
1/2 bay leaf
1/2 cup dry white wine or dry sherry
6 medium potatoes, peeled and cut into chunks
6 medium carrots, peeled and cut into 1-inch pieces
8 ounces green beans, ends trimmed, cut into 1-inch pieces

1. In a large, heavy pot, heat the oil and brown the meat, stirring to make sure each cube is browned on all sides. Using a slotted spoon, transfer the meat to a plate or shallow dish and sprinkle with the flour and salt and pepper. Stir the meat to coat each piece, and set aside.

2. Pour off most of the fat in the pan. Add the garlic, onion, beef broth, tomato sauce, peppercorns, cloves, parsley, bay leaf, and wine and bring to a boil. Scrape up any brown bits on the bottom of the pan.

3. Add the meat to the pan and simmer, covered, over low heat for about 1 hour.

4. Add the potatoes, carrots, and green beans and continue cooking, covered, until the vegetables and meat are tender, another 30 minutes or so. Remove the peppercorns, cloves, and bay leaf before serving.

TIPS AND TIDBITS
+ This is one of those dishes that taste better the next day, so if you are making it for company, it's best to make it a day ahead.

CHILI

from **ROSIE O'DONNELL**

Actress, Comedian, Author,
Winner of Six Emmy Awards

◆

SERVES 8 TO 10

1 large onion, chopped
³/₄ cup hot Italian sausage drippings
3 pounds ground beef
¹/₂ cup red crushed peppers
¹/₂ cup chili powder
Salt and pepper to taste
One 24-ounce can crushed tomatoes

1. Sauté the onion in the sausage drippings until soft.
2. Add the ground beef and cook, stirring to break up the beef as it browns.
3. Add the red crushed peppers, chili powder, and salt and pepper, and cook over medium heat for about 20 minutes.
4. Add the crushed tomatoes and simmer for 45 minutes.
5. Serve the chili over French fries that are sprinkled with seasoned salt and any type of cheese.

CHILI

◆

SERVES 6 TO 8

1 large onion, thinly sliced or chopped
2 tablespoons olive oil
1 large clove garlic, minced

1 to 2 small jalapeño peppers, seeded and diced (optional)
1/2 to 3/4 pound ground beef
Two 15-ounce cans red kidney beans (preferably S&W), rinsed
    and drained
2 cups fresh (4 ears), canned, or frozen corn
One 16-ounce can whole peeled plum tomatoes, coarsely
    chopped, or a 16-ounce can crushed tomatoes
One 8-ounce can tomato sauce
One 6-ounce can tomato paste
1 tablespoon chili powder, or more to taste
1 tablespoon dried oregano
1 tablespoon white vinegar
1 tablespoon brown sugar, or more to taste
1/2 teaspoon ground cumin
A dash of ground allspice
A dash of ground cloves
A dash of ground coriander
A dash of cayenne pepper, or more if you like a spicier chili

1. In a large, heavy skillet, slowly cook the onion in the olive oil until
   it softens, about 5 minutes.
2. Add the garlic and jalapeño pepper(s), if desired, and cook for another few minutes, stirring.
3. Add the meat and cook, stirring, until it breaks up into small bits and
   loses its red color. Remove from the heat and drain the fat by pouring the mixture into a colander. Wipe the pan with a paper towel.
4. Put the drained meat mixture back into the pan and add the beans,
   corn, tomatoes, tomato sauce, tomato paste, chili powder, oregano,
   vinegar, brown sugar, and remaining spices. Stir well.
5. Bring the mixture to a simmer, and continue cooking, covered, for
   about 1 1/2 hours.
6. Serve on a bed of yellow rice or with tortilla chips.

TIPS AND TIDBITS

✦ Wear rubber gloves when handling jalapeño peppers; the seeds and
   juice are *especially caustic*. And don't rub your eyes!

CHILI CON GOAT CHEESE

from **PERRI KLASS, M.D.**

Author, Assistant Professor of Pediatrics,
Winner of Five O. Henry Awards

◆

"This recipe, which is a major family favorite, turns into a mysteriously rich and creamy dish, deeply beloved by my children, especially my daughter, Josephine—and is unexpectedly successful with crowds. I have made this in vast quantity for a party and watched it disappear."

SERVES 4 TO 6

2 pounds beef (preferably round, chuck, or good stew beef),
   cut into ¼-inch cubes
3 large onions, coarsely chopped
1 to 3 cloves garlic, according to taste, minced
¼ cup chili powder, or more to taste
1 generous teaspoon dried oregano
½ teaspoon paprika
Salt to taste
1 teaspoon powdered cumin
1 cup tomato product (fresh chopped tomatoes, drained diced
   tomatoes, tomato puree, or tomato sauce)
4 to 6 ounces beer (optional)
Cayenne pepper to taste
¾ pound goat cheese, cut up
½ teaspoon cumin seeds

1. In a heavy casserole or kettle, brown the cubes of meat in vegetable oil, stirring often.
2. Add the onions and garlic, cook briefly, and add the chili powder, oregano, paprika, salt, powdered cumin, tomato product, and beer. Bring to a boil.

3. Reduce the heat to low, cover, and let it cook for a while, at least 1 hour.
4. Add the cayenne to taste, the goat cheese, and the cumin seeds, and simmer over low heat, stirring, until the cheese is melted and it is bubbling gently.

QUICK AND TASTY MEAT LOAF

SERVES 2

1 large egg
¹/₄ cup finely chopped onion
4 teaspoons white horseradish, drained
2 tablespoons old-fashioned rolled oats (not instant)
Salt and pepper to taste
³/₄ pound ground beef
1 tablespoon ketchup

1. Preheat the oven to 400°F.
2. In a bowl, stir together the egg, onion, horseradish, oats, and salt and pepper to taste.
3. Add the meat and combine well.
4. Form the mixture into a loaf about 5¹/₂ inches long and 3¹/₂ inches wide and place in a shallow baking pan. Spread the ketchup over it.
5. Bake for 30 minutes. When the meat loaf is done, allow it to stand for about 3 minutes before slicing.

TIPS AND TIDBITS

✦ When opening a package of chopped meat, don't be concerned if the meat is brown on the inside and red on the outside. The meat is naturally brown but turns red when exposed to the air.

CONCERT HAM LOAF

from **PAULA ZAHN**

CNN Television News Anchor and Host,
Winner of One Emmy Award

◆

"This recipe came from a family friend who was a violinist and who would serve this to the Zahn family and guests postconcert."

SERVES 4 TO 6

BASTING MIX

$^1/_2$ *cup brown sugar*

$^3/_4$ *teaspoon dry mustard*

$^1/_4$ *cup vinegar*

$^1/_4$ *cup water*

HAM LOAF

1 pound cooked lean ham, ground or finely chopped

1 pound lean ground pork

$^3/_4$ *cup milk*

1 cup bread crumbs, moistened in a small amount of milk

2 eggs, beaten

1. Preheat the oven to 375°F.
2. Prepare the basting mix by placing the brown sugar, dry mustard, vinegar, and water in a small pan and heating over a low flame, stirring until the sugar and mustard are dissolved. Set aside.
3. Mix the ham loaf ingredients together and shape into a loaf.
4. Place in a shallow baking pan.
5. Bake for 20 to 25 minutes, then reduce the oven temperature to 350°F and continue cooking, basting every 15 minutes.
6. Bake for a total of 1$^1/_2$ to 2 hours.

SPARERIBS

*1 rack of pork spareribs (allow ³/₄ pound per person; ask the
butcher to crack the rack but not cut the ribs)*
A pinch of dried rosemary (optional)
¹/₂ cup soy sauce
¹/₂ cup ketchup
¹/₄ cup honey
3 cloves garlic, crushed

1. Preheat the oven to 350°F.
2. Rub the spareribs with the rosemary and set aside.
3. In a small bowl, combine the soy sauce, ketchup, honey, and garlic and brush the ribs with this mixture.
4. Place the ribs on a wire rack set in a baking pan. Pour some water into the pan and place in the oven for 1 to 1¹/₂ hours. Baste the ribs frequently with the sauce, at least 4 or 5 times.
5. Before serving, cut the ribs all the way through.

CREOLE BLACK BEANS

from **CAROL MOSELEY BRAUN**
*Former U.S. Senator from Illinois, the First
African American Woman Elected to the Senate*

"You may add other meats, such as ham, pork, smoked meat, or even smoked turkey. This dish always tastes better if you let it settle overnight."

SERVES 4 TO 6

2 to 3 strips bacon (for rendering fat)

1 large green bell pepper, seeded and chopped

1¹/₂ large onions, chopped

³/₄ teaspoon minced garlic

3 cups cooked black beans (canned Goya beans), rinsed and
*   drained, or 1 cup dried beans, cooked according to package*
*   directions (preferably with a ham bone)*

1 cup extra-virgin olive oil

¹/₄ teaspoon ground cumin

¹/₂ pound cooked smoked or spicy meat (preferably tasso,
*   andouille sausage, or in a pinch, Italian sausage), cut into*
*   bite-sized chunks*

1 teaspoon vinegar

1. Slowly cook the bacon in a large, heavy pan to render its fat. Discard the bacon.
2. Add the bell pepper to the bacon fat and sauté for several minutes.
3. Stir in the onions and allow them to brown slowly.
4. Add the garlic and sauté for a few minutes more.
5. Mix in the beans, olive oil, and cumin, stirring well.
6. Add the cooked meat and simmer for a few minutes at low heat.
7. Add the vinegar and cook for about 5 minutes more.
8. To thicken the mixture, mash the beans with a fork.

KOLOZSVAR LAYERED CABBAGE

from **JUDITH LEIBER**

Designer;
Founder, Judith Leiber Inc.

SERVES 6 TO 8

2 to 3 red onions, chopped

½ cup Hungarian sweet paprika

4 pounds pork, cut into small squares

6 pounds sauerkraut, plus some of the juice

1 bottle champagne

¾ pound rice

3 cups meat or chicken stock

6 hard-boiled eggs, sliced

1 pound thinly sliced bacon, cut into small pieces

6 sausage links, sliced into rounds

4 to 5 cups sour cream

1. Preheat the oven to 400°F.
2. In a large pot, wilt the onions in a small amount of oil or lard until they turn golden.
3. Add the paprika, mix well, and add the pork. Mix together and cook slowly until the pork is soft.
4. Place the sauerkraut in a separate pot and barely cover with water. Add a little of its juice and the champagne, and bring to a boil. Cook until the sauerkraut is soft, about 20 minutes or more.
5. In another pot, cook the rice in meat or chicken stock until done.
6. Add the rice to the pork mixture and stir to combine.
7. Coat the bottom of a large casserole with oil or lard and cover with one-third of the sauerkraut.
8. Add a layer of half the egg slices, followed by a layer of half the meat-rice mixture and a layer of half the bacon pieces and sausage rounds. Top with one-third of the sour cream.
9. Repeat this procedure (sauerkraut through sour cream).
10. Top with the remaining one-third sauerkraut and cover with the rest of the sour cream.
11. Place in the oven and bake for 1½ hours, until the top gets a crust.

GREEK-STYLE LAMB

◆

SERVES 4

One 4- to 6-pound boneless leg of lamb, rolled and tied
4 to 5 cloves garlic, cut into slivers
Salt and pepper to taste
2 medium to large onions, sliced
³/₄ cup olive oil
¹/₄ teaspoon dried oregano
A pinch of ground cinnamon
1 pound fresh plum tomatoes, peeled, seeded, and coarsely
    chopped, or 2 cups canned whole peeled plum tomatoes
    (with liquid), coarsely crushed
1 cup dry white wine
2 cups chicken broth
1 cup orzo
¹/₂ cup freshly grated Parmesan cheese

1. Preheat the oven to 400°F.
2. Using a sharp knife, make thin slits in the meat and insert the garlic slivers. Season with salt and pepper to taste.
3. Place the lamb in a roasting pan and sprinkle the onion slices
   around and on top of the meat. Drizzle with the olive oil.
4. Roast the lamb for about 30 minutes, then sprinkle with the
   oregano and cinnamon and spoon the tomatoes around and on top
   of the meat. Pour the wine around the meat and return the pan to
   the oven and roast for about 45 minutes more.
5. Remove the lamb from the pan and set aside.
6. Add the chicken broth to the pan and stir in the orzo. Place the
   lamb back in the pan and baste with some of the broth.
7. Place the pan back in the oven and cook for about 15 minutes, or
   until the orzo is tender and nearly all of the liquid has been absorbed.
8. When the lamb is done, sprinkle with the grated cheese and serve.

OSSO BUCO WITH RISOTTO

from **SUE CLARK-JOHNSON**

Senior Group President, Gannett Co., Inc.;

Publisher and CEO, The Arizona Republic

◆

"I love to cook and I love to share recipes. This is one of our favorite recipes—just for us, and for company. Despite the hundreds of recipes I have collected (maybe thousands) and a plethora of cookbooks, we fall back on this one frequently."

SERVES 4 TO 6

2 tablespoons butter or margarine

5 to 6 pounds meaty veal shanks, cut 2 inches thick

Cognac, for deglazing

4 cups sodium-free chicken broth

1/2 cup white wine

1 cup combined diced carrot, celery, yellow onion

2 tablespoons grated lemon peel

1 tablespoon grated orange peel

2 anchovy fillets, chopped (optional)

1 bay leaf

Several fresh sage leaves

1 teaspoon dried thyme

1/4 teaspoon ground ginger

1/4 teaspoon ground cinnamon

2 cups water

2 cups medium-grain or short-grain white rice

1/4 cup minced fresh parsley

2 cloves garlic, minced

1/4 cup grated Parmesan cheese

Lemon wedges and fresh parsley sprigs, for garnish

1. Preheat the oven to 475°F.
2. Place the butter or margarine in a 17 × 11-inch roasting pan and place the pan in the oven until the butter or margarine sizzles.
3. Lay the shanks in the pan in a single layer and bake, uncovered, for 30 minutes.
4. Turn the shanks over and continue baking for another 30 minutes.
5. Deglaze the pan with a little Cognac.
6. Add to the pan: chicken broth, wine, diced carrots, celery, and onion, 1 tablespoon of the lemon peel, the orange peel, anchovies, bay leaf, sage leaves, thyme, ginger, and cinnamon.
7. Cover the pan tightly with aluminum foil and bake for about 1 1/2 hours, or until the meat is fork-tender.
8. Uncover the pan and remove the shanks. Put them on a warmed dish, cover, and keep warm.
9. Stir the water and the rice into the pan. Bake, uncovered, stirring occasionally, for 20 to 25 minutes, until the liquid has been absorbed and the rice is tender.
10. Mix together the remaining 1 tablespoon lemon peel, the minced parsley, and the garlic.
11. Transfer the shanks to a serving platter and sprinkle the meat with the parsley mixture.
12. Stir the cheese into the rice and spoon onto the platter alongside the meat or serve in a separate bowl.
13. Garnish with lemon wedges and parsley sprigs.

VEAL CHOPS

◆

SERVES 4

1 cup bread crumbs
1 tablespoon minced fresh parsley
1 teaspoon dried oregano
1/2 cup grated Parmesan cheese

4 thick loin veal chops
Salt and pepper to taste
1 egg, beaten
2 to 3 tablespoons vegetable oil or butter

1. Combine the bread crumbs, parsley, oregano, and cheese in a shallow dish.
2. Sprinkle the chops with salt and pepper.
3. Dip each chop in the beaten egg and then place in the bread crumb mixture, patting to make the crumbs adhere.
4. Heat the vegetable oil in a large, heavy pan and cook the chops until tender, about 10 minutes on each side. Drain on paper towels.

TIPS AND TIDBITS

✦ If you like a slightly tangier cheese, grated Romano (sheep's milk) is a tasty alternative to Parmesan (cow's milk). Sometimes you can buy a mixture of both. And, of course, freshly grated cheese is vastly superior to packaged.

VEAL MARSALA

◆

SERVES 2 TO 3

¹/₄ cup flour
Salt and pepper to taste
2 to 3 tablespoons olive oil
1 large clove garlic, crushed
4 thin veal cutlets (3 to 4 ounces each)
4 ounces white or shiitake mushrooms, sliced
2 tablespoons chopped shallots (optional)
1 cup dry Marsala wine

1. Place the flour in a shallow dish and season with salt and pepper.
2. Pour the olive oil in a large, heavy pan and add the crushed garlic.
3. Heat the oil and slowly cook the garlic until it browns. Remove the garlic from the pan and discard.
4. While the garlic is browning, dredge the veal cutlets in the seasoned flour, shaking off any excess flour.
5. After the garlic has been removed from the pan, sauté the cutlets in the hot oil, cooking them for just a few minutes on each side. Drain them on paper towels, and set aside.
6. Add the mushrooms and shallots, if desired, to the pan and cook for a few minutes, stirring, until the mushrooms are starting to brown and the shallots are translucent.
7. Place the cutlets back in the pan and pour in the Marsala. Cook for about 10 minutes, turning the meat once, and scraping up the brown bits on the bottom of the pan. Serve with noodles or rice.

TIPS AND TIDBITS

✦ Whenever you add wine to a pan, take the pan off the heat before pouring, to prevent the alcohol from catching on fire.

VEAL AND PEPPERS

◆

SERVES 4

3 to 4 large red or yellow bell peppers, each seeded and cut into
    8 sections
Two 14-ounce jars marinara or your favorite tomato sauce
2 tablepoons sugar
1¹/₂ to 2 pounds veal cutlets, cut into strips about ¹/₂ inch wide
8 to 12 ounces mushrooms, sliced or whole

1. Place the bell peppers in a large pot of boiling salted water. Cook for 3 minutes and drain.
2. Heat the tomato sauce in a large, heavy pan and stir in the sugar.
3. Over low heat, simmer the veal in the sauce for about 30 minutes.
4. Add the bell peppers and cook for another 15 minutes.
5. Stir in the mushrooms and cook for 15 minutes more. Serve with noodles or small pasta, such as penne or fusilli.

TIPS AND TIDBITS

✦ Be sure to drain the cooked peppers very well so that the added moisture doesn't water down the sauce.

RECIPE TITLE

FROM

SERVES

INGREDIENTS

INSTRUCTIONS

TIPS AND TIDBITS

RECIPE TITLE_____

FROM_____

SERVES _____

INGREDIENTS

INSTRUCTIONS

TIPS AND TIDBITS

SEAFOOD

Also check out:

TIPS AND HINTS ON...

BUYING AND STORING FISH AND SHELLFISH

✦ Fresh fish and shellfish (shrimp, lobster, clams, mussels, scallops) can be purchased at your local supermarket or fish store, but because they are so perishable, make sure they are displayed on a bed of ice or in a refrigerated case.

✦ Fish should have a mild, pleasant, slightly sweet aroma, a little like that of the ocean. The flesh should be moist, firm, and clear, without any dark or pinkish spots or areas.

✦ Some shrimp—often the brown shrimp caught in the Gulf of Mexico—have a very distinct iodine flavor that is impossible to disguise. If you don't care for this flavor, ask where the shrimp was imported from so you can avoid those from the Gulf of Mexico.

✦ If you buy frozen fish, avoid fish that looks dry or chalky—it may taste that way. Place frozen fish directly in your freezer unless you plan to use it the same day. Always follow the package directions when thawing frozen fish and shellfish.

✦ It is important to remember that fresh seafood spoils very quickly and should be kept in the coldest part of your refrigerator, usually the bottom shelf. Cook it the same day you buy it or, at the very latest, the next day.

✦ If you have to keep fresh seafood any longer, freeze it, but keep in mind that most kinds of fish and shellfish do not freeze well and will deteriorate in taste and texture, especially if kept more than a month or two.

✦ If you do freeze fish, rinse and dry it, then wrap it tightly in two layers of plastic wrap. To thaw it, take the wrapped fish out of the freezer the day before you plan to cook it and keep it on a plate in the refrigerator. To speed up the defrosting process, place the package of frozen fish in a bowl and cover with cold water, changing the water often.

COOKING FISH AND SHELLFISH

+ Fish and shellfish cook very quickly and can easily be overcooked.

+ Shellfish are often boiled or steamed, usually for just a few minutes.

+ To make a strongly flavored fish taste milder, soak it in milk for an hour or so in the refrigerator before cooking.

+ When cooking fish, it is a good general rule to allow three minutes per half inch of thickness, six or seven minutes per inch, unless you like your fish well done.

+ Once you remove the fish from the pan, it will continue cooking for a few minutes more. This is called carry-over cooking time. It's always better to remove the fish a little too early than too late.

+ Broiling is suitable for most cuts of fish as well as small whole fish (under 3 pounds).

+ Grilling is great for steaks or thick fillets of swordfish, salmon, or tuna. Small firm whole fish that won't fall apart when they are turned are also good for grilling. These include pompano, red snapper, and mackerel.

+ Sautéing and frying are quick, easy ways to cook fish fillets.

+ Baking and roasting are good methods for cooking whole fish as well as thick steaks and fillets. Thin fillets may dry out.

+ You can check for doneness by cutting a small slit in the thickest part of the flesh. If it flakes easily and appears opaque, it is done.

SHELLING AND DEVEINING SHRIMP

+ Although some recipes call for cooking shrimp in the shell, most often you have to remove the shell before cooking, simply by peeling it off with your fingers.

+ Once the shell is removed, you must also remove the threadlike "vein" that runs down the shrimp's back. (It is actually the intestinal tract, and when it contains food material, it appears as a thin black line.)

+ An easy way to remove the vein is to make a crosswise slit near the tail and pull the vein out from the other (front) end. You can also take it out by making a slit along the entire length of the back.

BOILING SHRIMP

+ Shrimp turn rubbery when they are overcooked, so it is important to cook them quickly.

+ While you are shelling and deveining them, bring a large pot of water to a boil and add a pinch or two of salt.

+ If you plan to serve the shrimp as a cold appetizer or an hors d'oeuvre with a dip, it is a good idea to add some seasoning to the water. A teaspoon of pickling spice, a chopped celery stalk, a few black peppercorns, or a few lemon wedges add a nice flavor.

+ Once the water is boiling, add the shrimp all at once and stir them to keep them from clumping.

+ Once the water returns to a boil, turn off the heat and drain the shrimp in a colander. If the shrimp are very large, let them boil for about thirty seconds before draining.

+ Cool cooked shrimp under cold running water. If you will be serving the shrimp cold, place them in a bowl with cold water, cover the bowl, and place it in the refrigerator. Don't forget to dry them before serving.

EASY FISH FILLETS

◆

SERVES 4

2 to 3 tablespoons butter, cut into several pieces
4 large sole or flounder fillets
Juice of ½ lemon, about 1 to 1½ tablespoons
⅔ cup Ritz cracker crumbs
Lemon wedges, for garnish

1. Preheat the oven to 450°F.
2. Place the pieces of butter in a 13 × 9-inch glass baking dish and place the dish in the oven until the butter is sizzling but not burned, just a few minutes.
3. While the butter is heating, sprinkle the fish fillets with the lemon juice.
4. When the butter is ready, remove the dish from the oven and place the fillets in the dish. Count to 60 and turn them over.
5. Sprinkle the fillets with the Ritz cracker crumbs and place the dish back in the oven for 3 to 5 minutes. Garnish with lemon wedges.

MONKFISH WITH FRESH TOMATO AND GARLIC

from **LILLIAN VERNON**
Founder, Lillian Vernon Corporation; Author

◆

"I found this dish in a seafood restaurant in Rome, Italy, and they gave me the recipe—it's delicious. Enjoy!"

SERVES 4

2 tablespoons olive oil

6 large cloves garlic, crushed or chopped

2 medium to large tomatoes, seeded and cut into small cubes

2 pounds monkfish fillets, cut into cubes

³/₄ cup white wine

Salt and pepper to taste

¹/₄ teaspoon red pepper flakes

2 tablespoons chopped fresh parsley for garnish

1. Pour the olive oil into a large skillet and cook the garlic until it starts to change color, about 2 or 3 minutes.
2. Add the tomatoes and cook for 3 minutes.
3. Add the fish and cook over high heat for 5 minutes, turning often.
4. Add the wine, salt and pepper to taste, and the red pepper flakes. Reduce the heat to medium, cover, and cook for 10 minutes. Sprinkle with the parsley and serve with toasted Italian bread.

SIMPLY SALMON

from **CAROLEE FRIEDLANDER**

Jewelry Designer; President and
CEO, Carolee Designs, Inc.

◆

"Serve with a salad of mixed field greens tossed with your favorite dressing."

SERVES 4

Four 6-ounce salmon fillet pieces (each about ¹/₂ inch thick)

4 teaspoons fresh lemon juice

2 tablespoons extra-virgin olive oil

2 red potatoes, boiled until tender, and sliced

1 cup snow peas, blanched in boiling water for 1 minute

SALMON IN PARCHMENT PAPER

from **PEGGY FLEMING**

*Figure Skater, Winner of the 1968 Olympic Gold Medal for
Figure Skating, Winner of Five Consecutive U.S. Skating Titles
and Three World Championships*

◆

SERVES 6 TO 8

2¹/₂ to 3 pounds fresh salmon fillets
¹/₄ cup chopped fresh dill and/or mint
A splash of Madeira wine
A splash of olive oil, preferably an herb-flavored oil
Juice of 1 lemon
2 tablespoons drained capers

1. Preheat the oven to 375°F.
2. Cut the salmon fillets into individual portions and cut circular pieces of parchment paper large enough to wrap each portion.
3. Place some of the chopped dill and/or mint in the middle of each parchment circle and place a portion of fish on top.
4. Add a splash of wine to each piece of fish, followed by a splash of olive oil.
5. Drizzle a few drops of lemon juice onto each piece of fish and sprinkle with a few capers.
6. Gather up the paper, twist to seal, and tie with a piece of kitchen string.
7. Bake for 13 to 15 minutes.

POACHED SALMON

◆

1 medium onion, peeled, with 2 or 3 whole cloves stuck in it
1 cup white wine
Several sprigs of fresh dill
2 bay leaves
10 black peppercorns
1 to 1¹/₂ pounds salmon fillet (1 large or 2 smaller ones)
Lemon wedges, for garnish

1. Place the onion, wine, dill, bay leaves, and peppercorns in a large stainless-steel or enamel saucepan. Add a few cups of water—there should be enough liquid to cover the fish when it's added—and simmer for 10 to 20 minutes to get a flavorful broth.
2. Gently add the fish and simmer for about 3 minutes. Remove the saucepan from the heat, cover, and allow it to stand for 1 hour.
3. Carefully drain the fish and refrigerate. When cool, remove the skin and the dark layer just underneath the skin.
4. Serve the salmon chilled or at room temperature, along with lemon wedges.

TIPS AND TIDBITS

✦ This salmon also goes well with a **green sauce**, which you can make by pureeing in a food processor 3 tablespoons mayonnaise, 3 table-spoons sour cream, 1 teaspoon Dijon mustard, 1 bunch fresh parsley, 1 bunch fresh dill, ¹/₂ teaspoon horseradish sauce (or to taste), and salt and pepper to taste.

GRILLED SWORDFISH

◆

SERVES 3 TO 4

2 swordfish steaks (about 2 pounds total)
Salt and pepper to taste
½ cup olive oil
1 to 2 cloves garlic, crushed
1 to 2 sprigs fresh rosemary or your favorite herb
A splash of fresh lemon juice

1. Sprinkle the swordfish steaks with salt and pepper to taste.
2. Combine the olive oil, garlic, rosemary, and lemon juice and pour into a Ziploc bag.
3. Add the fish to the bag and gently shake it so that the fish is well coated. Place the bag in the refrigerator and allow the fish to marinate for 1 hour before cooking.
4. When ready to cook, remove the fish from the bag and grill for 5 minutes on one side and 2 to 5 minutes on the other side, depending on the thickness of the steaks and the desired doneness.

TIPS AND TIDBITS

✦ This basic marinade is also nice with salmon and tuna.

GRILLED TUNA

◆

SERVES 2 TO 3

1 pound fresh tuna steak, preferably yellowfin
2 tablespoons ginger teriyaki marinade
Wasabi sauce (optional)

1. Coat both sides of the tuna with the marinade. Cover with plastic wrap and refrigerate for an hour or two.
2. When ready to cook, lightly oil a grill pan and heat it for several minutes before cooking.
3. Add the tuna to the pan and cook for 3 to 4 minutes on each side. To test for doneness, cut a small slit in the fish and peek inside. Don't overcook. Remember that there will be some carry-over cooking after you remove the fish from the pan.

TIPS AND TIDBITS

✦ Although this fish is delicious by itself, it goes very well with a tangy **wasabi sauce**, which you can make by combining ½ cup mayonnaise, 2 teaspoons soy sauce, 1 teaspoon sugar, 1 teaspoon fresh lemon juice, and 1 teaspoon wasabi paste.

NAME THAT TUNA

◆

Every family seems to have its own favorite tuna salad.
Here are ours:

◆

Each recipe starts with two 6.5-ounce cans of solid white tuna packed in water, well drained and separated into flakes. For more flavor, use light tuna instead of white. Also, fish packed in oil is tastier than fish packed in water, but it also has more calories. On the other hand, if you are watching your calories and want to use a low-fat mayonnaise, we have found that Hellmann's Light is just about as tasty as regular mayonnaise.

BASIC TUNA SALAD I

4 to 6 tablespoons mayonnaise
½ cup chopped celery or peeled diced cucumber
1 teaspoon lemon juice (optional)
Salt and pepper to taste

BASIC TUNA SALAD II

1 to 2 tablespoons regular or low-fat mayonnaise
2 tablespoons minced red onion or shallot
1 teaspoon sugar dissolved in 1 teaspoon lemon juice
Salt and pepper to taste

BASIC TUNA SALAD III

2 tablespoons regular or low-fat mayonnaise
1 tablespoon India or other sweet pickle relish, or more to taste
A splash of lemon juice

GRANDMA PEARL'S LOW-FAT TUNA SALAD

$1/4$ cup low-fat or nonfat cottage cheese
1 stalk celery, chopped
6 to 8 stuffed green olives, chopped
Pepper and/or garlic powder to taste
A few sprigs of fresh dill, chopped (optional)

TANGY LOW-FAT TUNA SALAD

2 teaspoons white horseradish, drained
1 teaspoon mustard
2 to 3 teaspoons low-fat mayonnaise
Salt and pepper to taste
1 to 2 tablespoons chopped red onion or scallion (optional)

VERY LOW-FAT TUNA SALAD

3 tablespoons capers, rinsed
$1/4$ cup peeled, diced cucumber
$1/2$ to $3/4$ cup chopped onions
2 tablespoons balsamic vinegar, or to taste

TIPS AND TIDBITS

✦ Grandma Pearl says that cottage cheese stays fresh longer if you keep the container upside down in the refrigerator. Try it; it works! And the cottage cheese doesn't leak out.

CRAB CAKES

from **BARBARA A. MIKULSKI**

U.S. Senator from Maryland,

Former Congresswoman from Maryland

◆

SERVES 6

1 egg
3 slices white bread
1 tablespoon mayonnaise, preferably low-fat
1 tablespoon Dijon mustard
2 teaspoons Old Bay or Wye River seasoning
1 tablespoon chopped fresh parsley (optional)
1 pound jumbo lump or backfin crabmeat
Vegetable oil (for frying) or olive oil or clarified butter
    (for sautéing)
Tartar sauce, mustard, or cocktail sauce

1. Beat the egg in a bowl.
2. Remove the crusts from the bread, break the slices into small pieces, and add to the egg.
3. Mix in the mayonnaise, Dijon mustard, Old Bay or Wye River seasoning, and parsley, if desired. Beat well.
4. Place the crabmeat in a separate bowl and pour the egg mixture over it. Gently toss or fold the ingredients together, taking care not to break up the lumps of crabmeat.
5. Form the crab mixture into cakes by hand or with an ice-cream scoop, making 8 rounded mounds about 3 inches in diameter and 3/4 inch thick. Do not pack the mixture too firmly; the cakes should be as loose as possible yet firm enough to hold their shape. Place the cakes on a tray or platter lined with waxed paper. Cover and refrigerate for at least 1 hour before cooking.
6. *To fry the cakes:* Pour vegetable oil into a heavy skillet to a depth of about 1½ inches. Heat the oil and fry the crab cakes, a few at a

2. When the rice is slightly al dente (tender yet still firm), and there is still a little bit of liquid in the pan, stir in the shrimp. Cook until they are pink, about 5 minutes.
3. Transfer to a serving dish and stir in the almonds, if desired. Sprinkle with the parsley and orange rind and serve hot.

TIPS AND TIDBITS

✦ You can substitute pineapple juice for the orange juice and use cut-up pineapple instead of the orange rind.

✦ Additions to the rice pilaf can include 1/2 cup shelled peas, corn niblets, or cut-up steamed asparagus.

SHRIMP SALAD WITH GRAPES

◆

SERVES 4

1 pound medium shrimp
1 cup seedless green or red grapes
1/2 cup sour cream or plain yogurt
1/2 cup mayonnaise
1/3 cup chopped fresh dill
Salt and pepper to taste

1. Shell and devein the shrimp.
2. Cook the shrimp by dropping them into a large pot of salted boiling water. When the water starts to come to a second boil, turn off the heat, drain the shrimp, and cool under cold running water. Drain on paper towels.
3. Cut the shrimp into bite-sized pieces.
4. Place the shrimp in a large bowl and add the grapes. (If the grapes are very large, cut them in half.)

Continued

5. In a small bowl, mix together the sour cream or yogurt, mayonnaise, and dill.

6. Pour about three-quarters of the dressing over the shrimp-and-grape mixture, mix well, and season with salt and pepper.

7. Refrigerate for several hours before serving. Add more of the dressing if needed.

TIPS AND TIDBITS

✦ If fresh shrimp isn't available, this recipe works equally well with chunks of cooked boneless, skinless chicken breast.

SHRIMP SALAD WITH ORZO AND FETA CHEESE

SERVES 4

1 pound large shrimp
³/₄ cup orzo
4 ounces feta cheese, crumbled or cut into very small pieces
¹/₄ cup minced scallion (green onion), white and some of the green
3 tablespoons canola or other light vegetable oil
2 tablespoons white wine vinegar
Salt and pepper to taste

1. Shell and devein the shrimp.

2. Cook the shrimp by dropping them into a large pot of salted boiling water. When the water starts to come to a second boil, turn off the heat, drain the shrimp, and cool under cold running water. Drain on paper towels.

3. While the shrimp are cooling, place the orzo in a pot of salted boiling water and boil just until the pasta is tender, about 10 minutes. Drain well.

4. Cut the cooled shrimp into thirds or quarters, depending on the size of your shrimp, and place in a bowl.

5. Add the orzo, feta cheese, and scallion.
6. In a separate small bowl, whisk together the canola oil and vinegar.
7. Pour the dressing over the shrimp mixture and add salt and pepper. Mix well and serve or refrigerate.

TIPS AND TIDBITS

✦ When a recipe calls for feta cheese, it usually means Greek feta. However, you might prefer another variety, such as French, which is milder and creamier.

✦ If your feta cheese is very salty, rinse it under cold running water and drain on paper towels.

VIVA NAPOLI

from **CLAIRE GAUDIANI**
Senior Research Scholar, Yale Law School;
President and Founder, New London Development
Corporation; Former President, Connecticut College

◆

"This wildly delicious meal-in-a-dish can be made a day or two ahead (don't add the seafood until it is ready to serve) or in less than an hour if you and your guests arrive home together and you bought the ingredients on your way home. It makes a full dinner served with hot bread and followed by a green salad and a sinful dessert."

SERVES 8 TO 10

3 *cloves garlic*
1/2 *cup olive oil, plus more as needed*
2 *onions, chopped*
6 *carrots, peeled and cut into* 1/2-*inch pieces*
2 *fennel bulbs or 1 head of celery, washed and chopped into*
    1/2-*inch pieces*

Continued

2 teaspoons dried thyme

*Rind of 1 orange, cut into thin slivers (peel the orange with a
    potato peeler, being careful to take as much of the orange
    skin and as little of the white as possible)*

2 teaspoons fennel seeds (optional)

2 ounces Pernod (optional)

A handful of finely chopped fresh parsley

One 35-ounce can Italian plum tomatoes

*Two 8-ounce bottles clam juice, or two 10- to 14-ounce cans
    chicken broth*

1½ pounds fresh shrimp, shelled and deveined

1½ pounds bay scallops

*1½ pounds fresh cod or other white fish (such as halibut or
    flounder), cut into 1½-inch cubes (you might want to try
    other seafood as available—orange roughy, sea bass, red
    snapper, or even fresh clams or mussels)*

1. In a large pot, sauté the garlic cloves in the olive oil until light brown.
2. Add the onions, carrots, fennel, thyme, half the orange rind slivers, the fennel seeds, and the Pernod. Stir gently and cook for 15 minutes over medium heat so that the vegetables soften and brown lightly but do not burn. Add additional olive oil if necessary.
3. Add half the chopped parsley, the tomatoes (breaking them up in the pot), and the clam juice or chicken broth. Cover the pot and cook on low heat for 30 minutes. You may continue cooking at this point or set the pot aside until your guests arrive.
4. Add the shrimp, scallops, fish, and most of the remaining parsley and orange rind slivers, saving a little for garnishing.
5. Bring to a low simmer and cook for 5 to 8 minutes, stirring every few minutes to assure even cooking. (If you are using clams or mussels, add them 6 to 7 minutes before the shrimp, scallops, and fish.) When all of the shrimp have turned bright pink, cover the pot and turn off the heat.
6. Reheat before serving, and garnish with the reserved parsley and orange rind slivers.

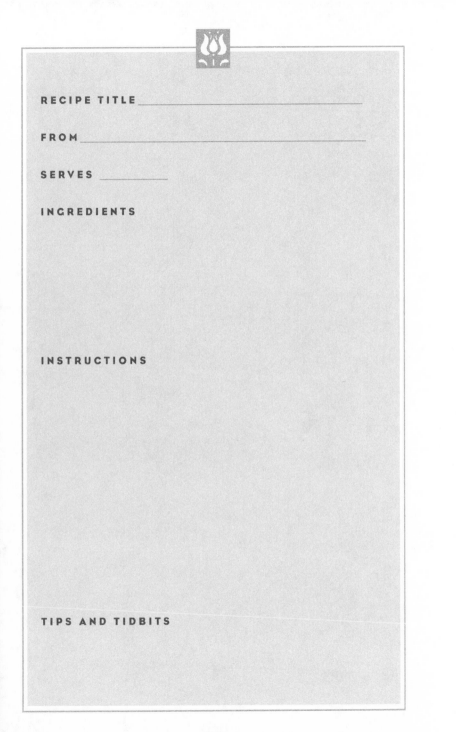

RECIPE TITLE

FROM

SERVES

INGREDIENTS

INSTRUCTIONS

TIPS AND TIDBITS

RECIPE TITLE_____

FROM_____

SERVES _____

INGREDIENTS

INSTRUCTIONS

TIPS AND TIDBITS

DESSERTS

Also check out:

MEASURING DRY INGREDIENTS FOR BAKING

+ It is particularly important to be accurate when measuring flour, sugar, and other dry ingredients for cakes and other baked goods.
+ Always work with a standard set of measuring spoons and cups and use the appropriate sizes.
+ To measure, lightly scoop or spoon your dry ingredient into the measuring cup or spoon, leaving a slight mound on the top. Then run a knife blade or other flat utensil across the top of the cup or spoon to remove the excess. The one exception to this method is brown sugar, which should always be packed firmly into the measuring cup.

BUYING AND STORING SUGAR

+ Three types of sugar are used most frequently in cooking:

—*White granulated sugar,* also called *white sugar,* is the standard table sugar and the one most often called for in recipes.

—*Confectioners' sugar,* also known as *powdered sugar,* is granulated sugar that has been pulverized to a fine powder and sometimes mixed with a small amount of cornstarch to keep it from caking. While confectioners' sugar should never be used instead of granulated sugar in baking, it can be used as a substitute in other kinds of recipes:

1¼ cups of confectioners' sugar = 1 cup of granulated sugar

—*Brown sugar* is white sugar to which molasses or other syrup has been added, and it is available in dark (strong) and light (mild) varieties. Unless a recipe specifies either one, use whichever you prefer. *Brownulated sugar* is a form of light brown sugar that pours easily but has a slightly different taste from regular brown sugar.

—*Special sugars* include Demerara and Barbados, which are brown in color but are actually raw sugars, not a form of brown sugar. Other special sugars include superfine, which dissolves faster than granulated sugar, sparkling white sugar, glazing sugar, burnt amber icing sugar, and colored sugars.

+ All types of sugar should be stored in sealed containers or plastic bags and kept at room temperature.
+ Because brown sugar has a tendency to dry out and harden into a solid mass, it is a good idea to wrap it tightly in its original inner plastic bag and place that bag inside a Tupperware or similar plastic container.
+ If your brown sugar does harden, you may be able to salvage it by removing it from its plastic bag, wrapping it in a damp (not soaking wet) paper towel, placing it in a small paper bag, closing the bag, and microwaving it for two to three minutes or heating it in a 200°F oven for twenty to thirty minutes. Once the sugar softens, use it as soon as you can; it will harden again as it cools.
+ Other sweeteners—honey, corn syrup, maple syrup, fructose (a natural by-product of fruits and honey), molasses—should never be substituted for sugar. Use them only when a recipe calls for them.
+ Similarly, never substitute an artificial sweetener, such as saccharine or aspartame, for sugar.

TESTING BAKING POWDER AND BAKING SODA FOR FRESHNESS

+ If your cakes, muffins, and other baked goods are not rising as high as they should, it may be that your baking powder or baking soda has lost its oomph. It's a good idea to test them every once in a while, especially if you don't use them very often.
+ To test baking powder for freshness, add about $1/2$ teaspoon to $1/4$ cup of hot water. If the water bubbles furiously, the baking powder is still fresh.
+ To test your baking soda, follow the same procedure, but use vinegar instead of hot water.

BUYING AND STORING BUTTER AND OTHER FATS

+ Butter is generally considered to have the best flavor for making cakes, cookies, and other baked products.

+ Butter is available as *salted butter* or *sweet butter* (sometimes called *unsalted*) and sold in packages of quarter-pound bars (sticks) or in tubs. Unless otherwise specified, the word *butter* in a recipe refers to sweet butter. If you have only the salted kind, be sure to reduce the amount of salt you add to the recipe.

+ When buying butter, check the label's expiration date and buy the freshest package you can find.

+ Store butter in the refrigerator, keeping it in its original box, and then wrapping it in plastic wrap or placing it inside a plastic bag. You could also store the wrapped butter in the freezer, which will extend its life but may also alter its flavor after a while.

+ Because butter easily absorbs odors, keep it well wrapped and as far away as possible from other foods. Land O' Lakes packages its sticks of butter in foil wrappers, which helps to keep odors from reaching the butter.

+ When making baked goods, never substitute whipped butter or any low-fat imitation spreads or liquids for the real thing.

+ You may substitute stick margarine for butter, but it will reduce the richness and slightly alter the flavor of the finished product. It is better to use a combination of margarine and butter. (Keep in mind, though, that butter and margarine have the same number of calories and the same fat content.)

+ Vegetable shortening, such as Crisco, is often preferred for making flaky pie crusts but should not be used in other baked goods because it adds little flavor.

+ When buying oil, unless a particular kind is specified in the recipe, the healthiest ones to chose are the polyunsaturated oils (safflower, sunflower, and corn) and the monounsaturated oils (olive and canola).

+ When a cake or cookie recipe calls for oil, use only a very light, mild vegetable oil, such as canola or safflower, never olive oil.

BUYING AND STORING CHOCOLATE

+ While there are a dazzling array of choices available to the chocolate lover, for cooking purposes, there are basically two types of chocolate:

—*Unsweetened chocolate,* which is also called *baking chocolate,* is usually sold in packages containing eight individually wrapped 1-ounce squares.

—*Sweetened chocolate* is available in several forms, chiefly squares, bars, and morsels (chips), and can range in flavor from sweet to extra bittersweet. Your choice should be based on convenience and your own personal preference.

—*White chocolate* is not considered to be real chocolate and should never be used unless specifically called for in a recipe. (Although it contains cocoa butter, it has no chocolate liquor, the primary ingredient in chocolate.)

✦ All types of chocolate should be stored at room temperature, not in the refrigerator.

✦ If chocolate gets too warm, it may turn an unappetizing gray color, but it is still fine to use.

MELTING CHOCOLATE

✦ Melting chocolate can be a little tricky. Because it burns easily, you shouldn't melt chocolate over direct heat. But if you do, be sure to use a heavy pan and a very low flame and to stir constantly.

✦ The easiest way to melt chocolate is in a microwave oven:

—Place the chocolate in a nonmetal bowl or measuring cup and microwave it at 50 percent (medium) power.

—Stir it after two minutes and continue microwaving for another minute or two.

✦ If you don't have a microwave oven, you can melt chocolate in a small, heavy pot placed over a second pot containing an inch of very hot—but not boiling—water. Stir it often and remove the pot from the heat just before the chocolate is completely melted, stirring it to complete the process.

✦ To make whipped cream, buy containers marked heavy or whipping cream. Do not use light or medium cream or half-and-half, which is made up of equal parts whole milk and light cream. Although half-and-half can be substituted for cream in many recipes, it cannot be used to make whipped cream.

✦ Here is a surefire way to make whipped cream:

—Make sure that the cream, the bowl, and the beaters are very cold. You can place them in the refrigerator or freezer for a few minutes before you begin.

—As you start beating the cream, watch it carefully to see when it starts to thicken. This is the point at which you would add any sugar and other flavorings.

—As you continue beating, be sure to move the beaters around the bowl.

—After a few minutes, the cream will develop soft, floppy peaks (which some people prefer) and then form firm peaks (which other people prefer).

—If you continue beating, the cream will stiffen and start to gather around the beaters. This is an excellent time to *stop*, because if you continue, you will be well on your way to making butter! If you think you are rapidly approaching this point, you may want to switch from your electric mixer to a hand whisk for the final few minutes.

✦ If you are making whipped cream ahead of time, underwhip it, put it in the refrigerator, and then finish whipping it with a hand whisk just before you need it.

SEPARATING EGG WHITES FROM YOLKS

✦ Although many experienced cooks have perfected their own methods of separating eggs, we prefer the tried-and-true way, aka Three-Bowl Monte:

—Start with cold eggs and three small bowls, one for the whites, one for the yolks, and one for "just in case."

—Crack open an egg by tapping it lightly against the side of bowl #1.

—Slowly pull the two halves apart. As you do so, some of the white will run out into the bowl.

—To collect the rest of the white, hold the two halves over the bowl and carefully pour the yolk back and forth between the two halves while more of the white spills into the bowl.

—When finished, pour the yolk into bowl #2 and the white from bowl #1 into bowl #3.

—Repeat this process with each egg, transferring the white in bowl #1 to bowl #3 each time.

✦ If you accidentally break a yolk and some of it—even just a drop or two—ends up in bowl #1, remove it with a spoon or paper towel. If you add it to the other egg whites, it will ruin the entire batch.

✦ Never use a piece of the egg shell to remove a drop of yolk, since the shell may be contaminated with harmful bacteria.

WHIPPING EGG WHITES

✦ Always whip egg whites just before you use them, since beaten whites will collapse fairly quickly.

✦ While it is easiest to separate egg whites while the eggs are cold, it is easiest (though not necessary) to whip egg whites while they are at room temperature.

✦ Use a glass, china, or stainless-steel bowl (never aluminum or plastic) large enough to accommodate the expanding volume.

✦ You may use an electric mixer or an eggbeater, but never a blender or a food processor.

✦ Make sure that the bowl and beaters are clean and dry. Any egg yolk, moisture, fat, or other substance will keep the whites from whipping properly.

✦ A good method for whipping egg whites:

—Begin beating on a low speed and slowly increase the speed while moving the beaters around the bowl to incorporate as much air as possible throughout the mixture.
—At first, the whites become *foamy,* and it is at this stage that you would add any salt, lemon juice, cream of tartar, or other ingredient called for in your recipe. (Many recipes add cream of tartar, which helps stabilize the whites but also slows the foaming process.)
—As you continue beating, you soon reach the *soft peak* stage, when lifting the beaters causes the mixture to flop over gently. It is at this stage that many recipes tell you to slowly add some sugar, which also reduces the volume but makes the mixture sturdier.
—Beating further makes the mixture glossy and produces *stiff peaks,* which are firm enough to hold their shape. This is the stage called for by most recipes.

✦ Be careful not to overbeat egg whites—they will become dry and start to collapse!

For tips and hints on buying and storing flour, see the chapter "Bread and Breakfast."

SLICED ALMOND COOKIES

◆

MAKES 35 TO 40 COOKIES

1 egg white
¹/₃ cup sugar
One 6-ounce package (about 2 cups) sliced almonds
¹/₃ cup semisweet chocolate chips, preferably Nestlé

1. Preheat the oven to 300°F.
2. Line a cookie sheet with aluminum foil, parchment paper, or a Teflon liner.
3. In a medium bowl, whisk together the egg white and sugar.
4. Add the sliced nuts and stir well to coat.
5. Using a spoon, make small mounds of the nut mixture on the cookie sheet. The mounds should be fairly dense and spaced close together, since they will not spread as they bake.
6. Top each mound with a few chocolate chips.
7. Bake for about 20 to 22 minutes, until the cookies are very lightly browned. When the cookies are done, carefully place them on wire racks to cool. Store in a cookie tin to keep crisp.

TIPS AND TIDBITS

✦ Store all nuts in the freezer to keep them from turning rancid—there's no need to defrost them. And just to be safe, taste them before using.

✦ A Teflon or silicone baking liner is a wonderful investment. It is great for baking cookies that are fragile or tend to stick to the baking sheet or pan.

BROWNIE COOKIES

◆

Six 1-ounce squares semisweet or bittersweet chocolate
Four 1-ounce squares unsweetened chocolate
6 tablespoons unsalted margarine or butter
1¹/₄ cups sugar
3 eggs, or 4 egg whites
2 teaspoons vanilla extract
1 cup flour
1 teaspoon baking powder
¹/₄ teaspoon salt
2 cups chopped walnuts

1. Preheat the oven to 325°F.
2. Melt the chocolate and margarine or butter together, either in a heavy saucepan on the stove or in a microwave oven. When melted, stir to combine.
3. Stir in the sugar until well blended.
4. Add the eggs and vanilla extract and mix well.
5. Stir in the flour, baking powder, and salt.
6. Add the nuts and stir to combine.
7. Drop the batter by teaspoonfuls onto an ungreased cookie sheet.
8. Bake for 12 minutes, remove from the oven, and allow the cookies to cool on the cookie sheet for 5 minutes before transferring them to wire racks. To keep the cookies crisp, store in a tin.

TIPS AND TIDBITS

✦ If you are not sure how fresh your baking powder is, add ¹/₂ teaspoon of it to ¹/₄ cup of hot water. If the water bubbles furiously, the baking powder is still active.

CHOCOLATE CHIP COOKIES

from **J U D Y   M A R T Z**

Governor of Montana, Member of the
1964 U.S. Olympic Speed Skating Team

♦

MAKES ABOUT 4 DOZEN COOKIES

1½ *cups Crisco*
8 *tablespoons (1 stick) margarine or butter*
1½ *cups brown sugar*
¾ *cup white sugar*
1½ *teaspoons vanilla extract*
3 *eggs*
3¼ *cups plus 2 tablespoons flour*
1½ *teaspoons salt*
1½ *teaspoons baking soda*
18 *ounces (1½ large packages) chocolate chips*

1. Preheat the oven to 350°F.
2. Cream together the Crisco, margarine or butter, brown sugar, white sugar, vanilla extract, and eggs.
3. Mix together the flour, salt, and baking soda.
4. Stir the dry ingredients into the creamed mixture.
5. Add the chocolate chips and combine.
6. Drop by teaspoonfuls onto an ungreased cookie sheet and bake for 12 to 15 minutes.

CHOCOLATE CHIP AND
RAISIN COOKIES

from **NADINE STROSSEN**

Professor, New York Law School;
President, American Civil Liberties Union

♦

"This recipe, one of my favorites, is from Delores Devito, Director, Deloitte Consulting. If you actually want to bake these, don't mix the dough when kids, big or little, are around. Or, you can double the recipe. Then you'll have a chance that some dough will actually make it into the oven. Enjoy with cold milk!

"For best results, bake on ungreased parchment paper placed on top of 'air bake'–type cookie sheets. This will keep the bottoms from burning before the tops are baked.

"For variety, use pecans instead of walnuts. Or leave out the raisins. For chewy cookies, make them larger. For crisper cookies, make them smaller.

"In general, cookie dough freezes well. Freeze this dough— in rounded teaspoon-sized lumps—in plastic Ziploc bags. Get as much air out of the bags as you can. Take the dough out of the freezer and place it in the refrigerator on the morning you plan to bake the cookies. This method lets you bake lots of cookies in a relatively short time.

"If you want homemade cookies really fast, freeze the dollops of dough on sheets of foil, spacing them as you would on a cookie sheet. Gently roll up the foil (with the dough inside) and freeze in a plastic bag. When you need warm cookies, just pop the foil onto a cookie sheet. The dough will be ready to bake by time the oven heats. Instant gratification with no work, no cleanup. Recycle the foil!"

MAKES ABOUT 100 2-INCH COOKIES

2¹/₄ cups flour

1 teaspoon baking soda

1 teaspoon salt

¹/₂ pound (2 sticks) sweet butter, softened to room temperature

*1¹/₂ cups blond (turbinado) sugar (Sugar in the Raw is a good
    brand that comes in 2-pound bulk packages)*

1 teaspoon vanilla extract

2 eggs, at room temperature

One 12-ounce package chocolate chips

1 cup coarsely chopped walnuts

1 cup raisins

1. Preheat the oven to 350°F.
2. In a medium bowl, mix the flour, baking soda, and salt. Set aside.
3. In a separate bowl, use an electric mixer to cream the butter. When it is fluffy, add the sugar and continue to cream.
4. Continue beating and add the vanilla extract.
5. Add the eggs, one at a time, beating well after each egg. Scrape the bottom of the bowl occasionally.
6. At very low speed, stir in the flour mixture. Do not overbeat or the cookies will be tough.
7. Combine the chocolate chips, walnuts, and raisins and stir into the dough, mixing just enough to blend.
8. Drop teaspoonfuls of the dough onto ungreased cookie sheets covered with parchment paper.
9. Bake for about 8¹/₂ to 10 minutes, depending on your oven, until the cookies are light golden brown and the nuts are just a tiny bit lighter than the dough.
10. Cool the cookies on the cookie sheets for 2 minutes, then transfer to wire racks. Store the cookies in airtight containers.

CHOCOLATE CHIP–BROWNIE COOKIES

◆

Six 1-ounce squares unsweetened chocolate
8 tablespoons (1 stick) butter, margarine, or a combination
  of both
1¹/₂ cups sugar
4 eggs, or 5 egg whites
1 teaspoon vanilla extract
1¹/₄ cups flour
One 12-ounce package (2 cups) semisweet chocolate chips,
  preferably Nestlé
¹/₂ cup chopped pecans

1. Preheat the oven to 350°F.
2. Grease 2 cookie sheets.
3. Melt the chocolate and butter together in a microwave oven, at 50 percent power, for a few minutes. You can also melt them in a heavy saucepan over very low heat, or in a metal bowl set over a pan of simmering water. Stir to combine.
4. Add the sugar and mix well.
5. Stir in the eggs and vanilla extract, followed by the flour, chocolate chips, and pecans. Mix well.
6. Drop by large spoonfuls onto the cookie sheets and bake for about 10 minutes, or just until the cookies have set.
7. Allow the cookies to cool on the cookie sheets for several minutes before transferring them to wire racks.

TIPS AND TIDBITS

+ These cookies are delicious and especially easy to make because you need only one bowl and do all of the mixing by hand.
+ For a special treat, use them to make "sandwiches" with vanilla (or your favorite flavor) ice cream or frozen yogurt. You might even want to top each "sandwich" with a drizzle of chocolate syrup!

CHOCOLATE CHIP MONDELBREAD

◆

3 cups flour

1 tablespoon baking powder

A pinch of salt

3 eggs

1 scant cup sugar

1 teaspoon vanilla extract

$^1/_4$ teaspoon almond extract (optional)

5 ounces canola or other light vegetable oil

One 6-ounce package (1 cup) semisweet chocolate chips,
preferably Nestlé

1. Preheat the oven to 350°F.
2. Lightly grease a cookie sheet or jelly-roll pan.
3. In a large bowl or on a piece of waxed paper, sift together the flour, baking powder, and salt. Set aside.
4. In another large bowl, beat the eggs until frothy.
5. Beat in the sugar, vanilla extract, almond extract, if desired, and oil.
6. Stir in the flour mixture.
7. Add the chocolate chips and combine well.
8. Turn the dough onto a floured surface and divide into 3 equal balls. (If the dough is too sticky, add more flour.)
9. Roll each ball into a log about 8 inches long.
10. Place the 3 logs on a cookie sheet (not too close together) and flatten each one a bit so that it is about 3 to 4 inches wide and 1 inch high. (They will rise a little as they bake.)
11. Bake about 40 to 45 minutes, until golden.
12. When the logs are done, remove the cookie sheet from the oven and increase the oven temperature to 400°F.

Continued

13. With a very sharp knife, cut each log into $1/2$-inch-wide slices, cutting slightly diagonally.
14. Lay the slices on the cookie sheet, with a cut side down. There should be just enough room to hold all of them.
15. Return the cookie sheet to the 400°F oven and bake for 10 minutes.
16. When the cookies are done, use a spatula to transfer the slices to wire cooling racks.

TIPS AND TIDBITS

✦ This recipe is a variation of traditional mondelbread, which contains coarsely chopped almonds instead of chocolate chips.

GINGER-MOLASSES COOKIES

◆

MAKES ABOUT 50 COOKIES

9 tablespoons unsalted butter, margarine, or a combination of
  both, at room temperature
1 scant cup sugar
1 egg
$1/4$ cup molasses
2 cups flour
1 teaspoon baking soda
1 teaspoon ground cinnamon
1 teaspoon ground ginger
$1/2$ teaspoon ground cloves
$1/4$ teaspoon salt
Sugar, for coating the cookies (regular white granulated sugar
  is okay, but large crystals—white, colored, or Demerara—
  make prettier cookies)

1. With an electric mixer, thoroughly combine the butter and sugar. Add the egg and molasses, mixing well.

2. Combine the flour with the remaining dry ingredients (except the sugar for coating) and gradually add to the butter-sugar mixture, using a very slow speed to combine them.
3. Cover the bowl with plastic wrap and refrigerate the dough for at least 1 hour.
4. Preheat the oven to 350°F.
5. Using your hands, scoop out chunks of dough and form into 1-inch balls.
6. Roll the balls in the sugar, making sure they are completely coated, and place them about 2 inches apart on ungreased cookie sheets.
7. Bake for about 8 to 10 minutes and promptly allow the cookies to cool on wire racks. The cookies should still be soft when you remove them from the cookie sheets; they harden as they cool. If you like very crisp cookies, bake them another minute or two. Store in a cookie tin.

TIPS AND TIDBITS

✦ Demerara is a brown large-crystal sugar available at specialty food stores and many supermarkets.

✦ Whenever you measure molasses or other sticky liquids (honey, maple syrup), lightly coat your measuring cup with cooking spray or vegetable oil. The molasses will pour more easily and won't stick to the cup, making cleaning easier.

MATZO BUTTER-CRUNCH COOKIES

MAKES ABOUT 2 DOZEN COOKIES

4 to 6 unsalted matzo boards
1/2 pound (2 sticks) unsalted butter or margarine
1 cup packed brown sugar
3/4 cup semisweet chocolate chips, preferably Nestlé, or coarsely chopped semisweet chocolate

1. Preheat the oven to 375°F.
2. Line a cookie sheet with aluminum foil. Then cover the foil with baking parchment.
3. Place a single layer of matzo boards on top of the parchment paper, cutting extra pieces of matzo to fill any empty spaces.
4. Place the butter and brown sugar in a heavy saucepan and cook, stirring constantly, over medium heat until the mixture comes to a boil. Continue cooking, stirring constantly, for 3 minutes more.
5. Remove from the heat and pour evenly over the matzo.
6. Place the cookie sheet in the oven and immediately reduce the heat to 350°F. Bake for 15 minutes, checking every few minutes to make sure the butter–brown sugar mixture is not burning. (If it seems to be browning too quickly, remove the matzo from the oven, reduce the heat to 325°F, and return the cookie sheet to the oven.)
7. Remove the cookie sheet from the oven and immediately sprinkle the matzo with the chopped chocolate or chips. Allow the matzo to stand for 5 minutes, then spread the melted chocolate over it.
8. While the matzo is still warm, cut into squares. Chill in the refrigerator until set.

TIPS AND TIDBITS

✦ If you like nuts, sprinkle ¹/₂ cup of chopped walnuts over the melted chocolate before it sets.

✦ A pizza cutter is a handy tool for cutting the matzo.

MERINGUE COOKIES

◆

MAKES ABOUT 50 COOKIES

2 egg whites, at room temperature
1 teaspoon vanilla extract
¹/₈ teaspoon salt
¹/₈ teaspoon cream of tartar

¹/₂ cup sugar

One 6-ounce package (1 cup) semisweet chocolate chips,
  preferably Nestlé

¹/₄ cup finely chopped walnuts (optional)

1. Preheat the oven to 300°F.
2. Cover 2 cookie sheets with aluminum foil or parchment paper.
3. With an electric mixer, beat the egg whites, vanilla extract, salt, and cream of tartar until the mixture forms soft peaks. Gradually add the sugar and keep beating until the mixture forms stiff peaks.
4. Gently fold in the chocolate chips and the nuts, if desired.
5. Drop by teaspoonfuls onto the cookie sheets and bake for 25 minutes.
6. With a spatula, gently transfer the cookies to wire racks. When the cookies are cool, store in a tin to keep them crisp.

TIPS AND TIDBITS

✦ Egg whites are easier to whip if they are at room temperature or even slightly warmer. Also, be sure to remove any yolk that may have gotten mixed in with the whites. The fat in the yolk will make it harder for the whites to foam.

✦ High humidity makes meringue soggy, so don't make these cookies on a rainy or humid day.

OATMEAL COOKIES

◆

MAKES ABOUT 50 COOKIES

1 cup raisins
1¹/₂ cups flour
1 teaspoon baking soda

Continued

1 teaspoon ground cinnamon

¹/₄ teaspoon salt (optional)

15 tablespoons unsalted butter, margarine, or a combination of
both, at room temperature

³/₄ cup packed brown sugar

¹/₂ cup white sugar

1 egg

1 egg white

1 teaspoon vanilla extract

3 cups rolled oats

¹/₂ cup chopped walnuts (optional)

1. Preheat the oven to 350°F.
2. Soak the raisins in hot water for 10 minutes, drain, and spread on a paper towel to remove the excess water.
3. Sift together the flour, baking soda, cinnamon, and salt, if desired, into a large bowl or onto a piece of waxed paper. Set aside.
4. With an electric mixer, combine the butter or margarine with the sugars. Beat well.
5. While still beating, add the egg, egg white, and vanilla extract.
6. On the lowest speed, gradually add the flour mixture and beat until well blended.
7. Stir in the oats, nuts, if desired, and drained raisins.
8. Drop rounded tablespoonfuls of the batter onto ungreased cookie sheets.
9. Bake for about 10 to 12 minutes, until golden. Allow to cool on wire racks.

TIPS AND TIDBITS

✦ Leftover batter, wrapped in aluminum foil, stays fresh for about a week in the refrigerator. It also freezes well.

PECAN ROLL COOKIES

from **ELIZABETH DOLE**

U.S. Senator from North Carolina; Former President,
American Red Cross; Former Secretary
of Transportation; Former Secretary of Labor

◆

MAKES ABOUT 50 COOKIES

¹/₂ pound (2 sticks) margarine, at room temperature
¹/₄ cup confectioners' sugar plus about ¹/₂ cup more for rolling
   the cookies
2 cups flour
1 tablespoon cold water
1 teaspoon vanilla extract
2 cups chopped pecans

1. Preheat the oven to 275°F.
2. Grease a cookie sheet.
3. With an electric mixer, beat the margarine and the ¹/₄ cup confectioners' sugar until creamy.
4. Add the flour, cold water, and vanilla extract and beat well.
5. Stir in the pecans.
6. Put some flour on your hands and shape the dough into small mounds about the size and shape of dates. Arrange them on the cookie sheet and crease each one lengthwise with a knife.
7. Bake for 1 hour. When done, roll the warm cookies in confectioners' sugar.

APPLE BROWN BETTY

from **LUCINDA FRANKS**

Journalist, Author, Winner of the 1971 Pulitzer Prize for National Reporting

◆

"My daughter, Amy, and I love to put on aprons, get all dusty-white as the flour flies around, and put together this old-time dish, which originated with our Jamaican housekeeper, Renia Hylton. It is yummy piled with vanilla ice cream or whipped cream and it is particularly fun to make when you slap the apple slices one on top of the other, make little dabs of butter with your fingers, and shake the flour mixture down to the bottom of the bowl while doing the Macarena."

SERVES 12

18 McIntosh apples, peeled and cored
Juice of 1 lemon (about 2 to 3 tablespoons)
Juice of 1 orange (about 6 tablespoons)
2 teaspoons vanilla extract
3/4 cup yellow raisins
1/4 cup flour
1 cup brownulated sugar
1 teaspoon ground cinnamon
1/4 teaspoon ground nutmeg
1 tablespoon margarine or butter

1. Preheat the oven to 350°F.
2. Butter a 13 × 9-inch baking pan or spray it with vegetable cooking oil.
3. Slice each apple into 6 or 8 pieces and place the slices in a bowl.
4. Sprinkle them with the lemon juice, orange juice, and vanilla extract. Add the raisins, mix, and set aside to marinate.
5. In a separate bowl, combine the flour with the brownulated sugar, cinnamon, and nutmeg.

6. Place the apple-raisin mixture in the bottom of the prepared pan and sprinkle the flour mixture over it. Shake the pan so the flour mixture settles around the apples.
7. Dot the top with the margarine or butter, and bake for about 1 hour, until the top is brown and the apples are cooked. Serve with whipped cream, crème fraîche, or vanilla ice cream.

DELICIOUS APPLE CAKE

◆

SERVES 10 TO 12

6 medium apples (preferably Fuji, Granny Smith, Golden
  Delicious, or a combination), peeled, cored, and sliced
Juice of ¹/₂ lemon
3 cups flour
¹/₂ teaspoon salt
3 teaspoons baking powder
4 eggs, or 2 eggs and 2 egg whites
1 cup canola, safflower, or other light vegetable oil
2 cups sugar
1 tablespoon vanilla extract
¹/₂ cup orange juice
1 teaspoon ground cinnamon

1. Preheat the oven to 350°F.
2. Butter and flour a 9- or 10-inch springform pan.
3. Place the apple slices in a large bowl and sprinkle with the lemon juice. Set aside.
4. Sift together the flour, salt, and baking powder into a bowl or onto a sheet of waxed paper. Set aside.

Continued

5. In a large bowl, beat the eggs until foamy, either by hand or with an electric mixer.
6. Add the oil and 1¾ cups of the sugar and continue beating.
7. Beat in the vanilla extract.
8. Alternately add the flour mixture and the orange juice to the egg mixture and beat until well blended.
9. Pour half the batter into the prepared pan and cover with half the apple slices.
10. In a small bowl, combine the cinnamon with the remaining ¼ cup sugar and sprinkle half the mixture over the apple slices in the pan.
11. Pour the remaining batter on top of the sugared apples and place the remaining apple slices on top. You can arrange them in concentric circles or any pattern you like.
12. Sprinkle the apples with the remaining sugar-cinnamon mixture.
13. Bake for about 1½ to 1¾ hours, until a toothpick inserted in the center comes out clean. If, after an hour or so, the top starts to get too dark, place a sheet of aluminum foil over the pan for the remaining cooking time.
14. Allow to cool completely before removing from the pan. You may have to use a sharp knife to loosen the cake from the sides of the pan.

TIPS AND TIDBITS

✦ A melon baller is a wonderful tool for coring apples. Cut each apple in half and scoop out the core.

APPLE CRISP

from **JEANNE SHAHEEN**

Former Governor of New Hampshire

♦

SERVES 6

4 cups sliced, peeled tart apples (about 4 medium)
²/₃ to ³/₄ cup packed brown sugar
¹/₂ cup Gold Medal flour
¹/₂ cup oats
³/₄ teaspoon ground cinnamon
³/₄ teaspoon ground nutmeg
¹/₃ cup butter or margarine, softened

1. Preheat the oven to 375°F.
2. Grease an 8 × 8-inch baking pan.
3. Place the apple slices in the prepared pan.
4. Mix together the brown sugar, flour, oats, cinnamon, nutmeg, and butter or margarine. Using a fork or your fingers, crumble the mixture until it forms large crumbs.
5. Sprinkle the crumbled mixture over the apples.
6. Bake for 30 minutes, or until the apples are tender and the topping is golden brown. Serve warm and, if desired, topped with light cream or ice cream.

APPLE PASTRY

from **CATHLEEN BLACK**
President, Hearst Magazines;
Former Publisher, USA Today

◆

"This dessert is always a hit—pretty and delicious."

SERVES 8

One 16-ounce package frozen puff pastry dough
5 to 6 Granny Smith apples or a mix of Red Delicious and
 Granny Smith
1 tablespoon fresh lemon juice

Continued

1¹/₂ tablespoons ground cinnamon, plus extra for sprinkling
¹/₄ cup sugar
8 tablespoons (1 stick) butter
Whipped cream or vanilla ice cream (Häagen-Dazs or an
*   equally good brand), for topping*

1. Defrost pastry dough according to package instructions.
2. Preheat the oven to 325°F.
3. Grease a cookie sheet.
4. Peel and core the apples and slice each one into thin sections. Place the slices in a bowl and sprinkle with the lemon juice to keep them from discoloring.
5. Gently toss the apples with the cinnamon and sugar, making sure they are well coated. Set aside.
6. Roll out both sheets of defrosted pastry dough according to package instructions, making each one 10 × 10 inches. Cut each sheet into 4 squares, each 5 × 5 inches.
7. Dot the center of each square with a small piece of butter (about 1 tablespoon) and cover it with about 4 tablespoons of the apples.
8. Pick up the 4 corners of the square and bring them to the center to make a pouch. Tightly pinch the seams together.
9. Place the 8 apple-filled pastries on the cookie sheet and bake for 45 minutes to 1 hour, until lightly browned.
10. Serve warm, topped with a scoop of vanilla ice cream or whipped cream and dusted lightly with cinnamon.

APPLE PIE

from **PATTY MURRAY**
U.S. Senator from the State of Washington

◆

"You'll love this apple pie made with fresh and delicious Washington apples. For a little extra treat, I recommend a Dutch apple pie.

Make your apple pie as usual, except make extra-large slits in the top crust. Five minutes before the end of baking, pour 1/2 cup heavy whipping cream through the slits. Enjoy."

SERVES 10 TO 12

CRUST

3 cups unbleached flour
1 teaspoon dry mustard
A pinch of salt
1/4 cup sugar
8 tablespoons (1 stick) unsalted butter
1/3 cup vegetable shortening
3/4 cup shredded sharp Cheddar cheese
8 tablespoons cold water

FILLING

9 tart Washington State apples, peeled, cored, and cut into
    1-inch chunks
4 tablespoons (1/2 stick) unsalted butter, melted
1 teaspoon ground cinnamon
2 tablespoons cornstarch
1/2 cup sugar
1 teaspoon grated lemon zest
1 teaspoon vanilla extract

TOPPING

1 teaspoon sugar
A pinch of ground cinnamon

1. Preheat the oven to 350°F.
2. *To prepare the crust:* Combine the flour, dry mustard, salt, and sugar in a mixing bowl and blend thoroughly. Using a pastry blender or your fingertips, cut in the butter and shortening until the mixture forms small clumps. Add the cheese and continue crumbling until the mixture resembles coarse crumbs.

Continued

3. Sprinkle the water, 2 tablespoons at a time, over the crumbled flour mixture, and toss with a fork until it can be gathered into a ball. Knead it once or twice in the bowl and divide it into slightly unequal halves. Place the bowl in the refrigerator.

4. *To prepare the filling:* In a large bowl, combine the apple chunks with the melted butter. Add the cinnamon, cornstarch, sugar, grated lemon zest, and vanilla extract, and toss until the apples are evenly coated. Set aside.

5. *To assemble the pie:* Roll the smaller portion of chilled dough on a floured surface to form a 12-inch circle. Transfer it to a 10-inch pie plate and press it into the bottom and sides. Trim the dough, leaving a 1-inch overhang. Save the extra dough.

6. Roll the larger portion of dough to form a slightly larger circle.

7. Fill the pie pan with the apple mixture, mounding it slightly. Brush the edge of the bottom crust with water and move the top crust over the apples, tucking it under the rim. Trim the extra dough, but allow for a 1-inch overhang. Seal and crimp the edges of the crusts with a fork, and remove any extra dough. Prick the top crust in several places with a fork and cut a small vent in the center.

8. *To make the topping:* Mix the sugar and cinnamon. Brush the top of the pie with water and sprinkle with the sugar-cinnamon mixture. Now get creative and decorate the top with the extra crust dough.

9. Bake for about 1 to 1½ hours, until the filling is bubbling and the top is golden. Serve warm.

APPLE PIE IN A BAG

◆

SERVES 8 TO 10

FILLING

5 to 6 apples (preferably Granny Smith or other tart variety), peeled, cored, and sliced (about 4 cups)

¹/₂ cup sugar

2 tablespoons flour

³/₄ teaspoon ground cinnamon

¹/₂ teaspoon ground nutmeg

TOPPING

¹/₂ cup flour

¹/₂ cup sugar

3 tablespoons margarine or butter, cut into small pieces

SHELL

1¹/₂ cups flour

1¹/₂ teaspoons sugar

1 teaspoon salt

2 tablespoons cold skim or low-fat milk

¹/₂ cup canola, safflower, or other light vegetable oil

1. Preheat the oven to 350°F.
2. Place the apple slices in a large bowl and toss with the other filling ingredients. Set aside.
3. In a small bowl, combine the topping ingredients with your fingers to make a crumbly mixture. Set aside.
4. In a separate bowl, mix together the dry ingredients for the shell.
5. Combine the cold milk with the oil and add to the dry shell ingredients. Mix with your hands and then press the dough onto the bottom and sides of a 9- or 10-inch pie pan, preferably one that is fairly deep.
6. Spoon the apples into the shell and sprinkle with the topping mixture.
7. Slide the assembled pie into a large brown paper bag (which keeps the pie very moist) and place on a cookie sheet.
8. Bake for 1¹/₂ hours—no peeking!

TIPS AND TIDBITS

+ Make sure the bag is 100 percent paper. If it says it is made of "recycled materials," don't use it; it may burn. Most brown bags you get in the supermarket are 100 percent paper, but check to make sure.

APPLESAUCE CAKE

1¹/₂ cups flour

¹/₂ teaspoon baking powder

¹/₂ teaspoon baking soda

¹/₂ teaspoon ground cinnamon

¹/₄ teaspoon ground nutmeg

¹/₈ teaspoon ground cloves

¹/₄ teaspoon salt

*8 tablespoons (1 stick) margarine or butter, at
    room temperature*

1 scant cup sugar

1 egg or egg white, at room temperature

1 teaspoon vanilla extract

1 cup applesauce, at room temperature

¹/₃ cup golden raisins

¹/₃ cup chopped walnuts

¹/₃ cup dried currants

1. Preheat the oven to 350°F.
2. Grease and flour an 8 × 8-inch baking pan.
3. Sift together the flour, baking powder, baking soda, cinnamon, nutmeg, cloves, and salt into a bowl or onto a sheet of waxed paper.
   Set aside.
4. With an electric mixer, beat the margarine or butter for about 30
   seconds. Add the sugar and continue beating for about 3 minutes
   more.
5. Beat in the egg or egg white and vanilla extract.
6. At a very low speed, add about one-third of the flour mixture, beat
   to combine, and add ¹/₂ cup of the applesauce. When blended, add
   another one-third of the flour and then the remaining ¹/₂ cup applesauce. Finish with the remaining flour.

7. Gently fold in the raisins, nuts, and currants and pour the batter into the prepared pan.
8. Bake for about 30 to 35 minutes, until the top is golden and springs back when lightly pressed. Allow to cool for about 10 minutes before inverting the pan to remove the cake.
9. Serve plain or topped with vanilla ice cream or frozen yogurt.

TIPS AND TIDBITS

✦ This cake is even better the next day, after the spices have had a chance to blend.

MELT-IN-YOUR-MOUTH BLUEBERRY CAKE

from **SUSAN M. COLLINS**

U.S. Senator from Maine

SERVES 8

$1^{1}/_{2}$ *cups fresh Maine blueberries*

1 to 2 tablespoons flour, for coating the blueberries

2 eggs, separated

1 cup sugar, plus some extra for sprinkling

$^{1}/_{2}$ *cup vegetable shortening*

$^{1}/_{4}$ *teaspoon salt*

1 teaspoon vanilla extract

$1^{1}/_{2}$ *cups flour, sifted*

1 teaspoon baking powder

$^{1}/_{3}$ *cup milk*

1. Preheat the oven to 350°F.
2. Grease an 8 × 8-inch baking pan.

Continued

3. Wash the blueberries, remove any stems, and place them in a bowl. Sprinkle with 1 or 2 spoonfuls of flour and shake the bowl to make sure the berries are well coated. Set aside.

4. In a small glass bowl, beat the egg whites with an electric mixer until stiff, gradually adding about 1/4 cup of the sugar to keep them stiff. Set aside.

5. In a separate bowl, beat the shortening and add the salt and vanilla extract. While still beating, gradually add the remaining 3/4 cup sugar.

6. Add the egg yolks to the shortening-sugar mixture and beat until light and creamy.

7. Combine the flour with the baking powder and add to the mixture, alternating with the milk. Beat well to combine.

8. Fold in the beaten egg whites and then the floured berries.

9. Turn the batter into the prepared pan and sprinkle the top with sugar.

10. Bake for 50 to 60 minutes.

BLUEBERRY CRUMB COFFEE CAKE

SERVES 12

TOPPING

1/2 cup flour

2/3 cup sugar

1 teaspoon ground cinnamon

3 tablespoons butter, cut into small pieces

1/2 cup chopped walnuts

CAKE

1 cup sugar

8 tablespoons (1 stick) unsalted butter or a combination of butter and margarine, at room temperature

2 eggs

1 cup regular or low-fat sour cream

1 teaspoon vanilla extract

Grated peel of 1 lemon, about 1 tablespoon

2 cups flour

1 teaspoon baking soda

2 cups blueberries tossed with 1 tablespoon flour

$^1/_2$ cup chopped walnuts

1. Preheat the oven to 350°F.
2. Lightly butter a 13 × 9-inch baking pan.
3. *To prepare the topping:* Combine the flour, sugar, and cinnamon in a small bowl.
4. Add the butter and mix with your fingers until it becomes somewhat crumbly.
5. Mix in the chopped nuts. Set aside.
6. *To prepare the cake:* Use an electric mixer to combine the sugar and butter. Beat until smooth.
7. Beat in the eggs, one at a time, followed by the sour cream, vanilla extract, and lemon peel.
8. Combine the flour and baking soda and gradually add to the batter.
9. Fold in the floured blueberries and chopped nuts.
10. Pour the batter into the prepared pan and sprinkle the topping mixture over it.
11. Bake for about 35 to 40 minutes, until a toothpick inserted in the center comes out clean.

TIPS AND TIDBITS

✦ The easiest way to grate lemon peel is with a microplane. It removes only the top yellow portion of the peel, leaving behind the bitter white layer underneath.

LOW-FAT BLUEBERRY TORTE

2 eggs

$^1/_2$ cup plain nonfat yogurt

$^3/_4$ cup sugar

1 cup flour

1 teaspoon baking powder

A pinch of salt

1 pint fresh blueberries, washed and stemmed

A few squeezes of lemon juice, preferably fresh

1 teaspoon ground cinnamon

1. Preheat the oven to 350°F.
2. Beat together the eggs, yogurt, and sugar until well blended.
3. Stir in the flour, baking powder, and salt.
4. Pour the batter into an ungreased 8-, 9-, or 10-inch springform pan.
5. Scatter the berries evenly over the batter and sprinkle with the lemon juice and cinnamon.
6. Bake for about 1 hour, or until a toothpick inserted in the center comes out clean. Remove from the oven and allow to cool.
7. Store in the refrigerator, but reheat to serve.

TIPS AND TIDBITS

+ This dessert is good to make during the summer, when fresh blueberries are the sweetest. If you can also get sweet raspberries, try using a combination of both.

+ If you would like to reduce the fat even more, substitute three egg whites for the two whole eggs.

RED, WHITE, AND BLUE COBBLER

from **BARBARA BUSH**

*Former First Lady; Founder, The Barbara Bush
Foundation for Family Literacy; Author*

SERVES 8

One 21-ounce can blueberry pie filling
One 21-ounce can cherry pie filling
1 cup flour
1 tablespoon sugar
1¹/₂ teaspoons baking powder
¹/₂ teaspoon salt
3 tablespoons butter or margarine, cut into small pieces
¹/₂ cup milk

1. Preheat the oven to 400°F.
2. Spread the blueberry pie filling evenly over the bottom of an 8 × 8-inch Pyrex baking dish.
3. Spoon the cherry pie filling on top, smoothing it to the edges of the dish.
4. Place the baking dish in the oven. While the pie filling is heating, make the topping batter.
5. To prepare the topping, combine the flour, sugar, baking powder, and salt in a bowl.
6. Drop in the pieces of butter or margarine and—using a fork or your fingers—crumble them until the mixture resembles coarse bread crumbs.
7. Stir in the milk.
8. Remove the baking dish from the oven and drop spoonfuls of the topping batter onto the hot pie filling.
9. Return the dish to the oven and bake for about 25 to 30 minutes, until the topping is brown. Serve with vanilla ice cream.

LEMON LOVES

from KATIE COURIC

*Coanchor, NBC News' Today; Contributing Anchor,
Dateline NBC; Cofounder, National Colorectal Cancer
Research Alliance; Winner of Two Emmy Awards and
a George Foster Peabody Award*

◆

MAKES 24 SQUARES

CRUST

> *¹/₂ cup confectioners' sugar, plus extra for sprinkling*
> *2 cups flour*
> *A pinch of salt*
> *¹/₂ pound (2 sticks) butter, cut into small pieces*

FILLING

> *4 eggs*
> *2 cups sugar*
> *6 tablespoons flour*
> *6 tablespoons lemon juice*
> *Grated rind of 1 lemon*

1. Preheat the oven to 350°F.
2. Lightly grease a 12 × 9-inch baking pan.
3. *To prepare the crust:* Blend the confectioners' sugar, flour, and salt. Add the pieces of butter and—using a fork or your fingers—crumble the mixture until it resembles coarse bread crumbs.
4. Press the crust into the prepared pan and bake for 20 minutes. While the crust is baking, make the filling.
5. *To prepare the filling:* Beat the eggs, sugar, flour, and lemon juice with an electric beater. Stir in the grated lemon rind.
6. Spread the filling over the baked crust.
7. Return the pan to the oven and bake for 25 to 30 minutes. Remove from the oven and allow to cool, then sprinkle with additional confectioners' sugar and cut into squares.

FRUIT CRISP

◆

SERVES 6

FILLING

> 5 to 6 cups fresh fruit, such as blueberries; raspberries;
>   strawberries; blackberries; nectarine, peach, or plum slices;
>   or a combination
>
> $^1/_4$ teaspoon ground ginger
>
> $^1/_4$ cup sugar, or more if your fruit is rather tart
>
> 3 tablespoons cornstarch or flour, or more if your fruit is
>   very juicy

TOPPING

> $^1/_4$ cup flour
>
> $^2/_3$ cup packed brown sugar
>
> 3 tablespoons chilled butter or margarine, cut into small pieces
>
> $^1/_4$ cup rolled oats (optional)
>
> $^1/_2$ cup chopped walnuts or pecans
>
> $^3/_4$ teaspoon ground cinnamon
>
> $^1/_2$ teaspoon ground nutmeg

1. Preheat the oven to 375°F.
2. Butter a baking dish, one that's 10 × 8 inches or 11 × 7 inches or of a similar size.
3. Place the fruit in a large bowl and gently toss with the ginger, sugar, and cornstarch or flour. Set aside.
4. Place the $^1/_4$ cup flour and the brown sugar in the bowl of a food processor and pulse until blended.
5. Add the butter or margarine and pulse until the mixture has the texture of coarse oatmeal.

Continued

6. Transfer to a bowl and stir in the oats, if desired, nuts, cinnamon, and nutmeg.
7. Pour the fruit into the prepared baking dish and cover it evenly with a thick layer of the topping.
8. Bake for about 25 to 30 minutes, until the fruit bubbles.
9. Serve warm.

TIPS AND TIDBITS

✦ If you don't have a food processor, you can combine the flour, brown sugar, and butter (steps 4 and 5) with your fingers. Don't worry if some of the clumps remain fairly large (dime-sized).

✦ Although this dessert is great by itself, it is even better topped with vanilla ice cream or yogurt.

FRUIT MERINGUE TART

◆

SERVES 6 TO 8

6 egg whites, at room temperature
¹/₂ teaspoon cream of tartar
About 2 cups sugar
3 to 4 cups fresh fruit, such as blueberries; raspberries;
  strawberry, peach, or kiwi slices; or a combination

1. Preheat the oven to 275°F.
2. Line a cookie sheet with aluminum foil or parchment paper.
3. Beat the egg whites with the cream of tartar until fluffy.
4. Beat in the sugar, 1 tablespoon at a time, until the mixture is stiff.
5. Spread 2 cups of the meringue into an 8-inch circle on the lined cookie sheet. Take the remaining meringue and spoon dollops around the edge of the circle. (If you have a pastry bag, you can make rosettes.)

6. Bake for 1 hour—keep the oven door slightly open so that moisture can escape.
7. When the meringue is done, remove from the oven and allow to cool. Place the fruit on the meringue just before serving.

TIPS AND TIDBITS

✦ If you forget to bring your eggs to room temperature, you can place them in hot tap water for five minutes.

✦ This dessert is especially colorful and attractive when a variety of fruits are arranged in concentric circles.

PEACHES IN WINE-CASSIS SYRUP

◆

SERVES 4

8 fresh small ripe peaches (do not use canned peaches)
1 cup red wine
¹/₂ cup cassis (black currant liqueur)
¹/₄ cup sugar
Vanilla ice cream, for topping

1. Bring a medium pot of water to a boil and add the peaches. Cook for 15 seconds, drain, and slip off the skins. Cut the peaches in half and discard the pits. Place in a bowl.
2. Combine the wine, cassis, and sugar in a saucepan and bring to a boil. Remove from the heat and allow to stand for 5 minutes.
3. Pour the mixture over the peaches and set aside for at least 2 hours.
4. Divide the peaches among 4 serving bowls and spoon the syrup over them. Top with vanilla ice cream.

ALASKA RHUBARB CRISP

from **LISA MURKOWSKI**

U.S. Senator from Alaska

♦

SERVES 8

4 cups rhubarb, cut into pieces
Several handfuls of fresh raspberries (optional, but preferred)
1¼ cups flour
1 cup white sugar
½ teaspoon ground cinnamon
½ cup rolled oats
1 cup packed brown sugar
8 tablespoons (1 stick) butter, melted

1. Preheat the oven to 375°F.
2. Combine the rhubarb, the raspberries, if desired, ¼ cup of the flour, the white sugar, and the cinnamon and place in an 11 × 9-inch baking dish.
3. Combine the remaining 1 cup flour, the oats, the brown sugar, and the melted butter and mix well.
4. Sprinkle the topping over the rhubarb mixture and bake for 35 minutes. Cool and serve with ice cream.

GRANDMA GERT'S PLUM CAKE

♦

MAKES 24 SQUARES

2 cups flour
1 tablespoon baking powder
1¼ cups sugar

²/₃ cup butter, cut into small pieces

2 eggs, beaten

¹/₂ cup milk

2 teaspoons vanilla extract

12 to 15 fresh small purple plums, each pitted and cut in half

6 to 8 tablespoons butter, melted

2 teaspoons ground cinnamon

1. Preheat the oven to 400°F.
2. Grease a 13 × 9-inch baking pan.
3. In a large bowl, combine the flour, baking powder, and ¹/₂ cup of the sugar.
4. Using a fork or your fingertips, cut in the pieces of butter.
5. Add the eggs, then the milk and vanilla extract, beating well after each addition.
6. Spoon the batter into the prepared pan and place the plums in a single layer on top.
7. Combine the melted butter, the remaining ³/₄ cup sugar, and the cinnamon.
8. Spoon the mixture over the fruit, and bake for 40 minutes.

CARROT CAKE

from **BRENDA CZAJKA BARNES**

*Business Executive; Former President and CEO,
Pepsi-Cola North America*

◆

"One of my mother's recipes!"

SERVES 10 TO 12

2 cups sugar

3 cups flour

1 tablespoon baking powder

2 teaspoons baking soda

$1^1/_2$ teaspoons salt

2 teaspoons ground cinnamon

$1^1/_2$ cups oil

4 eggs

2 junior-sized (6-ounce) jars carrot baby food

1 cup chopped nuts

FROSTING

One 8-ounce package cream cheese

8 tablespoons (1 stick) margarine

$3^1/_2$ cups (1 pound) powdered sugar

2 teaspoons vanilla extract

1 cup chopped nuts

1. Preheat the oven to 350°F.
2. *To prepare the cake:* In a large bowl, combine the sugar, flour, baking powder, baking soda, salt, and cinnamon.
3. Add the oil and mix well.
4. Beat in the eggs, one at a time.
5. Fold in the carrot baby food and chopped nuts.
6. Pour the batter into an angel food or tube pan and bake for about 1 hour or more, until a toothpick inserted in the center comes out clean. When the cake is done, place it on a rack to cool.
7. *To prepare the frosting:* Place the cream cheese and margarine in a bowl and blend well.
8. Stir in the powdered sugar, blending very well.
9. Add the vanilla extract and nuts. Mix well.
10. When the cake is completely cool, remove it from the pan and frost.

SAN FRANCISCO CHEESE PIE

from **DIANNE FEINSTEIN**

U.S. Senator from California,
Former Mayor of San Francisco

◆

"Due to my extraordinarily busy schedule, I rarely find time to bake. But when I do, I look forward to making this dessert (and eating it, too)!"

SERVES 6 TO 8

CRUST

> 1 *cup graham cracker crumbs*
> 6 *tablespoons (³/₄ stick) butter, melted*
> ¹/₄ *cup sugar*

FILLING

> 2 *eggs, beaten*
> ¹/₂ *teaspoon vanilla extract*
> ¹/₂ *cup sugar*
> *Four 3-ounce packages cream cheese, at room temperature*

TOPPING

> 1¹/₂ *cups sour cream*
> ¹/₂ *teaspoon vanilla extract*
> 2 *tablespoons sugar*

1. Preheat the oven to 375°F.
2. *To prepare the crust:* Combine the graham cracker crumbs, melted butter, and sugar and press the mixture onto the bottom of a round Pyrex pie pan.
3. *To prepare the filling:* Beat the eggs, adding the vanilla extract and sugar.

Continued

4. Beat in the cream cheese, 1 package at a time, until the mixture is thoroughly blended.
5. Pour the filling into the crust, and bake for about 35 minutes, or until lightly browned.
6. *To prepare the topping:* Beat together the sour cream, vanilla extract, and sugar until smooth.
7. When the filling has browned, pour the topping over it and put the pie back in the oven for 5 minutes more. When the pie is done, allow it to cool, and place in the refrigerator. Serve cold.

PUMPKIN CHEESECAKE

from **RUTH ANN MINNER**
Governor of Delaware

◆

SERVES 8

Graham cracker crust for an 8- or 9-inch springform pan
1 cup orange or pineapple juice
One 16-ounce can pumpkin
1 cup light brown sugar
3 eggs
1 teaspoon ground cinnamon
$\frac{1}{2}$ teaspoon ground ginger
1 envelope unflavored gelatin
Two 8-ounce packages cream cheese, at room temperature
1 tablespoon vanilla extract

1. Preheat the oven to 350°F.
2. Line the springform pan with the graham cracker crust and bake for 10 minutes.
3. Combine the juice with the pumpkin, brown sugar, eggs, cinnamon, ginger, and gelatin in a medium saucepan. Mix well. Cover and simmer gently, stirring occasionally, for 30 minutes.

4. Beat the cream cheese and vanilla extract until fluffy. Gradually beat in the warm pumpkin mixture until well blended.
5. Pour into the prepared pan. Cover and refrigerate overnight.
6. Remove the springform and serve with whipped cream.

FAT-FREE CHEESECAKE WITH FRUIT
◆

SERVES 12

2 tablespoons cornflake crumbs
24 ounces low-fat or nonfat cream cheese (bar type,
not in a tub), at room temperature
¹/₂ cup sugar
¹/₂ teaspoon vanilla extract
¹/₂ teaspoon almond extract
5 or 6 egg whites or ³/₄ cup egg substitute
2 cups fresh fruit, such as blueberries or sliced strawberries

1. Preheat the oven to 325°F.
2. Spray a 9-inch pie pan with vegetable-oil cooking spray. Sprinkle the bottom and sides of the pan with the cornflake crumbs.
3. With an electric mixer, beat at high speed the cream cheese, sugar, and vanilla and almond extracts until well blended.
4. Stir in the egg whites or egg substitute and beat again at high speed until the mixture is well combined.
5. Pour the cream cheese mixture into the prepared pan and bake for about 45 minutes, or until the center is somewhat firm.
6. Allow to cool, and refrigerate for at least 2 hours. Just before serving, spoon the fresh fruit on top.

TIPS AND TIDBITS
✦ Although the cornflake crumbs add a nice texture, they are not absolutely necessary. *Continued*

+ While storing this dessert in the refrigerator, cover the pan with aluminum foil, but be careful to keep the foil from touching the cake or the cake will stick to the foil when you remove it. Or try using special nonstick aluminum foil.

BROWNIES

from **KATHLEEN SEBELIUS**
Governor of Kansas

MAKES 32 BROWNIES

Eight 1-ounce squares unsweetened chocolate
³/₄ pound (3 sticks) butter
6 eggs
3 cups sugar
1¹/₂ cups flour
3 teaspoons vanilla extract
1 cup pecans

1. Preheat the oven to 350°F.
2. Grease and flour two 8 × 8-inch baking pans.
3. Melt the chocolate with the butter.
4. Beat the eggs and add the sugar.
5. Add the melted chocolate and butter, the flour, the vanilla extract, and the nuts.
6. Pour into the prepared baking pans and bake for 25 minutes.

DECADENT CHOCOLATE CAKE

from **DIANE VON FURSTENBERG**
Fashion Designer; Chairman and Founder,
Diane von Furstenberg Studio

◆

SERVES 8 TO 10

¹/₂ pound (2 sticks) unsalted butter, at room temperature,
  plus more for buttering the pan
Four 3¹/₂-ounce bars Lindt bittersweet chocolate, broken up
3 whole eggs
3 egg yolks
¹/₃ cup sugar
¹/₂ cup all-purpose flour

1. Preheat the oven to 350°F.
2. Butter an 8- or 9-inch baking pan and line the bottom with parchment paper. Butter the parchment.
3. Combine the ¹/₂ pound butter and the chocolate in a heat-safe bowl set over a pan of water. Place over medium heat, stirring until the mixture is melted. Remove the bowl from the heat and set aside.
4. In a separate bowl, beat the eggs and egg yolks with an electric mixer until frothy.
5. Beat in the sugar at medium speed until creamy.
6. Beat in the flour.
7. Fold the flour mixture into the chocolate mixture with a rubber spatula until blended.
8. Spread the batter in the prepared pan and bake for 40 to 50 minutes, until set in the center. Let cool, remove the cake from the pan, and peel off the parchment.

CHOCOLATE ANGEL FOOD CAKE

◆

5 *tablespoons unsweetened cocoa (preferably Droste), plus*
   more for sprinkling (optional)
¹/₄ cup boiling water
2 teaspoons vanilla extract
1¹/₄ cups sugar
1 cup cake flour
¹/₄ teaspoon salt
12 egg whites
1¹/₂ teaspoons cream of tartar
Confectioners' sugar, for sprinkling (optional)

1. Preheat the oven to 350°F.
2. In a medium bowl, dissolve the cocoa in the boiling water and stir in the vanilla extract. Set aside.
3. In a separate bowl, combine ³/₄ cup of the sugar with the flour and salt. Set aside.
4. Using an electric mixer, beat the egg whites and cream of tartar until they form soft peaks. Slowly add the remaining ¹/₂ cup sugar and continue beating until stiff peaks form.
5. Gently stir about 1 cup of the beaten egg whites into the cocoa mixture.
6. Gradually fold the flour mixture into the remaining egg whites, adding about ¹/₂ cup at a time. Fold the cocoa mixture in last.
7. Pour the batter into an ungreased 10-inch tube pan and run a knife through the batter to remove any air bubbles.
8. Bake for about 40 to 50 minutes, until the surface is somewhat crusty and cracked.
9. When the cake is done, invert the pan and allow to cool. To remove the cake, first loosen it by running a knife around the inside of the pan. Then invert the cake onto a plate. If you wish, sprinkle the top with confectioners' sugar or cocoa.

✦ This cake is great with **raspberry sauce**, which you can easily make by pureeing in a blender or food processor 1 cup raspberries, 1/4 cup powdered sugar, 1/2 tablespoon lemon juice, and 2 tablespoons amaretto liqueur (optional). Strain to remove the seeds. (If you cannot find sweet fresh raspberries, frozen berries are excellent and sometimes even better than the fresh ones.)

CHOCOLATE CHIP COFFEE CAKE

◆

SERVES 8 TO 10

TOPPING

1/4 cup sugar

1/2 teaspoon ground cinnamon

1/2 cup chopped walnuts

1 cup semisweet chocolate chips, preferably Nestlé

BATTER

2 cups flour

1 teaspoon baking soda

A pinch of salt

8 tablespoons (1 stick) margarine or butter, at room temperature

1 cup sugar

2 eggs, or 3 egg whites

1 cup regular or low-fat sour cream

1 teaspoon vanilla extract

1/8 teaspoon almond extract

1. Preheat the oven to 350°F.
2. Grease a 13 × 9-inch baking pan.
3. Combine the topping ingredients in a small bowl and set aside.
4. Sift together the flour, baking soda, and salt into a bowl or onto a large sheet of waxed paper. Set aside.
5. With an electric mixer, cream together the margarine or butter and the sugar. Beat until smooth.
6. Continue beating and add the eggs, one at a time, followed by the sour cream and the vanilla and almond extracts. Beat until smooth.
7. At a very low speed, stir in the flour mixture.
8. Pour half the batter into the prepared pan.
9. Sprinkle half the topping mixture over the batter.
10. Cover with the rest of the batter (it will be somewhat sticky) and sprinkle with the remaining topping, using the back of a spoon to lightly press the topping into the batter.
11. Bake for about 35 minutes, or until the surface is somewhat crusty and lightly browned.

DEVIL'S FOOD CAKE

◆

SERVES 12

2 cups cake flour

1³/₄ cups sugar

³/₄ cup cocoa

1¹/₄ teaspoons baking soda

¹/₂ teaspoon baking powder

1 teaspoon salt

³/₄ cup vegetable shortening

1¹/₄ cups milk

1 teaspoon vanilla extract

3 eggs

1. Preheat the oven to 350°F.
2. Grease two 9-inch round baking pans or one 13 × 9-inch pan and line with waxed paper.
3. Sift together the cake flour, sugar, cocoa, baking soda, baking powder, and salt into a large bowl.
4. Add the shortening, and pour in ³/₄ cup of the milk and the vanilla extract. Using an electric mixer, beat at low to medium speed for 2¹/₂ minutes, scraping the bowl and beaters often.
5. Add the remaining ¹/₂ cup milk and the eggs. Beat for another 2¹/₂ minutes.
6. Pour the batter into the prepared pans and bake for 35 minutes.
7. When the cake is done, allow to cool for 10 minutes before removing from the pans. Allow the cake to cool completely on wire racks before frosting with your favorite icing.

HOT-FUDGE-SUNDAE CAKE

from **ALMA J. POWELL**
*Vice Chairman of the Board, John F. Kennedy Center
for the Performing Arts; Author*

◆

SERVES 8 TO 10

1 cup flour
³/₄ cup sugar
6 tablespoons cocoa
2 teaspoons baking powder
¹/₄ teaspoon salt
¹/₂ cup milk
2 tablespoons salad oil
1 teaspoon vanilla extract
1 cup pecans

Continued

1 cup packed brown sugar
1³/₄ cups very hot tap water—the hottest you can get
Ice cream, for topping

1. Preheat the oven to 350°F.
2. In an ungreased 9 × 9 × 2-inch baking pan, stir together the flour, the sugar, 2 tablespoons of the cocoa, the baking powder, and the salt.
3. Mix in the milk, salad oil, and vanilla extract and stir with a fork until smooth.
4. Stir in the pecans and spread the batter evenly in the pan.
5. Sprinkle with the brown sugar and the remaining 4 tablespoons cocoa.
6. Pour the hot water over the top and bake for 40 minutes.
7. When the cake is done, remove the pan from the oven and let stand for 15 minutes.
8. Spoon the cake into dessert dishes and top with ice cream and the sauce. (The cake makes its own hot-fudge sauce.)

CHOCOLATE POTS DE CRÈME

◆

SERVES 4 TO 6

1¹/₄ cups light cream
One 6-ounce package (1 cup) semisweet chocolate chips,
*   preferably Nestlé*
2 egg yolks
2 to 3 tablespoons brandy (optional)
Whipped cream and shaved chocolate, for garnish (optional)

1. Pour the light cream into a saucepan and heat until scalded.
2. While the cream is heating, put the chocolate chips, egg yolks, and brandy, if desired, in a blender.

3. Add the scalded cream and blend until smooth, about 10 seconds.
4. Pour into individual glasses or ramekins, cover with plastic wrap, and refrigerate for several hours or overnight.
5. Before serving, top with the whipped cream and shaved chocolate, if desired.

FIVE-MINUTE DESSERT
(Chocolate Ricotta)

♦

SERVES 4

1 pound ricotta cheese

2 tablespoons sugar

1 teaspoon vanilla extract, or $^1/_4$ cup light rum

One 6-ounce package (1 cup) semisweet chocolate chips, preferably Nestlé, finely chopped in a food processor or blender

1. Beat the ricotta with a fork until soft.
2. Stir in the sugar, vanilla extract or rum, and chocolate.
3. Spoon into 4 dessert dishes and serve or keep chilled in the refrigerator.

TIPS AND TIDBITS

✦ If you like a crunchier texture, save some of the whole chocolate chips and stir them in with the other ingredients.

✦ If you're a real chocoholic, increase the chocolate chips to 1 $^1/_4$ cups.

CHOCOLATE SOUFFLÉ

from **MARLO THOMAS**

Actress; Producer; Author; Winner of Four Emmy Awards,
One Golden Globe Award, and a George Foster Peabody Award

◆

SERVES 6

2 tablespoons butter
2 tablespoons flour
³/₄ cup milk
A pinch of salt
Two 1-ounce squares unsweetened chocolate
¹/₃ cup sugar, plus some for sprinkling
2 tablespoons cold coffee
¹/₂ teaspoon vanilla extract
3 egg yolks
4 egg whites
Whipped cream, for topping

1. Preheat the oven to 375°F.
2. Butter a 2-quart casserole and sprinkle it with sugar.
3. In a saucepan, melt the butter and add the flour, stirring with a wire whisk until blended.
4. Meanwhile, bring the milk to a boil and add it all at once to the butter-flour mixture, stirring vigorously with the whisk. Add the salt and set aside.
5. Slowly melt the chocolate with the sugar and the coffee over hot water.
6. Stir the melted chocolate mixture into the butter-flour mixture, and add the vanilla extract.
7. Beat in the egg yolks, one at a time, and cool.
8. In a separate bowl, use an electric mixer to beat the egg whites until stiff. Gently fold them into the chocolate batter.

9. Turn the mixture into the prepared casserole and bake for 35 to 45 minutes, until puffed and brown. Serve immediately with whipped cream.

BAKLAVA

from **OLYMPIA J. SNOWE**
U.S. Senator from Maine;
Former Congresswoman from Maine

◆

"This recipe is one of my personal favorites. It is a traditional family recipe that has been passed on through generations. While it can be difficult to prepare, it is very tasty and worth the effort."

SERVES 24

1 pound (4 sticks) butter, melted
1¹/₂ pounds walnuts, chopped
³/₄ cup sugar
1 teaspoon ground cinnamon
Grated rind of 1 orange
One 16-ounce package phyllo dough (strudel leaves)
2 cups water
2 cups sugar
¹/₂ cup honey
1 cinnamon stick
3 lemon slices

1. Preheat the oven to 400°F.
2. Brush some of the butter on the bottom of a 13 × 9-inch pan.
3. In a bowl, mix together the chopped nuts, sugar, cinnamon, and orange rind. Set aside.

Continued

4. Place 1 sheet of the phyllo dough in the pan, allowing the ends to extend over the sides. Brush the dough with the melted butter.
5. Repeat this process with 4 more sheets of phyllo dough, buttering each one. Heavily sprinkle the top sheet with the nut mixture.
6. Add another layer (4 buttered sheets of phyllo), and sprinkle the top sheet with the nut mixture.
7. Reserve 4 sheets of the phyllo for the top of the pastry and keep repeating this process (step 6) until the remaining phyllo sheets and nut mixture are used up.
8. Take the 4 phyllo sheets you have set aside and place them, one at a time, on top of the nut mixture, brushing each one with butter.
9. Brush the top surface with the remaining butter and trim the edges with a sharp knife. Cut diagonal lines in the top surface, creating a diamond pattern.
10. Bake at 400°F for 15 minutes, lower the oven temperature to 300°F, and continue baking for about 40 minutes, or until golden brown.
11. While the baklava is baking, make a syrup by combining the water, sugar, honey, cinnamon stick, and lemon slices and boiling the mixture for 10 minutes.
12. Once the baklava is done but still hot, cover it with the syrup and let it stand overnight. (It should rest for 24 hours before being removed from the pan.) It can be kept for weeks in the refrigerator or stored for longer periods in the freezer.

HAZELNUT MERINGUE CAKE
◆

SERVES 14 TO 16

MERINGUE LAYERS
5 egg whites, at room temperature
1¼ cups sugar

1 cup ground hazelnuts
¹/₂ teaspoon vanilla extract
2 tablespoons unsalted butter, at room temperature
2 tablespoons flour

CHOCOLATE CREAM

6 ounces semisweet chocolate (a bar, squares, or chips)
2 cups chilled heavy cream

1. Preheat the oven to 250°F.
2. *To prepare the meringue layers:* Beat the egg whites with an electric mixer at high speed until they begin to make medium soft peaks. Continue to beat, gradually adding the sugar, until the mixture forms very stiff peaks.
3. Fold in the hazelnuts and vanilla extract, gently distributing them throughout the mixture.
4. Cut three 9-inch rounds of waxed paper or baking parchment. If using waxed paper, coat the rounds with the butter and dust with the flour. Place the rounds on one or more baking sheets and spoon the meringue onto them, smoothing the surface of each one.
5. Bake for 45 to 60 minutes, until the meringue layers are very dry to the touch and can be nudged off the paper rounds. (If you are using more than one baking sheet, exchange their shelf positions after about 25 minutes.) As soon as the meringues are done, carefully peel off the paper rounds and place the meringues on cooling racks. If you are making the meringues ahead of time, let them rest on racks in the turned-off oven, even overnight.
6. *To prepare the chocolate cream:* Melt 5 ounces of the chocolate in the top of a double boiler set over barely simmering water. Reserve the remaining 1 ounce.
7. Beat the heavy cream until very stiff and fold most of it into the chocolate. Reserve a few tablespoons for garnish.
8. *To assemble the cake:* Spread each of the 3 meringue layers with one-third of the chocolate cream, then carefully stack the layers.

Continued

9. Garnish with the remaining chopped chocolate or chocolate chips and dollops of whipped cream.
10. Chill and serve within an hour or so.

SODA CRACKER PIE

SERVES 6

3 egg whites
$^1/_2$ teaspoon cream of tartar
1 cup sugar
1 teaspoon vanilla extract
16 soda crackers, crushed
$^1/_2$ teaspoon baking powder
$^3/_4$ cup chopped walnuts

1. Preheat the oven to 325°F.
2. Using an electric mixer, beat the egg whites and cream of tartar until they form stiff peaks.
3. Gently add the sugar, vanilla extract, crushed crackers, baking powder, and nuts.
4. Pour into an ungreased 8-inch round pie pan and bake for about 35 minutes, or until slightly brown. Allow to cool.
5. Serve topped with ice cream, frozen yogurt, or fresh berries.

ROCKY ROAD CANDY SQUARES

Two 7-ounce Hershey bars
One 12-ounce package semisweet chocolate chips
²/₃ cup crunchy peanut butter
Two 10-ounce packages marshmallows
One 6-ounce package chopped pecans

1. Line a 13 × 9-inch metal pan with waxed paper. (Use 2 sheets of waxed paper and overlap them.)
2. Melt the Hershey bars, chocolate chips, and peanut butter in a heavy saucepan over low heat. You can also melt them in a microwave oven.
3. Pour half the chocolate mixture into the prepared pan and spread evenly.
4. Add a layer of marshmallows.
5. Add the pecans to the remaining chocolate mixture and pour over the marshmallows. Make sure to spread the chocolate mixture all the way to the sides.
6. Refrigerate until hard. Cut into squares and serve.
7. Store in the refrigerator. These also freeze very well.

LOW-CAL "ICE CREAM"

SERVES 6 TO 8

4 cups frozen strawberries
6 tablespoons sugar, or to taste
1¹/₃ cups low-fat cottage cheese
3 tablespoons lemon juice, or to taste

1. Place all of the ingredients in a blender and process until smooth.
2. Pour into a container or individual bowls and freeze.

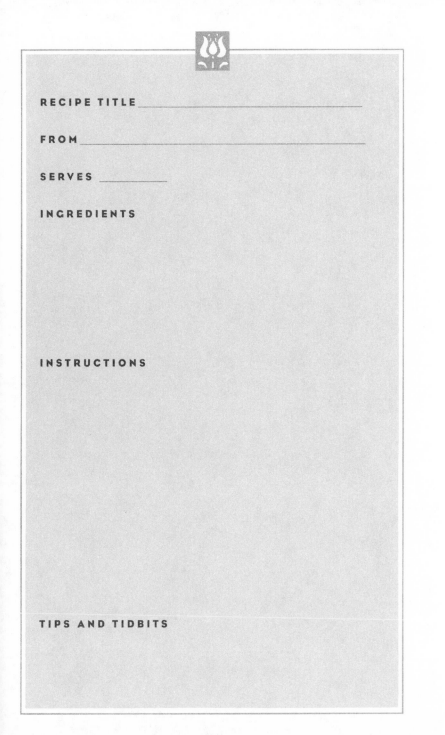

RECIPE TITLE

FROM

SERVES

INGREDIENTS

INSTRUCTIONS

TIPS AND TIDBITS

RECIPE TITLE_____

FROM_____

SERVES_____

INGREDIENTS

INSTRUCTIONS

TIPS AND TIDBITS

HELP!

TROUBLESHOOTING

or "WHAT CAN I DO IF IT'S..."

...TOO SALTY?...TOO SPICY?

If you're cooking a sauce, soup, or stew and it's too salty, peel a large white potato, cut it into chunks, and simmer it in the pot until soft, about fifteen minutes. Don't forget to throw away the potato.

It's also possible to reduce the saltiness by adding some lemon juice or vinegar. However, if this makes the dish too tart, add a little sugar.

If you've overdone the hot pepper or chili powder in a dish with a tomato sauce, try adding a bit of brown sugar and some additional tomatoes or tomato sauce. You can also add a peeled potato, whole or in chunks, and cook it until it softens. Discard the potato when you're done.

The easiest way to cool down a dish with too much curry is to add 3 tablespoons of cream or sour cream or 1 tablespoon of butter for each cup of the dish. You can make a low-fat alternative by heating 1 to 2 tablespoons of flour in 1 cup of skim or low-fat milk until the mixture thickens. Add 1 to 2 tablespoons of this mixture for each cup of the dish.

To reduce the spiciness even more, you can add 1 to 2 tablespoons of orange marmalade or 1/4 teaspoon of ground cinnamon for each cup of the spicy mixture.

...TOO THICK?...TOO RUNNY?

Adding some water or chicken broth is the best way to thin a sauce or soup that's too thick. If wine is one of the original ingredients, try adding a little more of it. If your sauce is made with tomatoes, add some tomato juice.

If a sauce is too thin, simmer it for a while, uncovered. Sauces and soups can also be thickened with some flour or cornstarch. But don't pour it directly into the sauce. Remove about a quarter cup of the sauce from the pot and dissolve 2 tablespoons of flour or cornstarch in it. Then gradually add the thickening mixture to the pot.

To slightly thicken a clear soup, mix 1 tablespoon of cornstarch with 2 tablespoons of cold water. Add this mixture to the soup and stir over medium heat until the soup thickens. A half cup of cooked rice or beans may be used to thicken a sauce or soup that will be pureed. If a stew isn't thick enough, try adding some grated raw potato.

MEASUREMENTS AND EQUIVALENTS

or

"I WAS NEVER GOOD AT NUMBERS!"

◆

The only tricky thing to keep in mind is that some ingredients are measured by weight and some by volume and that the term *ounce* is used in both kinds of measurements. Liquids are always measured by volume, as are many other ingredients, including flour, sugar, rice, and seasonings. Poultry, seafood, and meat are measured by weight. Butter and margarine are measured both ways.

VOLUME MEASUREMENTS

1 cup	=	8 ounces	=	16 tablespoons
3/4 cup	=	6 ounces	=	12 tablespoons
2/3 cup	=	5 1/3 ounces	=	10 tablespoons + 2 teaspoons
1/2 cup	=	4 ounces	=	8 tablespoons
1/3 cup	=	2 2/3 ounces	=	5 tablespoons + 1 teaspoon
1/4 cup	=	2 ounces	=	4 tablespoons
1/8 cup	=	1 ounce	=	2 tablespoons
1 tablespoon	=	1/2 ounce	=	3 teaspoons

Also, keep in mind:

1 pint	=	2 cups	=	16 ounces
1 quart	=	4 cups	=	32 ounces
1 gallon	=	4 quarts	=	128 ounces

Liquids, such as *milk, oil, chicken broth,* and *water,* should be poured into a glass measuring cup and held up to your line of sight. Small amounts should be measured in measuring spoons.

Dry ingredients, such as *flour, sugar, rice,* and *dried beans,* should be measured in measuring spoons or cups, which should be filled to the very top. In baking, it's particularly important to use just the right amounts, so be sure to run a knife blade or other flat object across the top of the measuring spoon or cup to remove any extra.

Dried herbs and spices, salt, pepper, and other seasonings are also measured by volume (teaspoon, tablespoon) and amounts less than 1/8 teaspoon are referred to as "a pinch" or "a dash."

WEIGHT MEASUREMENTS

The most important measurement to keep in mind is:

$$1 \text{ pound } = 16 \text{ ounces}$$

Margarine and *butter* come in handy sticks, often with the measurements marked right on the paper wrapping. Although most recipes list them by volume (tablespoons, cups), the packages are sold by weight:

1 stick	= 1/2 cup	= 8 tablespoons	= 1/4 pound
2 sticks	= 1 cup	= 16 tablespoons	= 1/2 pound
4 sticks	= 2 cups	= 32 tablespoons	= 1 pound

POT AND PAN SIZES

When you don't have the exact size pan a recipe calls for, you can substitute a similar size, but choose one with the same volume and a similar depth. (To measure the volume, fill the pan with water and then pour the water into a measuring cup.) Keep in mind, though, that a deeper pan will require a slightly longer baking time, and, likewise, a shallower one will require less time.

When a pan's dimensions are given, remember that *the width is measured across the inside of the pan. The depth is measured from the inside bottom of the pan to the rim.*

Here are some of the most commonly used sizes:

SIZE	VOLUME
6-inch round skillet	2 cups
5 1/2 × 3 × 2 1/2-inch loaf pan	2 cups
8 × 1 1/4-inch pie pan	3 cups
1-quart soufflé dish	4 cups
8 × 1 1/2-inch round cake or pie pan	4 cups
11 3/4 × 7 1/2 × 3/4-inch jelly-roll pan	4 cups
8 1/2 × 4 1/4 × 3-inch loaf pan	5 cups
9 × 1 1/2-inch pie pan	5 cups
8 × 2-inch round cake pan	6 cups
9 × 1 1/2-inch round cake pan	6 cups
10 × 2-inch pie pan	6 cups
8 × 8 × 2-inch square cake pan	8 cups
9 × 5 × 3-inch loaf pan	8 cups
9 × 2-inch round cake or pie pan	8 cups
9 × 9 × 2-inch square cake pan	10 cups
9 1/2 × 2 1/2-inch springform pan	10 cups
15 1/2 × 10 1/2 × 1-inch jelly-roll pan	10 cups
10 × 2-inch round cake pan	11 cups
10 × 3 1/2-inch tube pan	12 cups
10 × 2 1/2-inch springform pan	12 cups
13 × 9 × 2-inch pan	15 cups

SOME OTHER USEFUL MEASUREMENTS AND EQUIVALENTS

Fruits

Apples	1 lb.	3 cups peeled and sliced
Bananas	1 lb.	2 cups sliced
Cherries	1 lb.	2 1/2 cups pitted
Cranberries	12 oz.	3 cups
Currants, dried	1 lb.	3 cups
Dates	1 lb.	2 1/2 cups pitted

Grapes	1 lb.	2 1/2 cups
Lemon	1 medium	2 to 3 tablespoons juice
Lemon	1 medium	1 tablespoon grated peel
Lime	1 medium	1 1/2 to 2 tablespoons juice
Lime	1 medium	1 to 1 1/2 teaspoons grated peel
Orange	1 medium	6 tablespoons juice
Orange	1 medium	2 tablespoons grated peel
Peaches	1 lb.	2 cups sliced
Pears	1 lb.	2 cups sliced
Prunes	1 lb.	2 1/2 cups pitted
Raisins	1 lb.	3 cups

Vegetables

Asparagus	5 oz.	1 cup sliced
Avocado	1 lb.	2 1/2 cups cubed
Green beans	8 oz.	2 cups cut
Broccoli	6 oz.	2 cups florets
Cabbage	8 oz.	3 cups shredded
Carrots	8 oz.	2 cups sliced or shredded
Celery	2 stalks	1 cup sliced
Eggplant	1 lb.	3 cups chopped
Garlic	1 med. clove	3/4 teaspoon minced
Garlic	3 large cloves	1 tablespoon minced
Kidney beans	1 lb. dried	2 cups uncooked
Kidney beans	1 lb. dried	5 to 6 cups cooked
Lentils	1 cup	3 cups cooked
Mushrooms	8 oz.	2 1/2 cups chopped
Onion	1 small	1/4 to 1/3 cup chopped
Onion	1 medium	1/2 to 2/3 cup chopped
Onion	1 large	1 cup chopped
Parsley	1 oz.	1 cup chopped
Peas	1 lb. unshelled	1 cup shelled
Peppers	6 oz.	1 cup chopped
Potatoes	1 lb.	3 cups sliced
Spinach	1 lb. fresh	6 to 8 cups chopped
Split peas	1 cup	2 1/2 cups cooked

Tomatoes	8 oz. fresh	1 cup chopped
Tomatoes	35 oz. can	2 1/2 cups (drained)
Zucchini	6 oz.	1 cup sliced or diced

Dairy Products

Butter	1 stick	1/2 cup (8 tablespoons)
Butter	1 lb.	2 cups (4 sticks)
Cheese, hard	1/4 lb.	1 cup grated
Cheese, hard	1/4 lb.	1 to 1 1/3 cups shredded
Cottage cheese	1 lb.	2 cups
Cream, heavy	1 cup	2 cups whipped
Eggs	2 large	1/2 cup
Egg white	1 large	2 tablespoons
Egg whites	8 to 10	1 cup
Margarine	1 stick	1/2 cup (8 tablespoons)
Margarine	1 lb.	2 cups (4 sticks)
Milk, powdered	1 to 1 1/3 cups	1 quart milk

Dry Ingredients

Bread	1 slice	1/2 cup bread crumbs
Chocolate chips	6 oz.	1 cup
Coffee	1 lb. ground	40 cups brewed
Flour, all-purpose	1 lb.	4 cups
Flour, cake	1 lb.	4 1/2 cups
Graham crackers	15	1 cup crumbs
Nuts	1 lb. in shell	1/2 lb. shelled
Nuts	1/2 lb. shelled	2 cups
Pasta	1/2 lb. uncooked	4 cups cooked
Rice	1 lb. uncooked	2 1/2 cups uncooked
Rice	1 cup uncooked	3 cups cooked
Rice, wild	1 cup uncooked	4 cups cooked
Sugar, brown	1 lb.	2 1/2 cups packed
Sugar, confectioners'	1 lb.	3 1/2 cups
Sugar, white	1 lb.	2 cups

SUBSTITUTIONS

or

"UH-OH, I'VE RUN OUT OF..."

♦

Sometimes you can substitute one ingredient for another without drastically affecting the final result. Here is a list of common cooking substitutions.

INSTEAD OF...	YOU CAN USE...
Allspice	Cloves
Baking chocolate, unsweetened, 1 ounce	3 tablespoons unsweetened cocoa powder plus 1 tablespoon of either butter, margarine, oil, or vegetable shortening
Baking powder, 1 teaspoon	1/2 teaspoon cream of tartar plus 1/4 teaspoon baking soda
Bread crumbs, 1 cup	3/4 to 1 cup cracker or cereal crumbs
Brown sugar, 1 cup	1 cup white sugar plus 1/4 cup light molasses
Capers	Chopped pickles
Cayenne pepper, 1/8 teaspoon	4 drops Tabasco red pepper sauce
Chives	Scallion tops (green part)
Corn syrup, 1 cup	1 cup sugar plus 1/4 cup water
Cream for thickening sauces, stews, soups	Skim or low-fat milk combined with a small amount of flour or cornstarch
Cumin seeds	Caraway seeds
Currants, dried	Chopped raisins
Fines herbes	Equal amounts of chopped parsley, tarragon, chervil, and chives
Flour, all-purpose, 1 cup	1 cup plus 2 tablespoons cake flour
Flour, cake, 1 cup	7/8 cup all-purpose flour
Garlic, 1 clove	1/8 teaspoon garlic powder or 1/4 teaspoon minced dried garlic

Ginger, grated, 1 teaspoon	$1/4$ teaspoon ground ginger
Herbs, 1 tablespoon chopped fresh	$1/2$ to 1 teaspoon dried
Honey, 1 cup	$1 1/4$ cups sugar plus $1/4$ cup water
Lemon juice, 1 teaspoon	$1/2$ teaspoon vinegar
Marjoram	Oregano
Mayonnaise in salads and dressings	Plain nonfat yogurt
Mustard, dry, 1 teaspoon	$2 1/2$ teaspoons prepared mustard
Nutmeg	Mace
Onion, 1 whole	1 tablespoon onion powder or $1/4$ cup minced dried onion
Oregano	Marjoram
Raisins	Dried currants
Rice vinegar	Cider vinegar
Rosemary	Basil or oregano
Saffron	Turmeric
Sage	Thyme
Sour cream	Plain yogurt
Sugar, 1 cup	$3/4$ cup honey
Tabasco red pepper sauce, 4 drops	$1/8$ teaspoon cayenne pepper
Tarragon	Anise or fennel leaves
Thyme	Sage
Tomato juice, 1 cup	$1/2$ cup tomato sauce plus $1/2$ cup water
Tomato paste, $1/2$ cup	1 cup tomato sauce simmered until reduced by half
Tomato sauce, 1 cup	$1/2$ cup tomato paste plus $1/2$ cup water
Vinegar, 1 teaspoon	2 teaspoons lemon juice
Yogurt, plain	Sour cream

STORAGE

or

"HOW LONG CAN I KEEP IT IN THE REFRIGERATOR? THE FREEZER?"

◆

Here is a table listing the maximum length of time you should keep a food in the refrigerator or freezer. (Be sure to put a date on each wrapped package before putting it in the freezer!) It's also a good idea to get a refrigerator thermometer, so you can make sure the refrigerator compartment is kept at 40°F and the freezer at 0°F.

Always let hot foods cool before putting them in the refrigerator. And keep in mind that the rear portion of each shelf is colder than the front, so that if you store milk, orange juice, and other liquids back there, they may freeze.

FOOD	REFRIGERATOR (40°F)	FREEZER (0°F)
Beef, chopped	1 to 2 days	3 to 4 months
Beef, steaks	3 to 5 days	6 to 12 months
Cheese	3 to 4 weeks	Freezing affects taste and texture
Chicken, parts	1 to 2 days	9 months
Chicken, whole	1 to 2 days	12 months
Eggs	5 to 6 weeks	Do not freeze
Fish, fatty (tuna, salmon)	1 to 2 days	2 to 3 months
Fish, lean (cod, haddock)	1 to 2 days	6 months
Gravy	1 to 2 days	2 to 3 months
Soups	3 to 4 days	2 to 3 months
Stew	3 to 4 days	2 to 3 months

DIETING

or

"HOW CAN I REDUCE THE FAT IN A RECIPE?"

◆

There are a number of commonsense things you can easily do to reduce the amount of fat in a recipe, such as trimming the fat from meat and chicken, removing the skin from chicken and turkey, and substituting nonfat or low-fat milk, cottage cheese, sour cream, and mayonnaise for their richer counterparts. However, do keep in mind that these substitutes will alter the flavor a bit and that you may have to compensate by adding extra seasoning.

HERE ARE A FEW OTHER TIPS

✦ Use nonstick frying pans so you can greatly reduce the amount of oil needed for sautéing meats and vegetables.

✦ Using a grill pan is also a good idea. The ridges on the bottom of the pan keep the food slightly elevated so that it doesn't sit in (and absorb) the fat.

✦ When using stainless-steel or other types of pans, try using only half the amount of oil called for in the recipe. Sometimes you can get away with using as little as 1/2 teaspoon of oil, but be sure to spread it around the pan with a brush or paper towel. Or you can spray the pan with a cooking spray, such as Pam or I Can't Believe It's Not Butter!

✦ If you get the oil very hot before sautéing meat or vegetables, the cooking time will be slightly shorter and less fat will be absorbed.

✦ Sometimes you can brown sliced or chopped onions in a small amount of chicken broth. Or simply add them raw to a dish that will be further cooked. They may not be as tasty, but you'll avoid the extra fat.

✦ You can "brown" chicken by putting it under the broiler for a few minutes rather than cooking it in oil.

+ When a recipe calls for eggs, substitute one or two egg whites for each whole egg. A single egg yolk has about 5 grams of fat, while an egg white has none.

+ You can easily remove the fat from canned chicken broth by storing the cans in the refrigerator and spooning off the floating clumps of fat just after opening the can. Although you can buy nonfat chicken broth, it is also low in salt and therefore low in taste.

+ To remove fat from a gravy, sauce, stew, or soup, refrigerate it for at least several hours and then skim off the layer of fat that has hardened on the surface. If you don't have the time to allow it to cool completely, you can try "wiping" the surface with a paper towel.

+ Bouillon cubes (chicken, beef, or vegetable) contain no fat and are easy to use when a recipe calls for broth. However, they do contain a lot of salt, so you may want to dilute them by doubling the amount of water. Maggi is a brand we prefer.

+ Instead of using cream or milk to thicken a sauce or soup, use skim milk or buttermilk in which you have dissolved a small amount of flour or cornstarch.

+ When preparing salad dressing, you can sometimes substitute fruit juice or chicken broth for some of the oil. Or a few splashes of good balsamic vinegar may be all the dressing you need.

+ Orange, pineapple, and other fruit juices can be used as tasty marinades for poultry and fish.

+ Try using a dry wine to flavor a sauce; it adds no fat and most of the alcohol evaporates during cooking.

+ When buying cheese, keep in mind that cheeses made from sheep's milk are lower in fat than most cheeses made from cow's milk. Popular sheep's milk cheeses include Pecorino Romano, Roquefort, and most types of feta. Goat's milk cheeses are also lower in fat.

+ Some cow's milk cheeses, such as Parmesan, are made from skim milk or partly skim milk and are thus low in fat. When making a homemade pizza, you can leave out the mozzarella but still get the taste of cheese by sprinkling the surface with grated Parmesan.

+ To reduce the fat in cakes, brownies, or other baked goods, try substituting an equal amount of applesauce for the butter, margarine, or oil in the recipe. However, keep in mind that the texture and taste will be affected.

+ When choosing a menu, remember that skinless turkey breast is just about the leanest meat you can find. If you're serving beef, the leanest cuts include eye round, flank steak, and sirloin. And instead of using ground beef for hamburgers or chili, try substituting ground chicken or turkey breast.

+ If you decide to serve fish or shellfish, choose clams, cod, crabmeat, flounder, haddock, halibut, lobster, scallops, shrimp, and sole instead of salmon, mackerel, and swordfish, which are much fattier. Tuna and bluefish are only moderately fatty.

+ And choose canned fish—such as tuna and sardines—that are packed in water or sauce, not oil.

SOURCES

or

"WHERE CAN I FIND IT?"

◆

Here are some mail-order and Internet sources for cooking tools and accessories as well as ingredients, including some unusual spices, oils, vinegars, and other hard-to-find products:

A Kitchen Emporium
84 East Avenue, Westerly, RI 02891
Tel.: (401) 596-5588; Fax: (401) 596-4872
Website: www.kitchenemporium.com

American Spoon Foods (dried fruits, nuts, preserves)
P.O. Box 566, 1668 Clarion Avenue, Petoskey, MI 49770
Tel.: (800) 222-5886, (616) 347-9030
Website: www.spoon.com

Broadway Panhandler
477 Broome Street, New York, NY 10013
Tel.: (212) 966-3434
Website: www.broadwaypanhandler.com

Bridge Kitchenware
214 East 52nd Street, New York, NY 10022
Tel.: (212) 688-4220; Fax: (212) 758-5387
Website: www.bridgekitchenware.com

Chef's Catalog
P.O. Box 620048, Dallas, TX 75262-0048
Tel.: (800) 967-2433; Orders: (800) 338-3232; Fax: (800) 967-3291
Website: www.chefscatalog.com

Chefshop.com
1435 Elliot Avenue West, Seattle, WA 98119
Tel.: (877) 337-2491
Website: www.chefshop.com

Cooking by the Book
11 Worth Street, #8, New York, NY 10013
Tel.: (212) 966-9799; Fax: (212) 925-1074
Website: www.cookingbythebook.com

D'Artagnan
280 Wilson Avenue, Newark, NJ 07105
Tel.: (973) 344-0565; Fax: (973) 465-1870
Website: www.dartagnan.com

Dean & Deluca
P.O. Box 20810, Wichita, KS 67208
Tel.: (800) 221-7714
Website: www.deandeluca.com

Gold Mine Natural Food Company
3419 Hancock Street, San Diego, CA 92110
Tel.: (800) 475-3663
Website: www.goldminenaturalfood.com

Kitchen Market (Mexican ingredients)
218 Eighth Avenue, New York, NY 10011
Tel.: (212) 243-4433
Website: www.kitchenmarket.com

La Cuisine
323 Cameon Street, Alexandria, VA 22314
Tel.: (800) 521-1176; Fax: (703) 836-8925
Website: www.vmcs.com/lacuisine

Mozzarella Company
2944 Elm Street, Dallas, TX 75226
Tel.: (800) 798-2954, (214) 741-4072
Website: www.mozzco.com

New York Cake & Baking Distributors
56 West 22nd Street, New York, NY 10011
Tel.: (212) 675-2253; Fax: (212) 675-7099
Website: www.nycake.com

Oriental Pantry
423 Great Road, Acton, MA 01720
Tel.: (800) 828-0368
Website: www.orientalpantry.com

Penzey's Spice House
P.O. Box 924, Brookfield, WI 53008
Tel.: (800) 741-7787
Website: www.penzeys.com

Seeds of Change
P.O. Box 15700, Santa Fe, NM 87506
Tel.: (888) 762-7333
Website: www.seedsofchange.com

Sur La Table
1765 Sixth Avenue South, Seattle, WA 98134-1608
Tel.: (800) 243-0582; Fax: (206) 682-1026
Website: www.surlatable.com

Williams-Sonoma
P.O. Box 7456, San Francisco, CA 94120-7456
Tel.: (800) 541-1262; Orders: (800) 541-2233; Fax: (702) 363-2541
Website: www.williams-sonoma.com

Zabar's
2245 Broadway, New York, NY 10024
Tel.: (212) 787-2000; Orders: (800) 697-6301; in New York State only:
(212) 496-1234; Fax: (212) 580-4477
Website: www.zabars.com

Zingerman's
422 Detroit Street, Ann Arbor, MI 48104
Tel.: (888) 636-8162; (313) 769-1625
Website: www.zingermans.com

CONTACTS

or

"WHO CAN I CALL WHEN YOU'RE NOT HOME?"

◆

Here are some important websites and telephone numbers to keep handy:

BAKING

American Institute of Baking	(785) 537-4750; www.aibonline.org
Home Baking Institute	www.homebaking.org
Land O' Lakes Holiday Bakeline	(800) 782-9606

CHEESE

American Cheese Society	www.cheesesociety.org

CHOCOLATE

Chocolate Manufacturers Association	www.candyusa.org
Hershey Food Corporation	(800) 468-1714; www.hersheys.com

DAIRY

National Dairy Council	(708) 803-2000; www.nationaldairycouncil.org
Dairy Hotline	(800) 343-2479

FOOD SAFETY

National Food Safety Data Base	www.foodsafety.org
Foodborne Illness Line (CDC)	(404) 332-4597

MEAT

American Meat Institute   www.meatami.org
Meat and Poultry Hotline   (800) 535-4555; www.usda.gov
National Live Stock and Meat Board   www.beef.org

PASTA

National Pasta Association   www.ilovepasta.org

POULTRY

American Poultry Association   (503) 630-6759
Meat and Poultry Hotline   (800) 535-4555; www.usda.gov
Butterball Poultry Consumer Information (800) 288-8372

SEAFOOD

American Seafood Institute   (800) 328-3474
FDA Seafood Hotline   (800) 332-4010
National Fisheries Institute   www.nfi.usda

NUTRITION

Food and Nutrition Information Center   www.nal.usda.gov/fnic
Consumer Nutrition Hotline   (800) 366-1655

GLOSSARY

or

"WHAT DOES IT MEAN WHEN
THE RECIPE SAYS...?"

◆

al dente refers to pasta that is cooked just until it is tender yet still firm, but not hard, when you bite into it. Check the recommended cooking time on the pasta box, as this will vary depending on the shape and thickness of the pasta. It's always a good idea to taste a piece of the pasta while it is cooking to make sure it is not too hard or too mushy.

bake to cook using dry heat, in an oven or a covered barbecue grill. Most foods may be cooked by this method, either uncovered to produce a dry, crisp surface or covered to retain moistness. Always be sure to preheat the oven to the desired temperature before baking.

baste to drip, spoon, drizzle, brush, or pour a liquid (sauce, melted butter, pan juices) over food as it is cooking, usually roasting. Basting keeps food moist and also adds flavor.

batter a mixture of flour and other ingredients, such as shortening, eggs, and baking powder. Batter has a semiliquid consistency and can be poured or spooned, as opposed to dough, which is thicker.

blanch or parboil to place food in boiling water, usually for just a minute or two, to preserve its color, texture, and nutritional value. This preliminary cooking technique is also used to loosen or remove the skin of a fruit, vegetable, or nut.

boil to heat a liquid, usually water or broth, until it bubbles vigorously and gives off steam.

braise to brown food quickly in a small amount of fat and then cook slowly in a covered pan to which a small amount of liquid has been added. This is a moist-heat method of cooking.

broil to cook directly under the fire or heat source. This method generally creates a crisp outside while the inside, which cooks more slowly, remains moist. It is best to broil meat or other food that is less than 2 inches in thickness. Grilling is a similar process, but the heat source is below, not above, the food.

brown to cook quickly to achieve a brownish outside while the inside remains moist. Using a hot skillet on the top of the stove works best, but browning can also be done in a very hot oven.

Bundt or tube pan a round metal baking pan with high sides and a hollow funnel in the center. In a Bundt pan, the sides are fluted or decorated, while in a tube pan, they are plain. Tube pans are used for making angel food cakes and have little metal "feet" attached to the rim to make it easy to invert the pan while the cake is cooling.

caramelize to melt sugar slowly over low heat, stirring very carefully, until it turns into a golden brown syrup. Or, you can first dissolve the sugar slowly in water and then heat the mixture until it becomes a golden brown syrup. Caramelized sugar is also known as burnt sugar.

chop to cut food into small pieces, using a knife, a food processor, or a single or double-edged chopping tool. The chopped pieces usually range in size from $1/4$ to $1/2$ inch in diameter.

colander a perforated bowl-shaped container for draining foods. It is particularly handy for draining cooked pasta.

core to remove the center of an apple, pear, or other type of fruit. A melon baller is especially handy for coring apples once they have been cut into halves.

dash a very small amount—less than $1/8$ teaspoon—of an ingredient, usually salt, pepper, Tabasco, or other seasoning, added quickly.

deep-fry or French-fry to cook food submerged in a large amount of hot oil.

deglaze to make a sauce by heating and dissolving with wine, stock, or other liquid the tiny browned bits of food left in a skillet after cooking meat or other food.

dice to cut food into very small, uniform cubes.

dissolve to mix a dry ingredient, such as sugar, salt, or gelatin, into a liquid (often boiling) until the dry ingredient is completely incorporated into the liquid.

dot to dab or drip small pieces of an ingredient randomly over the surface of a food. Many casseroles are dotted with butter before baking.

double boiler a two-pot arrangement in which one pot rests partway inside the other. A small amount of simmering water in the lower pot heats the food in the upper one. It is generally used for melting chocolate and warming custards and other heat-sensitive foods. If you don't own a double boiler, you can easily improvise one using two of your own pots or a pot and a bowl.

dough a thick, pliable mixture of flour, liquid, and other ingredients (often including a leavening agent), which can be kneaded, rolled, or spooned to make bread, pie crust, or cookies.

drain to pour off liquid, usually using a colander or strainer. If you wish to save the liquid, place the strainer in a bowl or other container.

dredge to sprinkle or lightly coat with flour or bread crumbs before frying.

drizzle to slowly pour a topping in thin lines over food, such as drizzling icing over cake.

dry sauté to cook food over very high heat using no oil or other fat in either a nonstick pan or in a hot skillet that has been sprinkled with salt or other seasoning.

Dutch oven a large, heavy pot with a tight-fitting lid that prevents steam from easily escaping. It is often used for making stew or for braising large cuts of meat, such as brisket.

flake to gently break a food into thin pieces using a fork.

fold to incorporate one mixture into another—usually a light airy one, such as beaten egg whites, into a heavier one, such as cake batter. The lighter mixture is gently lifted up and mixed into the heavier one, usually with a spatula.

fry to cook food in hot oil, butter, or other fat.

garnish small, often flavorful accompaniments used to decorate a plate of food. Parsley sprigs, lemon wedges, chocolate curls—even edible flowers—are used as garnishes.

glaze a shiny coating that is brushed or drizzled on a food, such as a cake or pastry.

grate to reduce a food to fine particles. Hand graters are available as flat, cylindrical, or box-shaped tools with sharp-edged holes or slits. A microplane, a rasplike tool, is particularly good for very fine grating. You can also use a food processor for grating.

grease to rub or spread butter, margarine, or other shortening on a surface, such as on a cookie sheet to prevent the cookies from sticking, or on a turkey to add flavor and seal in moisture.

griddle a flat, rimless pan often used for cooking pancakes.

grill to cook food on a rack directly over the flame or other heat source. Meat, chicken, and vegetables are often cooked this way.

grill pan a heavy ridged pan used for cooking a variety of foods, such as steaks, hamburgers, chicken breasts, fish, and vegetables.

grind to crush or pulverize food into tiny bits or particles. You can use a food processor or an electric grinder or do it by hand with a chopper or mortar and pestle. If you use your electric grinder to grind coffee or a spice, be sure to clean it thoroughly before using it for anything else. A good way to clean a grinder is to put a piece of bread in it and grind away!

hull to remove the outer covering of a fruit or seed, or in the case of strawberries, to remove the stem and any leaves attached to it.

infuse to steep or soak tea leaves or herbs in water or other liquid to extract the flavor into the liquid.

insulated baking sheet a wide, flat metal baking sheet, sometimes with a low lip on one side or on all four sides. Unlike a regular cookie sheet, an insulated sheet is made of two layers of metal with an airspace between them. It is used for making soft cookies or other baked goods that you don't want to get crisp or brown on the bottom.

jelly-roll pan a flat, rectangular metal baking pan with a low rim, about 1 inch high. It is often used for baking the thin sheet of cake that is rolled into a jelly roll. The most commonly used size is 15¹/₂ × 10¹/₂ × 1 inch, although both larger and smaller versions are available.

julienne to cut a vegetable or other food into very thin strips of equal length. Potatoes cut this way are often called matchstick potatoes.

knead to work a pliable dough with your hands so that it becomes a smooth, elastic mass. You can also use an electric mixer with a dough hook or a food processor fitted with a plastic blade.

loaf pan a narrow rectangular pan with high straight sides, used mostly for making bread, meat loaf, and pound cake. It may be made of glass or metal; the most commonly used sizes are 9 × 5 × 3 inches and 8¹/₂ × 4¹/₂ × 2¹/₂ inches.

macerate to soak berries or other food in a liquid, often a juice or liqueur, to soften and flavor the fruit while releasing its juices into the liquid.

marinate to soak meat or other food in a seasoned liquid, such as wine or lemon juice, to add flavor. Marinating is also used to tenderize tough cuts of meat.

mash to crush food into a soft mushy mixture, such as mashed potatoes.

melt to heat a solid food, such as chocolate or butter, until it becomes a liquid. Melting can be done over low heat on top of the stove or in a microwave oven. Remember, though, that as the melted food begins to cool, it will start to harden.

microplane a thin rasplike tool for fine grating. It is particularly useful for grating lemon zest because it removes the outer layer of the peel but not the underlying white bitter layer (pith). It is also often used for grating nutmeg and Parmesan cheese.

mince to chop a food into very tiny pieces.

parboil see *blanch.*

pinch a tiny amount—typically so tiny that it can be held between the tips of your thumb and forefinger. It is generally about 1/16 teaspoon.

pipe to squeeze a softened mixture, such as icing or whipped cream, through a pastry bag, usually to decorate a cake or serving platter.

poach to simmer a food, such as fish, chicken, or eggs, in water, broth, wine, or other liquid that is heated to just below the boiling point.

puree to reduce food to a very smooth, creamy texture using a food processor, food mill, or blender.

reconstitute to add liquid to dried food, such as dehydrated mushrooms, in order to restore it to its original form or consistency.

reduce to cook a liquid, such as broth or a sauce, over high heat in order to thicken it and intensify its flavor. It is important to "watch the pot" to make sure the liquid doesn't completely boil away.

render to cook meat or other food over low heat to release its fat.

roast to cook with indirect, dry heat in an oven.

sauté to cook quickly in an open shallow pan, using a small amount of fat and tossing frequently.

scald to heat milk or other liquid until almost boiling. Tiny bubbles will appear around the edge of the saucepan, and in the case of milk, a thin skin will form on the surface.

score to cut shallow slits (about 1/4 inch deep) into the surface of a food. This is often done to tenderize it or to hasten the absorption of a marinade.

sear to cook meat or other food quickly over high heat in order to form a brown crust. Searing can be done in the oven, under the broiler, on a grill, or in a skillet on top of the stove. As the food cooks further, the seared surface helps seal in the natural juices.

shred to cut into very narrow strips. Many foods, including carrots, cabbage, and cheese, are easily shredded with a grater or food processor. Cooked meat can be shredded with two forks.

sieve a perforated or mesh bowl-like utensil used for draining, straining, and sifting.

sift to shake a dry ingredient, such as flour or sugar, through a sieve or sifter to eliminate any lumps and to incorporate air. In many baking recipes, dry ingredients are sifted together to combine them.

simmer to cook food in liquid that is heated to just below the boiling point. A simmering liquid has small occasional bubbles, as opposed to a boiling liquid, which has larger, vigorous bubbles.

skillet a long-handled, often round, frying pan with low, gently sloping sides.

spatula a flat, usually flexible, long-handled utensil used for scraping, stirring, spreading, folding, and lifting. It is available in many sizes, shapes, and materials.

springform pan a round metal baking pan with a special clamp that allows you to remove the sides (and more easily remove the cake). It is used mostly for making cheesecakes and other cakes that would otherwise be difficult to remove from the pan. It is generally available in 8-, 9-, and 10-inch sizes.

steam to cook food in vapor produced by boiling water. The food is usually placed on a rack or in a basket just above the water's surface and the pot is tightly covered. This method helps retain the food's nutrients.

steep to soak in boiling water for a few minutes. Steeping releases flavors in the food and also softens it.

stew to slowly cook a combination of meat and vegetables in broth or other liquid for several hours in a tightly covered pot. Stewing tenderizes the meat and also produces a flavorful sauce that is served with the dish.

stir-fry to cook small pieces of food over very high heat in a small amount of fat, stirring continuously, until tender but still crisp. This is a popular cooking method for many Asian dishes and can be done in a wok or a standard skillet.

strain to pour a liquid or soft food through a strainer, sieve, or cheesecloth to remove solid particles. Raspberry sauce, for example, is often strained to remove the seeds.

tea infuser a small perforated basketlike container with a hinged lid used for steeping tea leaves, herbs, or spices.

toast to brown food in an oven or under a broiler, or in a skillet on top of the stove. Nuts and spices are often toasted to bring out their flavor.

tube pan see *Bundt pan.*

whip to mix ingredients by vigorously beating. You can use a hand whisk or an electric mixer.

zest to remove the outermost layer of the skin of a citrus fruit, leaving behind the bitter white layer (pith) underneath. This is easily done with a sharp paring knife or a citrus zester. A microplane is an excellent tool to use if the recipe calls for grated zest. The term *zest* also refers to the outermost skin layer of a citrus fruit.

EPILOGUE

MY FAVORITE RECIPE

from **WENDY WASSERSTEIN**
Novelist, Playwright, Screenwriter,
Winner of the 1989 Pulitzer Prize for Drama,
the First Woman to Win a Tony Award for Best Play

◆

The phone number for Shun Lee West is (212) 595-8895.

"That is truly my favorite recipe."

INDEX OF RECIPES
AND COOKING TIPS

(See also Index of Contributors, page 347)

◆

baking (*cont'd*):
  buying and storing sugar for, 240–41
  measuring dry ingredients for, 240
  melting chocolate for, 243
  reducing fat in, 313
  separating egg whites from yolks for,
    244–45
  testing baking powder and baking
    soda for freshness for, 241
  whipping egg whites for, 245–46
baking liners, Teflon or silicone, 247
baking powder, 6
  Biscuits, Gamoo's, 18–19
  testing for freshness, 241
baking soda, 6
  testing for freshness, 241
Baklava, 293–94
balsamic vinegar, 117
banana(s), 26
  Delicious Healthy Breakfast Drink, 7
  Muffins, 19–20
  ripening, 20, 66–67
  storing, 66
barbecued:
  Brisket, 193–94
  Chicken, 158
bars, *see* squares
basil:
  chopping, 90
  Pesto, 133
  pesto, in Pasta Genovese, 138
  Tomato Sauce, Fresh, 132
bean(s):
  canned versus dried, 46
  Chicken Chili, 160–61
  Chili, 200–201
  dried, soaking methods for, 46–47
  Three-, Salad, 69
  see also black bean(s); chickpeas;
    lentil(s)
beef, 187–203, 313
  Brisket, Barbecued, 193–94
  Brisket with Cranberries, 194–95
  with Broccoli, 196–97
  buying, 187–88
  Chili, 200–201
  Chili con Goat Cheese, 202–3
  cooking, 189–90
  Corned, Glazed, 192–93
  Fillet of, Elegant and Easy, 191

Flank Steak, Glazed, 192
freezing and thawing, 188
ground, 188, 189, 190
Horseradish Sauce for, 191
marinating, 189
Meat Loaf, Quick and Tasty, 203
Meaty Cocktail Sandwiches, 37
Pepper Steak, 195–96
Provençal, 197–98
roast, in Chef's Salad, 72–73
serving size for, 188–89
Stew, 198–99
storing, 188, 310
berry(ies):
  Sauce, 15
  -Stuffed French Toast, San Fran-
    cisco–Style, 14–15
  see also specific berries
Betty, Apple Brown, 260–61
biscuit cutters, substitute for, 6
Biscuits, Baking Powder, Gamoo's, 18–19
Bisque, Tomato-Dill, 60
black bean(s):
  Corn, and Feta Salad with Pita, 71
  Creole, 205–6
  Hummus, 40
  Oberlin Perfectionist Pasta, 135
  Salad, 70
blenders:
  caution for hot liquids in, 165
  immersion, 46
blueberry(ies), 26
  Cake, Melt-in-Your-Mouth, 269–70
  Crumb Coffee Cake, 270–71
  Red, White, and Blue Cobbler, 273
  Soup, 49
  Torte, Low-Fat, 272
Blue Mashed Potatoes, 109–10
bottled foods, safety concerns and, 68
bouillon cubes, 312
breads:
  Baking Powder Biscuits, Gamoo's,
    18–19
  Banana Muffins, 19–20
  Berry-Stuffed French Toast, San Fran-
    cisco–Style, 14–15
  Cranberry, 20–21
  Crème Brûlée French Toast, 16
  Egg Soufflé, Easy, 13–14
  Monkey, 21–22

quick, making, 6
whole grain, 26
yeast, making, 5–6
see also pita
breakfast, 3–22
Baking Powder Biscuits, Gamoo's, 18–19
Banana Muffins, 19–20
Berry-Stuffed French Toast, San Francisco–Style, 14–15
Cranberry Bread or Muffins, 20–21
Crème Brûlée French Toast, 16
Drink, Delicious Healthy, 7
Dutch Babies, 8–9
Egg Soufflé, Easy, 13–14
Granola, 7–8
Grape-Nuts Pudding, 12
Huevos Rancheros (Ranch-Style Eggs), 13
Lemon–Poppy Seed Pancakes, 10–11
Monkey Bread, 21–22
Pancake, 9–10
Sausage and Apple Pudding, Baked, 17–18
Working Mom's, xvii
brisket:
Barbecued, 193–94
with Cranberries, 194–95
broccoli:
Beef with, 196–97
Cream of, Soup—with No Cream, 50
Rice Casserole, 79
with Ziti, 146–47
Brownie Cookies, 248
Chocolate Chip, 252
Brownies, 284
reducing fat in, 313
brown sugar, 240
light vs. dark, 16
measuring, 240
storing, 241
brownulated sugar, 240
bulgur (cracked wheat):
Tabbouleh, 123–24
Tabbouleh with Currants and Pine Nuts, 125
butter:
buying and storing, 241–42
-Crunch Cookies, Matzo, 255–56
measuring, 304

C
cabbage:
Coleslaw, 74–75
grating, 75
Health Slaw, 75
Layered, Kolozsvar, 206–7
Napa, in Crunchy Chinese Salad, 76–77
Penne with Sausage and, 139–40
Vegetable Soup, Grandma Pearl's Healthful, 61
Cacciatore, Chicken, 158–59
cakes:
Apple, Delicious, 261–62
Applesauce, 268–69
Blueberry, Melt-in-Your-Mouth, 269–70
Blueberry Crumb Coffee, 270–71
Blueberry Torte, Low-Fat, 272
Carrot, 279–80
Cheesecake with Fruit, Fat-Free, 283–84
Chocolate, Decadent, 285
Chocolate Angel Food, 286–87
Chocolate Chip Coffee, 287–88
Devil's Food, 288–89
Hazelnut Meringue, 294–96
Hot-Fudge-Sundae, 289–90
Plum, Grandma Gert's, 278–79
Pumpkin Cheesecake, 282–83
reducing fat in, 313
canned foods, safety concerns and, 68
canola oil, 67
capons, 156
carrot(s):
Cake, 279–80
Coleslaw, 74–75
Glazed, 80
grating, 75
Health Slaw, 75
Ring, 80–81
Roasted Vegetable Medley, 87–88
Vegetable Soup, Grandma Pearl's Healthful, 61
Cashew Chicken, Thai-Style, 172–73
casseroles:
Artichoke and Spinach, 78
Broccoli-Rice, 79
Eggplant, 82–83
Noodle Pudding, 103

INDEX OF CONTRIBUTORS

(See also Index of Recipes and
Cooking Tips, page 329)

❖

ABOUT THE AUTHORS

NAOMI NEFT and CYNTHIA ROTHSTEIN met when their daughters Debbie and Lori entered kindergarten, and they have remained close friends ever since. They both enjoy cooking and continue to share many of their favorite recipes and cooking tips.

Naomi, a former encyclopedia editor for two major publishing companies, has also coauthored a reference book, *Where Women Stand: An International Report on the Status of Women in 140 Countries* (Random House, 1997). She lives in New York City with her husband, David.

Cynthia has worked as an investment research analyst and has taught in the New York City public school system. She lives in New York City with her husband, Jerry, and her younger daughter, Meryl, a college student who will soon enter the world of young career women, for whom this book was created.

Debbi and Lori, the inspiration for this book, are now in graduate school, living in New York City and still using their well-worn loose-leaf copies of "Recipes for Our Daughters."

DISCARD